DAVID TO DELACROIX

DAVID TO DELACROIX

BY WALTER FRIEDLAENDER

Translated by Robert Goldwater

HARVARD UNIVERSITY PRESS
CAMBRIDGE • MASSACHUSETTS
LONDON • ENGLAND

Eighth Printing, 1977

ISBN 0-674-19401-2
Library of Congress Catalog Card Number 52-5395
Printed in the United States of America

PREFACE

The German edition of this book was published in 1930 as a volume in a series of philological handbooks destined for use in colleges and universities. The special feature of the book is its emphasis on the historical structure of French painting from the time of David to that of Ingres and Delacroix. This most interesting and important period of French painting has been treated mostly by art critics who have specialized in the art and culture of the nineteenth century and who reduced the art of the period to two main tendencies, classicism and romanticism. Such terms, however, are unsuitable to contrasts of style or technique, whether in painting or in literature, because they refer to different levels of aesthetic experience; the one implies an ideal of form directly or indirectly dependent upon the antique, while the other describes the mood or sentiment which a creative artist expresses through the medium of his work. One can very well speak of a romantic classicism, for example in certain works of Ingres or Girodet, or of a classicistic romanticism in such a painting as Delacroix's "Medea." Such terms tend to confuse rather than to clarify the artistic situation of the period.

To my mind, a clearer idea of this situation can be gained by studying, more than has been done in the past, the historical sources of the various stylistic and intellectual currents of the time. Naturally these sources are to be found, to a large extent, in the art of the preceding period, the eighteenth century. I have therefore begun by outlining in an introduction (which because of lack of space is somewhat schematic) the main trends that lead up to David. Of equal importance, however, is the art of the sixteenth and seventeenth centuries, and significant parallels can be drawn between these periods and the early nineteenth century — parallels which are made particularly meaningful by the strongly and consciously retrospective element in the artistic intellect of the time from David to Delacroix. The art of David is largely based on that of Poussin, and Ingres proclaims his interest in Bronzino and his passionate concern with Raphael. Prud'hon was called the French Correggio with good reason, and Delacroix was an ardent follower of Rubens. Therefore, if I apply such terms as classic, mannerist, early baroque, and high baroque — terms which are generally applied to the sixteenth and seventeenth centuries — to the art of the early nineteenth century, it is because I believe that there are specific common denominators in the phases of these two periods and in the way in which these phases succeed one another. On the other hand, in tracing the historical developments, I have tried not to lose sight of the artistic integrity of the various artists who effected these developments, and it surely does not detract from the individuality of an artist to understand his work in an art-historical context. Indeed, an artist manifests his individuality partly through the force with which he reacts to his artistic inheritance.

The present English translation is a recent revision by Dr. Robert Goldwater of a translation he made in 1939. Except for minor corrections and omissions, it follows exactly the original German text. I am especially grateful to Dr. John Coolidge, Director of the Fogg Museum of Art in Cambridge, and to Dr. Sidney Freedberg of Wellesley College, without whose loving interest in the book this edition would never have been published. I would also like to thank Dr. Jane Costello, Mr. Irvin Lavin, and Mr. William Crelly for their enthusiastic assistance in preparing the manuscript for the press. I am greatly indebted to Mr. George Wildenstein, Mr. Richard Goetz, and Mr. Henry McIlhenny for giving me photographs which I was unable to obtain elsewhere, and to the administrations of the following museums for permission to reproduce paintings from their collections: the Walters Art Gallery in Baltimore, the National Gallery in Washington, D.C., the Metropolitan Museum of Art in New York, the Museum of Fine Arts in Boston, and especially the Fogg Museum, whose photographic collection was generously placed at my disposal.

WALTER FRIEDLAENDER

May 1952

CONTENTS

ILLUSTRATIONS

DAVID TO DELACROIX

THE ETHICAL AND FORMAL BASES OF CLASSICISM IN FRENCH PAINTING

Two main currents appear in French painting after the sixteenth century: the rational and the irrational. The first is apt to be moralizing and didactic; the second is free of such ethical tendencies. The rational trend stems from France's classical epoch, the seventeenth century, and continues, with more or less strength, throughout the eighteenth; the irrational current is less constant, but appears most splendidly in the first half of the eighteenth century. Both, though in a variety of transformations and mixtures, can be recognized in the complicated structure of French painting of the nineteenth century and continue even to our own day.

The moralizing bias is more evident in French painting than in that of any other European nation, north or south. Early in the seventeenth century there appears in France an attitude primarily concerned with the ethical and didactic content of a work of art and, of course, exerting a specific influence upon the form as well. The pioneer was Nicolas Poussin. His famous painting "Et in Arcadia ego" is a symbol of the transitory. Shepherds read on a grave monument the melancholy inscription, "I too am in Arcadia." The "Testament of Eudamidas" is a symbol of puritan rectitude; the only legacy that virtuous but poor citizen of Corinth left to his friends was the burden of caring for his mother and daughter. Such moralistic epigrams are conceivable only in the artistic and emotional milieu of France. Although the formal character of Poussin's art is based entirely on Italian, especially Roman, prototypes, no Italian artist would have chosen such didactic subjects. This moralizing element is even present in genre painting; Louis Le Nain's peasants are dignified and significant, unlike the drunken rustics of Brouwer and other Netherlands artists. Because of these ethical and didactic factors religious painting, too, acquired a typical sober character, very different from the fanciful brilliance of religious paintings produced in Italy and Spain in the wake of the Counter Reformation. In France, there was a new emphasis upon the individual's spiritual life and practical salvation, so that ethical and didactic concerns were more predominant than ever before. From the circle of "The Virtuous" of Port-Royal issued the serious but humanly and psychologically sensitive work of the Frenchified Fleming, Philippe de Champaigne. Eustache Le Sueur can also be placed in this category. What the French called the *grand goût* was, for the most part, permeated with this strongly didactic atmosphere. This is also true of the academic spirit so characteristic of France, a spirit that is closely related to the moralistic, or would like to appear so. The emphasis on *ratio*, a fundamental idea of the academic, is so closely related to the moralistic that the two can hardly be separated. When Boileau sets up his aesthetic rules, they are morally obligatory because they are built upon the rock of *raison* and *bon sens.* Similarly in Poussin and his great literary contemporary, Corneille, the elements of the rational are fused with those of the moral. *Raison* and didactic morality formed the *méthode classique*, represented in the seventeenth century by Poussin and Corneille, with whom the name of Descartes is associated as the rationalistic theoretician. This classical method provides an unshakable basis for the entire later development of French painting.

Sharply opposed to this moral and rational attitude is the second main current of French painting, the irrational. It does not attempt to build on the basis of human or superhuman truth or reason, but simply on taste — something that is neither rationally nor morally tangible. A real definition of taste can hardly be formulated; quite early one spoke of the imponderable fineness of *delicatesse* or, with complete subjectivity, of a certain *je ne sais quoi.* These antitheses — extreme rigidity and extreme laxity — are reflected in artistic and especially in literary theories. Against the strictly moralist and militantly classicist ideas of Boileau, who wanted to establish eternally valid rules of poetry confirmable in the works of antiquity, there appeared, at the beginning of the eighteenth century, a movement to make *sentiment* the criterion for artistic judgment. *Coeur* and *esprit* were catchwords of the literary salons around 1720. Thus arose an artistic mentality, unburdened by moral or academic tradition, that did not wish to live in the rarefied atmosphere of reason and morality, but at the same time had no desire to descend into the depth of emotion. It attempted rather to capture the attractive surface of reality, in both the objective and the psychological sense, and concerned itself with the facile and scintillating phenomena of life, treating them in a joyous and always technically masterful manner. *Charme* and *esprit*, the hallmarks of the style, are imponderables, pure elements of a taste whose extreme refinement and elegance could only have been developed in a metropolis such as Paris; they thoroughly defy reason. Moreover, these elements defy all morality; they are by definition amoral and this amorality was easily turned into immorality, frivolousness, and often overt eroticism. Thus, the whole movement became still more strongly opposed to the Academy, the stern guardian of morality.

The taste for the sensuously superficial and the charmingly elegant produced so many delightful works of art that there has been a tendency to forget everything in French art except these sparkling masterpieces of French eighteenth-century *esprit*. The wonderful decorations, large and small, of Watteau, Lancret, Pater, de Troy, etc., with their softly colored and yet brilliant lacquer tones and their captivating eroticism, covered the *rocaille* walls and ceilings of Parisian *hôtels* in the first half of the eighteenth century. They were the delight of connoisseurs and amateurs and enchanted the whole of Europe. But in spite of our pleasure in the finesse and quality, the spirit and charm of this art, we should not forget that this uninhibited and purely painterly attitude represents only one side of French art, as it were, the verso, the extreme, the beloved exception. From a certain point of view, this sensual and decorative art was tolerated merely as a passing phenomenon; for the intellectual and judicious Frenchman of the advancing eighteenth century, at least, it belonged only to the *petite manière*. Even its finest and earliest exponent, Watteau, was considered only an accident in the development of moralistic and rationalistic French art. Only the *grand goût* claimed unchallenged leadership; even such careful and penetrating critics as Diderot made no exceptions in this respect.

The great moral-classic attitude had been the dominant note in the history of French painting since the seventeenth century, but only with the inclusion of the free and optically sensitive manner could the structure be complete. Joyous and uncalculated melody is a fundamental element in the life and manner of the French people and their artistic culture, but it can never suppress the enduring rational keynote which, related to the high ideals of Italian classicism and antiquity, expresses the Latin intellect and is therefore a major component of the French spirit. Out of the conflict of these opposites, their alternation of leadership, and their partial interpenetration, French art develops. The battle between the *Poussinistes* and the *Rubénistes* which around the end of the seventeenth century produced a whole literature of bitter diatribes (more than the famous *querelle des anciens et des modernes* of the literary world) is a part of this greater struggle, really the first open conflict. For though the discussions were apparently concerned with the technical and the visual — drawing versus color, calm versus movement, sharply focused action of a few figures versus scattered crowding — the real battle was between discipline and morality on the one side and amoral slackening of rules and subjective irrationality on the other. The continuation of this deep cleavage even in the nineteenth century is seen in the bitter rivalry between Ingres and Delacroix. Even for them the real question was not one of mere formal laws. For Ingres, Delacroix, as the representative genius of colorism, was manifestly the Devil; "it smells of brimstone," he once said when he came upon Delacroix in a Salon. Ingres was the self-appointed protector not only of linearism and classical tradition, but of morality and reason as well. Strangely enough, in the most extreme academic credo, line and linear abstraction embodied something moral, lawful, and universal, and every descent into the coloristic and irrational was a heresy and a moral aberration that must be strenuously combatted. Similar though less sharply expressed oppositions are to be found in later French painting.

This continued battle of opinions, the constant friction in which a partial interpenetration of opposites was unavoidable, played an important part in the formation of French artists. Because of this the nineteenth century produced that extraordinary richness of individual artistic personalities and variety of schools and tendencies which distinguished French art from that of all other countries. Although the rationalistic element, characteristically and closely related to the moral, was always greatly in evidence in French art, the irrational component was of almost equal importance. The most subjective French artist was, in technique and compositional approach, partly dependent upon reason and even upon the Academy, and it is just this that in the midst of all excess still gave French art some measure of formal restraint.

Viewed historically, the freer manner appeared at the beginning of the eighteenth century primarily as a reaction. The classic epoch of the seventeenth century, in which Poussin, Descartes, and Corneille were representatives of the French mentality, was long past. Louis XIV and his ministers, especially Colbert, had gone to the utmost extremes of administrative concentration; they had bridled the classic spirit and had forced even art into the service of absolute monarchy. The result was an all-pervasive artistic sterility. The Academy, under Lebrun, with its verbose aesthetic speeches and discussions, took the lead in codifying and mummifying all vitality. The reaction that took place during the Regency toward complete freedom from any kind of academic limitation — in technique (the new colorism) as well as in subject matter (genre) — was anything but surprising. However, the dominance of the *peinture galante* lasted only a relatively short time. Watteau was active only during the first two decades of the century, and his true followers, Pater and Lancret, did not last beyond the middle of the century. Boucher, to be sure, lived on until

1770, but he was comparatively unappreciated in his last years. Only Fragonard, unique among these great names, carried on the line and worked in the freer manner into the new century, and even he had to make concessions to the *grand goût* as early as his diploma picture of 1765. What we generally call "the spirit of the eighteenth century" should properly be limited to its first half. The style which saw its highest development during the Regency and the early years of Louis XV's reign (when, as La Mettrie writes, it was as though one were constantly immersed in a *mer de volupté*) had not been entirely extinguished by 1750, but the severe and moralizing tendencies which then reappeared were constantly limiting it and forcing its retreat. The same development occurred in decoration when the *rocaille*, that flickering and facilely capricious ornament, gave way to an ever more sober stylization.

The strong reactionary tendency which now opposed the undisciplined mentality of the salons and the multitude of the *petits maîtres* was basically only a return to the rational and moralizing keynote of French art which had culminated in the classic epoch of the seventeenth century. The governing principle involved here — as is so often the case in the evolution of art forms — is, so to speak, the "grandfather law." A generation consciously and bitterly negates the efforts of its elders and returns to the tendencies of a preceding period; these tendencies had continued in more or less hidden undercurrents and had taken on a slightly different coloration through contact with the opposing tendencies. This was indeed the situation around the middle of the eighteenth century: a neoclassic, one might say a neo-Poussinist current returned and the *grand goût* was once more dominant. However, the character of the current had been significantly changed by fifty years of subjection to the irrational rococo, and a powerful effort was needed to strengthen and purify it. The chief complaint of the opposition around 1750 was against the superficiality in the period from Watteau to Boucher. One regretted the absence of grand action, of strong composition, of impassioned expression, but above all the lack of that ethical content which had pervaded the works of Poussin. Rousseau declaimed bitterly against the pictures in the galleries and the statues in the gardens, because instead of showing virtuous people they portrayed *les égarements du coeur et de la raison*. It was believed that the merely visual, the melting colors, delicate values, and attractive surfaces which charmed the amateurs and pleased the salons should be secondary to more spiritual emotion. "First move me, astonish me, break my heart, let me tremble, weep, stare, be enraged — only then regale my eyes" was Diderot's appeal to the artist.

The classicism which now began to reappear, with a new manner of adoring and emulating the antique, was to a very large extent a moral affair. Antiquity was no longer simply an ultimate teacher whom one followed unquestioningly. Rather, it was felt that man had found in himself lofty and valid rules for human morality which were rediscoverable, as nowhere else, in the history, literature, and art of antiquity, and that from them one could derive maxims for one's own conduct. Thus it was not simply the formal solutions of Greek and more especially Roman art which were emulated; the important thing was the ethical value which could be extracted from antique art. The heroic was now associated with the virtuous. The Hero — preferably clothed in antique drapery — was not merely someone who performed great deeds of physical prowess and before whose muscular strength and bodily beauty one stood in wonder. He was primarily someone — and this was the moralized conception of Hercules — whose noble body sheathed a soul shining with virtue and whose exploits could serve as a model and as an ideal. He had to be a paragon of magnanimity, high-mindedness, self-control, righteousness, human dignity, and self-sacrifice — in short, he was to possess every conceivable human virtue. The stronger the contrast to the effeminate and frivolously skeptical representatives of contemporary society, the more radiantly virtuous a hero seemed. Above all, the king and his entourage were to be confronted with a luminous example of Roman Republican decency and Spartan simplicity and stoicism.

Thus, this ethical classicism took on an eminently political character and, along with literature and moralizing philosophy, paved the way for the Revolution. It was no accident or mere historicism that the Revolution utilized classicistic forms. David in his "Oath of the

Horatii" — the classicistic painting par excellence — reached the summit of this development four years before the storming of the Bastille and became the great painter of the Revolution. Important also in heralding a new classical era was the influence of Winckelmann's ideas, especially his concept of "quiet" or "tranquillity" as the proper condition of beauty. For Winckelmann this concept had an ethical and almost religious character; it added something new to the "noble simplicity" and the *goût de grandeur* which already characterized the classicistic attitude. A real moral effect of these ideas was not felt until they met with the doctrines of Rousseau, which had begun to stimulate a new emotionalism in France about the same time that Winckelmann's ideas were becoming popular. The return to nature, from which civilization had removed mankind, the simple grandeur and beauty of "citizens of Sparta," was sought in the noble figures of the Roman Republic as they were described by Plutarch, one of the most popular antique writers of the time. The great myths which had decorated walls and ceilings, with their erotically colored Triumphs of Venus and their pale allegories, were now neglected or scarcely noticed. Cincinnatus with the plow, Manlius who condemned his own son, Arria who cried to her husband, *Paete, non dolet* ("it doesn't hurt"), as she stabbed herself — the new ideal, in brief, was the stoic dignity of man.

However, the development of the new *grand goût*, this elevated neo-Poussinist classicism, did not proceed quickly or smoothly. The path to a definitive resolution, to David's "Horatii" of 1785, was long, difficult, and not very glorious. Certainly the spirit was willing; themes of an antique, heroic, and moral nature abounded, and there was energetic competition in collecting and inventing them, even such men of letters as Diderot taking part. The formal problems of picture structure were also reworked in accordance with the new requirements of simplicity and clearly understandable staging. Poussin's "laconicism" was revived and painters began to follow his rule of *rareté*, on which Winckelmann had also insisted. This demanded that as few figures as possible be placed on the pictorial stage, whereas the decorative artists and the Rubenists were much more concerned with picturesque effects than with concentration on individual actions. Unlimited vistas of perspective depth were given up in favor of an effort to achieve a stage for the main action through parallel spatial planes placed one behind the other. Foreshortenings, accessories, and anything else which might distract the eye from the essence of the picture — i.e., the action — were strenuously avoided. But all of these technical classicistic regulations came into being only gradually. For the most part they remained mere beginnings or compromises and only with David were they sharply, clearly, and directly realized. Although there were real talents, hard-working and even very able men, none except David, the youngest of them, was a leading figure. Thus, though the names of the members of David's and the preceding generation are known, their works are partly lost or buried in obscure museums and, for the most part, rightly forgotten. In the ingenious and frequently enthusiastic analyses of their pictures in the *Salons* of Diderot, one often has the feeling, despite the vitality of his diction, that one is dealing with shadows. For it was more the attitude of these artists, their relation to actuality or nature (which included something of sentiment), than the qualities of the productions that Diderot and the other critics were praising. But even this attitude is often unclear and undecided. Fundamentally, it is still a matter of what one may call a pseudo or rococo classicism; the subject matter alone, heroically moralizing and taken from the antique, is in the *grand goût*. Everything is haunted by an effete and washed-out rococo which, in ridding itself of overt eroticism, had produced a more painful *volupté décente*, a kind of lascivious chastity. Chastity and the related virtues were portrayed with half-nude bosoms and draperies clinging to the body in the manner of the antique. Greuze's innocently voluptuous young maidens are typical examples of this sort of erotic prudery.

The indirect influence which the leader of the neoclassic eclectics, the Germano-Roman Anton Raphael Mengs, exercised on French art was not without importance. He was the most intimate friend and the ideal of Winckelmann, although his art was really only a watered-down version of Italy's continuing classicistic and antibaroque movements. It was, in fact, composed of reminiscences of Raphael and the

Bolognese-Roman school, with a touch of the antique and faded rococo coloring. His art and ideas had more influence on the countless French painters who were *pensionnaires* of the Académie de France in Rome than those of the director, the still very rococo Natoire, so that the authorities had to warn the students against the influence of Mengs. His numerous English pupils — and with them the Swiss-born Angelica Kauffmann — also helped to spread his artistic ideas. They created many historical pictures in this pseudoclassic manner which were disseminated in the form of engravings and became very popular in France. In spite of their weaknesses their heroic subject matter contributed much to the strengthening of the *grand goût*.

Moral virtuousness is frequently associated with sentimentality. In this respect, English influence is unmistakable in the eighteenth century; from England a wave of sensibility spread out over all of Europe (consider, for example, Richardson's *Clarissa Harlowe*). Without this almost neurotic sensitivity, a kind of hypertrophy of the emotions, the paintings of Greuze would not have received such enthusiastic and undivided applause. "Never have I seen truer color, more moving tears, more noble simplicity," said a critic of his "Maiden Mourning over a Dead Bird" (Salon of 1765). It is characteristic that Greuze was considered a painter of true nature, with reference not to the accurate delineation of details, which actually he valued greatly, but rather to just that sentimental expression which today seems somewhat dishonest and lachrymose. Moreover, it is worth while to notice that Greuze constructed his large compositions, such as "The Father's Curse" (Louvre), in a classicistic, Poussinist way, with additive planes and a curtain closing off the background; only the virile conviction is lacking.

This sensitive naïveté could also clothe itself in fashionable antique drapery, with titles to match: "Vestals Approaching the Fire," "Virtuous Athenians" (Vien), "Cupid Drilling a Squad of Little Amori" (Carle Van Loo, 1763), and the most famous of these subjects, "Merchant of Loves," taken from a mural in Herculaneum.

This *savante simplicité* and *pureté ingénue* were specialties of Joseph-Marie Vien, the teacher of David. "The Love Merchant" was painted by him, as was the "Ladies of Corinth Decorating a Vase of Flowers," and with such subjects he earned extraordinary acclaim. Diderot says of one of his sentimental and neo-Grecian ladies: "One would not wish to be her lover but her father or mother. Her head is so noble; she is so simple and naïve." It is obvious that the heroic and moral tendency had not yet rid itself of the *petite manière*; only the antique drapery and sober restraint in drawing and color added something new. However, the sentiment is fundamentally the same. Also, it should be remembered that the coloristic current had by no means disappeared at this time. A picture technically as well as morally so loose as Fragonard's "The Swing" was produced in 1766, contemporary with the sentimental heads of Greuze and the virtuous antique maidens of Vien. And even Diderot, the staunchest moralistic critic, admired the beautiful and sensitive still-life and genre painting of Chardin (d. 1779) although he regretted that Chardin's scenes of domestic life were not in themselves interesting. The great religious masterpiece of Vien, the "Sermon of St. Denis" of 1767, had its counterpart in another "machine" at St. Roch in Paris, the "Miracle des Ardents" by the Rubenist and colorist Doyen; both of these paintings were loudly applauded. According to Diderot, Vien was "a new Domenichino and Le Sueur," and his coloristic antagonist "a Rubens." The balance, however, finally turned in favor of the more severe attitude of Vien and his sympathizers, and their new "sublime" style was praised by critics and public alike. It contained the seeds of the future, even though its moral will was stronger than its rather unsubstantial artistic performance. It was David who created the real revolutionary classicism.

CHAPTER ONE

CLASSICISM AND MINOR TRENDS IN THE ART OF DAVID

Vien could teach Jacques-Louis David the externals of classicistic composition. While "the patriarch," as Vien was later called, was far from being a distinguished artist, he was a very sound draftsman in an academic sense and, as the leader of the Ecole de France he had achieved a considerable reputation as a teacher both in France and in Rome. Even Boucher, Vien's exact antithesis in painting, advised the young David as a family friend to get his training under Vien, because the latter was a master craftsman. Of course Boucher added that Vien's art was perhaps a little cold, and that should David find the atelier down there too boring, he had only to drop in from time to time and he would make good Vien's shortcomings, *en vous apprenant à mettre de la chaleur et à casser un bras avec grâce*. David, to be sure, had *chaleur* enough in his own right, if not the sort that Boucher meant. It was just because of his passionate temperament that he was to outstrip both Vien and his own contemporaries. He learned quite a bit from Boucher, as his early works show, and he was never to become an outspoken anticolorist; even in the severity of his later years he still revered Rubens. But Boucher's art to David was, or was to become, something outmoded and dead, belonging to a different age, and from his point of view embodying a false sentiment. In the historical sense, however, David takes on importance for us and for the new development only as a man in his late thirties, when he executed those decisive and characteristic works — above all the "Horatii" — with which he brought the endeavors of his youth to a triumphal close.

His early pictures were still very much in the spirit of the eighteenth century: painterly, somewhat soft, with blue and rose tones. For example, in "The Battle of Minerva and Mars," his competition piece of 1771, Venus borne on clouds is still very reminiscent of Boucher. Similarly, the painting with which he finally obtained the Prix de Rome in 1774, "Antiochus and Stratonice" (Fig. 2), was a favorite subject of the period, at once sentimental, erotic, and moralizing, and one that Ingres was later to recast in hard and frozen forms. The sketch for this picture (formerly in the Chéramy Collection) is fresh in color and filled with painterly qualities; reminiscent of Fragonard, it belongs essentially to the taste of the eighteenth century. In the abundance of details and figures, foreshortenings, and lifeless architecture, it is still far from the typical classicistic ideal of subject and form.

David, stubborn and self-sufficient by nature, was not yet completely won over to the antique. Shortly before his departure for Rome he declared himself opposed to Roman antiquity — *L'antique ne me séduira pas, il manque d'action et ne remue pas* — a position which, in view of what David knew of the classic through his teacher Vien, was easily understandable. And in Rome as a pensioner of the Academy, David did not immediately give himself up heart and soul to antiquity. Like all of the school of Vien in Rome, he was much influenced by the classicism, or pseudoclassicism, of Mengs. The theories of Winckelmann may have contributed much to decide those who still wavered. But already some of his contemporaries (for example Peyron, at whose grave in 1820 David said, *il m'a ouvert les yeux*), were as decidedly modern in their simplified compositions and their nudes as in their neoclassic convictions. David sought his own way slowly, but came eventually to an unequivocal stand.

In Rome, contact with sculptors and continued study of classical sculpture greatly heightened his feeling for three-dimensional form. The treatment of the back of a male nude done in 1777 and usually called "Patroklus" (Cherbourg) already reveals this sense of plasticity. But the Roman-Bolognese school of the seventeenth century, which was still in high favor, also had its effect upon David. His presentation piece for the Academy, "Andromache Bewailing Hector," was criticized because the Andromache had too much of the softness of a Reni Magdalene. It is more significant that an artist such as Caravaggio, reviled though he was by the idealists for his "naturalism," undoubtedly influenced the future leader of the classicists. David's "St. Roch Visiting the Plague-Stricken" (1779, Maison de Santé, Marseilles) is unthinkable without Caravaggio or his followers, among whom Valentin would have been particularly accessible to a Frenchman. The influence of Caravaggio or the Caravaggisti makes itself felt in the simplification and virility of the general tonality. An artist like David, trying to free himself from the luxurious and varied colors of the rococo, must have been greatly attracted by just these particular qualities.

On David's return to Paris his *romance sentimentale*, "Belisarius Asking Alms" (Fig. 3), was much admired. The picture is impressive, warm in tone, and in its formal character strongly suggestive of the seventeenth century. Justinian's general, blind and unjustly exiled, is recognized by one of his former soldiers from whom he begs alms. *Sic transit gloria mundi* is a stirring social theme with a moralizing motto, and therefore a favorite of the period. David was praised because, in contrast to the overcrowded and confused representations of his predecessors, he reduced his composition to four figures only; their severe and noble bearing was admired, as well as the "discretion" with which the great man's "extremely respectable" misfortune was presented. Commenting on this Belisarius in his *Salon*, Diderot said of David: *Ce jeune homme a de l'âme.*

But all this excitement was lost in the tremendous sensation caused by David's "Oath of the Horatii" (Fig. 1). Toward the end of 1782 the Comédie Française put on Corneille's *Horace*. Corneille, like Poussin, filled the need of the prerevolutionary period for a classic yet heroic style. The last act of the play made a strong impression upon David, especially the aged Horace's speech to the people in defence of his accused son, victor over the Curatii. He attempted to portray this scene in a powerful sketch (Louvre; Fig. 5) showing the old man on the platform, his arm around the shoulder of his rigidly erect son, and below, the barely indicated crowd. D'Angiviller, the Minister of Fine Arts, immediately ordered the execution of this sketch. David himself was not satisfied with his own concept. The epigrammatic edge was still missing, and it seemed to him that the portrayal of a "discourse" which one could hear but not see destroyed the unity of the painting. He therefore decided to depict a more precise scene, the oath of the Horatii (drawn, not from the play, but from a classical history of the period), and to show only a few figures, sharply and unambiguously posed. A sketch of this, containing the essentials of the composition we know, was soon completed. But David wanted to produce something uniquely genuine and convincing, to throw his whole personality into the conception. It was as if he wished to fulfill the demand that Diderot had already set forth in his *Salon* of 1771: *Le peintre qui n'a pu dans le moment se faire lui-même ni Romain, ni Brutus, n'a point senti ce que c'est que d'être Brutus et de voir Tarquin sur le trône.* And so, believing that not in Paris but only in Rome could he paint a picture of Roman virtue and patriotism, he proceeded to the Eternal City. There he finished it.

When the work was finally displayed in David's atelier on the Piazza del Popolo, it aroused tempestuous admiration. The aged Battoni, the best-known Italian painter of the time, was as enchanted as David's teacher, Vien, who explained to him that of all his (Vien's) achievements, David was *le plus précieux.* David's atelier was stormed; the press of people had to be regulated by the *carabinièri.* Angelica Kauffmann, Wilhelm Tischbein (Goethe's friend), everyone was enthusiastic. When shown in Paris in 1785, the picture was greeted with the same enthusiasm. All eyes were upon David, and a whole generation suddenly saw an omen in the "Horatii." The critics were united in the most exaggerated praise; David was called the "Athlete" and the "Messiah"; the "Oath of the Horatii" passed for "the most beautiful picture of the century," a *merveille*; one talked of "David's revolution."

In contrast to such delirium, the reaction of a later time is mild. Posterity no longer grasps (unless by a conscious effort of historical orientation) how this picture suddenly rallied the unfulfilled ideals, political, moral, and aesthetic, the hopes, the half-realized tendencies of the period. One sees a yellow-brown canvas, the quiet colors flatly applied, set off only here and there (as in the cloak of the father) by a powerful local red; a composition in part pathetic and declamatory, in part empty: the three Horatii, arrayed one behind the other in profile, step forward, their arms raised in oath towards the three swords which their father, the ancient Horace, holds out toward them. In contrast to this altogether manly, strongly expressed, and plastically executed group, the two women, broken by their conflicting emotions, are pushed to one side as a quiet, prettily stylized foil. These few figures, plus the small background group of the children and their nurse, are placed on a wide stage, closed at the back by arches on heavy, baseless, Doric columns. Surely, despite certain dry passages and an occasional mistake (such as the not altogether resolved perspective of the three warriors), this is still an impressive picture. But why did it seem to satisfy all the artistic longing of the time? Everything else exhibited at the Salon of September 1785 disappeared in the shadow of this one painting. This same Salon was characterized by the critics as the "most imposing in some time," and they emphasized the *ton sévère et soutenu* that dominated many of the large paintings. But in spite of their heroic subjects, neither Vien's "Return of Priam," nor Peyron's "Dying Alcestis," nor Berthélemy's "Manlius Torquatus," could vie with the "Oath of the Horatii."

Artists, critics, and the public were enchanted by David's picture because here for the first time exalted and patriotic feeling had achieved a concentration of form which satisfied the demands of classicistic theory. No one else would have dared to draw the axes so strongly and simply, to put the swordhilts so strikingly in mid-axis as a center of attention, to consummate the action so clearly by formal and artistic means. The serious, sober coloring is to be understood as Spartan and manly. Everything is precise and unambiguous; unity of place, unity of time, unity of treatment — all have been observed. Here is a paradigm of the neoclassic or the neo-Poussinist style, improving on its model in tightness and laconic manner. All the efforts of the previous thirty years to revivify and reform the *grand goût* have here been brought to finished expression. But above all, these technical means allow the idea of the picture to hit one squarely between the eyes. In their oath the Horatii express a patriotism above and beyond everything personal. They are even unconcerned with the lament of their own women, weeping at the fate of brothers and husbands. Thus, they create an extremely masculine image and raise a moral light — inspired and inspiring — against anything feminine, weak, and personal. This is a Spartan and Roman heroism, united with the highest civic virtue. Here is created a highly political symbol at an extremely agitated moment — four years before the outbreak of the Revolution.

With this picture David became the true painter of the new France, and the head of a powerful school that spread far beyond France's borders. "Socrates Drinking the Hemlock" (Salon of 1787; Fig. 4) increased his fame still further. Again this was not a new subject, but one that was closely allied to the new neoclassic sentiment. Socrates is shown sacrificed to class justice. Once more there is a union of moral message and emotion, as the philosopher, all his *grandes pensées* sacrificed, calmly grasps the cup of hemlock. Reynolds, an excellent connoisseur, collector, and theoretician, and at that time an old man, seeing this picture at the Salon, did not hesitate to compare it with the greatest that he knew, "the Sistine Chapel and the Stanze." "This canvas would have gained all honour in Athens at the time of Pericles," he said, and after ten days' close examination he pronounced his verdict: "This picture is in every sense perfect."

In these early works David was not rigid, or at least not as narrowly classicizing and archaizing as one might suppose from these themes and the similar ones to follow. Granted that he attains his impact through this active neoclassic manner; his portraits bear witness that his natural strength really lay more in the direction of realism. At the same time typically romantic features also made their appearance. Long before the German "Nazarenes," David admired Fra Angelico and the sculpture of the Middle Ages. Not only had he studied Poussin, the Bolognese, and Caravaggio, but in his teaching he also praised the artists of an opposite tendency — the Flemish, and above all Rubens, whom he went to Flanders especially to study. Perhaps influenced by the English "gothic revival" that favored legendary and terrible subjects, David painted at this time "The Death of Ugolino" (1786, Valence Museum), a theme of preromantic storm and stress. It was a subject drawn from Dante, known in Germany through Gerstenberg's drama and painted by Reynolds in the early seventies.

Through the study of the Flemings David sought to brighten his palette, which Roman influence had darkened. This he tried to carry out in one of the least "likeable" pictures he ever painted, "Paris and Helen" (1788; Fig. 6). For once there is no sententious and moralizing theme. The definition of the space by successive parallel planes, cut off, as so often in this style, by great hangings, is in the spirit of Poussin. The portico in the background stems from the sixteenth century; these are Goujon's famous caryatids of the Louvre. The other accessories, couch, brazier, etc., are for the first time archeologically exact. The two figures — Paris nude (the first nude that David put into a picture) with his Phrygian cap and his lute on his arm and rosy Helen leaning towards him — are in the prettifying poses of Hellenistic art. In spite of its formal strength, the sentiment of the picture recalls the vanished eighteenth century of Boucher, or the attempts of Vien and the other pseudoclassicists to call forth a new and graceful antique rococo. This *genre agréable* only partially satisfied the real essence of David's genius, and so he turned back to his proper calling, the style *tragique et historique.*

The key picture of the year of the Revolution is altogether in his own style: "Brutus and the Bringing Home of the Bodies of His Sons" (1789; Fig. 7). Brutus, the founder of the Roman Republic, drove out the kings and allowed his own sons to be put to death because they had betrayed the Republic. This was certainly a very dangerous theme for a former *pensionnaire du roi* to send to an exhibition sponsored by the king. In spite of efforts to have it withdrawn, it was shown, and created a tremendous sensation. But even less than with the "Horatii" did the furor it aroused depend upon any appreciation of artistic values, for the picture is much less well knit and falls to pieces as a composition. It was the picture's antiquarianism and the careful observance of what was called "costume" that was admired. The head of Brutus is taken from the Capitoline bust, the statue of Roma from an antique original; as for the interior decoration, the furniture (for which special models were made) and the dresses all claim archeological correctness. Delécluze, the pupil of David, writing later, tells us that the fashions of the Revolution, then being born, were decisively influenced by the details of this picture. Not only was the furniture imitated, but the dresses too, and the flattering coiffure derived from a Roman bacchante which the daughters of Brutus exhibit became fashionable among Parisiennes. It need not be emphasized that the picture would not have been so exhaustively studied if its political character had not made it the sensation of the day. "Through his Brutus as through his Horatii, David talks to the people more directly and more clearly than all the inflammatory writers whom the regime has confiscated and burned." So wrote a contemporary.

In this fashion David, a painter, became the man of the Revolution, dictator of the artistic realm of his time. Out of a long and gradual development, in close rapport with tendencies which a previous generation had prepared, his native impulse and his impetuous temperament succeeded in fusing the moralistic and the antiquarian into a political creation — a living thing that was part of an extraordinary time. Of all the creative artists of Europe, who could say as much? Perhaps Schiller with his *The Robbers*, bearing the motto *in Tyrannos* and written only about a decade before the Revolution. Or Rousseau — but less through his imaginative works than through the influence of his principles (his *Confessions* were not published until 1782, four years after his death). Nor are there real parallels to David's exciting and concentrated creation in French poetry, at least nothing of a similar intensity. The political poems of the half-Greek André Chénier, himself a martyr to the Revolution (one, the "Jeu de Paume," begins with a glorification of David), did not inflame the people. In the plastic arts there seems to have been no one to contest

David's "popularity" — his flair for the need of the historic hour. Beside him the others are only artists. The impetus to action developed out of a moralizing point of view and operated through the medium of a severe and quasi-abstract artistic style. It not only followed the trend of the time, rather it added as well its own momentum and became decisive for the future — this is the significance of the *révolution Davidienne.* Though in the social and literary fields this change had already been prepared in the eighteenth century, if not earlier, it reached its full and evident artistic fruition only with David, and did not quickly disappear from French art of the nineteenth century. In this sense David became a modern artist — the artist with whom the painting of the nineteenth century began.

David did not confine his political activity to artistic fields alone, and so created for himself a difficult personal destiny. A similar participation in politics was later to make life hard for Courbet. David took an active part in the Revolution and, consonant with his temperament, enlisted on the extreme wing of the Jacobins under Robespierre. It was only natural that he should have been sucked into their downfall, since he had many enemies, particularly among the members of the old Academy, which he hated bitterly and whose abolition he had brought about. Only thanks to the great respect for his art — placed so decisively at the service of the Revolution — did he escape with his life. He was twice imprisoned, but his sentences were mild and allowed him a chance to paint.

David has often been reproached because he, the painter of the Revolution par excellence, went over to Napoleon without hesitation. He served the Empire and glorified the "tyrant" with the same zeal he had displayed for the Revolution. It must be remembered, however, that Napoleon's Empire was not a continuation of the old royal line, but was born of the Revolution and unimaginable without it. The Revolution not only marked a social process, the rise to power of the *tiers état*, it had also a strongly nationalist and patriotic side. How deeply this had penetrated moralistic-artistic thought has been seen in the sentiment preferred, and above all in the themes chosen, by David and his like-minded contemporaries before the Revolution.

Napoleon was the most complete embodiment of this aspect of the people's longing. It was, therefore, altogether natural that, like countless others, David should have been completely taken in and enchanted with the "heroism" of his personality. Upon Napoleon's return from Elba, David, disregarding any personal danger, outspokenly and unconditionally declared himself for the Emperor, and against the Bourbons. And after the Restoration, he scorned seeking mercy from the legitimist ruler, although it was suggested that such a plea would fall on favorable ears. Because he was faithful to his ideals he had to expiate in his old age the sins he had committed when, as the man of the Revolution he had been more impressionable than steadfast. For these sins he was bitterly reproached, both during his lifetime and after. The old artist and fighter had to flee to Brussels and was exiled from France; not even the corpse of the greatest heroic painter of modern France was allowed to return home.

David's artistic and historic significance lies wholly within two closely connected heroic epochs: the Revolution and the Empire. What he did before 1785 was essentially preparation; what he did after 1815 was only a weary echo. Whenever the demand arose, his capacity as a painter was entirely at the service of the cause. In addition, by virtue of his extraordinary skill in the administration and politics of the arts he played a significant public role, especially during the critical period of the Revolution. Though he did not have, or wish to have, the title *premier peintre* which was Lebrun's under Louis XIV, yet his sphere of power was just as all-inclusive and the rules he laid down just as dictatorial. They were directed against the slovenliness, the factional tyrannies, the mediocrity and arrogance of the Academy, in general against all those who were responsible for the training given in art. He proclaimed penalties for restorers who, as a profession and with the protection and favor of the authorities, destroyed the finest works of art. In brief, he tried to put through a whole mass of reforms, most of which, unfortunately, did not last beyond the period of his own unlimited power. He also controlled the artistic arrangements of the great festivals of the "Etre Suprême" and the "Régénération," and the solemn funeral processions of Marat and others. In imitation of the Greeks and Romans he had medals struck to commemorate important events. He had obelisks erected in the provinces decorated with bronze obtained by melting down Parisian statues, the *débris du luxe des cinq derniers despotes français.* These things and many more he carried out, the inevitable accompaniment of such political revolution.

The more immediate the problem, the more significant and meaningful was David's own creation. In the fall of 1790 he was commissioned to eternalize "The Tennis Court Oath." On June 20, 1789, the representatives of the "third estate," meeting in the hall of the Jeu de Paume, had sworn never to part until they had accomplished their ends, a memorable occasion which constituted the opening act of the Revolution. The realistic representation of a contemporary event was, in a certain sense, a novelty. To be sure, the deeds of Louis XIV were chosen by Lebrun and others as preferred subjects for pictorial narrative, but generally they were given allegorical dress. So too in the eighteenth century realistic representations of contemporary happenings were rare, if we except pictures of particular battles.

It was typical of that sense of workmanship and of reality, which, in spite of all classicistic theories, were fundamental to David that he succeeded in mastering such a living theme, even though the project was not carried beyond the preliminary sketches (Figs. 9–11). Here the painter of the stylized "Horatii" and "Paris and Helen," pictures limited to a few plastically conceived figures, was confronted with the problem of gathering together in a unified scene one hundred excited, gesticulating men, all dressed in contemporary costume. More than that, he had to paint them as heroes without losing realistic accuracy, either in such details as the portraitlike main figures or in the whole. David knew how to combine exact observation with a feeling for the monumental sharpened by a study of the antique and of the art of the seventeenth century. By this combination he achieved a style of great breadth. The most surprising quality of the picture is its representation of space, the feeling of depth in this great, dreary tennis court. The gray walls rise large and bare, broken simply by broad surfaces of light. The whole upper space, nearly two thirds of the area of the picture, is enlivened only by high-set windows and by draperies which the storm blows into the room. One can see the crowd, excited auditors of the gathering, pushing in at the windows. The vacuum above effectively sets off the multitude below; in the main group Président Bailly is raised high above the rest on a table, his arm uplifted. The delegates surround him on all sides, their arms outstretched as they call to him and take their oath. It is the gesture of the Horatii, multiplied and freed from its stiffness. Of course, certain statuelike poses, heroic and stylized in character, do remain, but everywhere the individual form breaks through.

No one but David, "the author of the Brutus and the Horatii, this patriotic Frenchman, whose genius foreshadowed the Revolution" could have been chosen to solve this problem. As David's commission continued, "his energetic brush may record for our great-grandchildren what, after centuries of oppression, France has done for them." Unfortunately the picture, projected on a tremendous scale, was not executed; it exists only in an accurate study (well known through engravings). This was exhibited in the Salon of 1791 and is now in the Louvre.

The three pictures David painted of the "martyrs" of the Revolution are as large in conception and as new. Conceived as portraits, they rise above the representational sphere into the domain of universal tragedy. The first was that of Lepeletier de Saint-Fargeau, who was murdered early in 1793 by a counterrevolutionary — *assassiné lâchement pour avoir voté la mort du Tyran* — that is to say, Louis XVI. In David's original picture this sentence could be read on a piece of paper stuck to the royalist sword near the wound of the victim. The upper part of the body is bare; the head lies upon a thick pillow as if in sleep. The drawing is vigorous, and the whole seems as monumental as a marble statue on a tomb. The painting has been destroyed and is known only through an engraving (Fig. 12) that was made at the request of the Revolutionary Convention.

Much more famous, above all for its tremendous power of suggestion, is the representation of the murdered Marat (1793; Fig. 14). David does not depict the actual murder of Marat by Charlotte Corday. According to his own statement, he shows us Marat as he had seen him the day before his death when, on the instructions of the Jacobin Club, he had gone to visit the sick man. "I found him in a striking pose. Next to him was a block of wood, on which were paper and ink. Out of the bathtub his hand wrote down his last thoughts for the good of the people. . . . I thought it would be interesting to show him in the attitude in which I had discovered him."

Once more David's inherent power of realism, his faculty for seizing a likeness, was combined with that ability to stylize and to simplify which his classical education had taught him. A direct, convincing impression has been fixed in the simplest of forms and with a minimum of means. Again the whole upper section of the picture surface is left impressively empty — a method David had learned from the study of Caravaggio or his school. The space where the action takes place is indicated concisely and with utmost sincerity. A great wooden block or box laconically inscribed À MARAT DAVID is pushed forward right to the picture frame; behind it, in the second and last plane extends the gray-brown bathtub, three quarters of it covered by a wooden board. The head and shoulders of the murdered man rise out of the long, narrow box like Lazarus from his coffin. The breast with its tiny wound is placed in shadow. Marat's head is thrown back in death agony, and twisted around it is a kind of gray-white turban. From under this his face emerges half in light and half in shade, the eyes closed, the mouth anguished yet partly smiling; it has extraordinary plastic force, and is a striking likeness; it is also infinitely moving. Such grand simplicity is attained only by masterly composition. The gray, brown, and stone-green tones applied in flat planes are likewise simple; in their austerity, in their calculated overlapping, they too stem from the school of Caravaggio. It is precisely by these very delicate values and by the varying but moderate contrasts of light and shade that a painterly and colorful impression is achieved, in spite of the reticent handling. The essential fact is that all these accomplishments are only the means by which David expresses a spiritual concept. In these "martyr" canvases he portrays the tragedy of the patriot (and later in life David still viewed Marat as such) who, in the midst of carrying out his patriotic duties, falls a victim to the dagger.

The third picture of this series is the unfinished "Bara" (Fig. 13). Of the three representations of lives sacrificed to the Revolution, this is the tenderest, the most graceful, and therefore the least striking. The youth, who took part in the war in the Vendée as a drummer boy and was shot by the legitimists, lies with his fine, long-limbed body completely naked, his head leaning against the hillside and his somewhat feminine hips bent sharply out. His eyes half closed, he presses the national cockade to his breast. He might be a Narcissus seeking his own image in the spring — and indeed he bears a distant resemblance to Poussin's famous picture in the Louvre. David's usual pathos is altogether missing. This is no more than a nude youth, beautiful, if somewhat hermaphroditic.

David considered the "Marat" and the "Lepeletier" his best works, and when they were given back to him in 1795 kept them near him in his atelier, in spite of worth-while offers. As a matter of fact, these pictures of the Revolution are painted with a freshness and a clairvoyant naïveté that is more and more lacking in his constructed compositions; even Delécluze said of the former that they were created as if in a trance. One can see in them the fever that shook these passionate men and artists during those terrible, immeasurably wrought-up years.

David was deeply affected by the fall of Robespierre, for whom only a few days before he had interceded warmly. Moved and broken, he closed his stuttered speech of defence with the assurance that henceforth he would attach himself *aux principes et non pas aux hommes*. Political interests had given life to his art. Once he had to renounce these, his principles could only be applied to purely artistic problems. Thus, the more rigorously he held to these principles the more aesthetic and empty they became.

This is demonstrated in his major work of this period, "The Rape of the Sabines" (Fig. 8), begun when the Directory released him from prison, and completed in 1799 after unrelenting labor. This picture was to surpass all his previous attainments in its adherence to those principles demanded by the *beau idéal.* David himself was no longer altogether pleased with his earlier achievements, not even with the "Horatii." He found them (in his own words) too "small" and "mean" in drawing, too deliberately anatomic, and so calculated in their color arrangement that they neglected the power of local tones. He also felt that they were too much influenced by Roman antiquities, the only monuments to which anyone had paid any attention during his Italian sojourn. He regretted having lost so much time upon them. Now, after nearly a quarter of a century, ancient art was much better and more intimately understood. In the "Sabines" he wanted to create a work "in the Greek style" — that is, a work of increased refinement and abstraction. The single figures were to be given a greater emphasis, and they are in fact executed with much more refinement and painterly restraint. The figures of the "Horatii" are crude in comparison to the protagonists in the "Sabines," the spear-swinging Romulus and his opponent, the bearded Sabine king. One striking innovation is that both are naked. They are modeled after famous classical types and their elegant proportions recall Hellenistic statues like the Apollo Belvedere, brought back to Paris at this time as part of Napoleon's booty. The women who have thrown themselves between their struggling husbands and brothers are particularly lovely. The one-sided emphasis on plasticity found in the "Horatii" is lessened and the figures are more successfully disposed upon the picture plane.

The painting called forth enthusiastic applause which this time could contain no extra-artistic elements. It was particularly admired in those elegant upper strata of Directoire society which had once more become extremely "aesthetic." David's position and fame were altogether reëstablished. The only people to take exception were a small but very interesting group among David's troop of pupils. For them David's new stylizing effort was not nearly radical or abstract enough, not sufficiently Greek or "Etruscan," and in general did not satisfy their archaizing ideals. We will return to them later.

Obviously nothing so thoroughly consistent could be asked of

David; his innate plastic realism made it impossible. As a matter of fact, in this picture David was not moving toward the Greek, but (perhaps unconsciously) in the direction of seventeenth-century painting. His model was not Poussin's laconic, dramatic, style with a few nudes on a narrow stage, but rather the early Poussin who filled his scenes with many active figures. The second version of Poussin's "Rape of the Sabines" (New York, Metropolitan Museum) had a great influence on David's picture, not merely because of its similar theme, but even more particularly through its composition and details (children crawling about on the ground among the combatants, horses without bridles in misinterpretation of the antique, etc.). In comparison with Poussin, despite the multitude of his figures David displays a much greater simplification and subtlety in the relations of the picture plane to the three-dimensional picture space. There is an intimation here of a new stylistic tendency, but fresher energies than David's were needed to carry it to completion.

Under Napoleon David retained the outstanding social and artistic position which the "Sabines" had reconquered for him during the Directory. His atelier became famous all over Europe. *Voilà mon héros*, David said to his pupils when General Bonaparte, only twenty-eight years old but already glorious, visited him in his atelier for the first time. His hero worship had at last found its object. And Napoleon valued David; he had even secretly offered him a refuge in his Italian camp when the painter was in a dangerous political position due to his intercession for Robespierre. For Napoleon needed artists to glorify his name, and could not afford to let such an important man escape him.

But neither at the time of their first meeting, when Bonaparte was received with all pomp in Paris after the peace of Campoformio, nor later, did David manage to obtain a long portrait sitting from his much preoccupied subject; an oil sketch from nature was all he ever managed. Nevertheless, an idealized picture has become famous: "Napoleon at St. Bernard." David had originally wanted to show the general on the battlefield, sword in hand. Napoleon dryly replied that this was not the pose in which battles were won. He wanted to be shown *calme sur un cheval fougueux*. Therefore, David could only heroize the scene and its accessories: the rearing steed at the edge of the rocks and the gray cloak blown out by the wind. Napoleon himself, with his quiet face and calm gesture, shows the army its way forward and upward. His silhouette is set sharply against a sky broken by clouds and lightning; barely suggested snowy peaks rise into the clouds. On a jagged rock are cut the words BONAPARTE, HANNIBAL, CAROLUS MAGNUS.

Named *premier peintre* of the Empire, an honor which he had refused during the Consulate, David was once more given the most important commissions. They were far removed from his theorizing ideals; instead, to his good fortune, they led him back to the living present. His realistic sense, otherwise condemned to find expression in frozen forms, regained the upper hand. The significance of these works surpressed his own intention. To his surprise, he discovered in the great official pictures that he was required to do for the Emperor *plus de ressources pour l'art qu'il n'y serait attendu*. Only two of the four great commissions in commemoration of Napoleon's coronation were carried out: the famous "Sacre" (or, "Napoleon Crowning Josephine") and the "Distribution of the Eagles" (Figs. 15–18). The "Reception of Napoleon at the Hôtel de Ville" exists only in a fine large sketch.

These ceremonial representations of contemporary events were the continuation of what David had begun at the start of the Revolution in his "Jeu de Paume." The compositions he now created point the way for a whole genre (most subsequent coronation and ceremonial pictures are unthinkable without David). In the study for the "Jeu de Paume" David had already shown a striking exactness in detail. All the chief actors, at least, are rendered with characteristic features and gestures. In spite of this, the unity, the movement and excitement of the whole could not at any price be lost. In Napoleon's official commissions nearly everyone had to be recognizably portrayed, yet at the same time it was imperative to preserve the impression of a great ceremony. Even the sketches were submitted to the censorship of the Emperor and the court. Each figure was studied for action by a sketch in the nude (for this purpose David was given soldiers as models), and finally for its details of clothing and portraiture.

The compositions, likewise, had to pass the censors. David had made a very striking sketch of the famous precedent set at the coronation. Napoleon, instead of bowing humbly to receive his crown from the Pope, stood proudly erect and with an imperious gesture set it upon his own head, while the Pope sat quietly behind him, as if intimidated. It did not seem wise to Napoleon, or perhaps to his counselors, to show this historic scene in a public picture; it would have proclaimed *urbi et orbi* the ruler's usurpation. So it was replaced by a much less Napoleonic and also less Davidian scene: the Emperor holding the crown in his upraised arms over the kneeling Josephine. Similarly in the "Distribution of the Eagles" an important passage in the original composition was changed in accordance with the desires of the rulers, this time, to be sure, for artistic reasons. David had placed over the group of the flag bearers a laurel-throwing Winged Victory, which was needed to tie together two separated groups. This figure was found to be *vieux jeu*, a relapse into the sort of eighteenth century allegory which David himself had fought. In the suppression of this figure, the patrons were, for once, more modern, and more realistic, than the artist — although the composition certainly suffered.

But it is clear that David achieved neither of the two great ceremonial pictures for Napoleon through realism alone. Obviously his extraordinarily strong sense of reality was, here as elsewhere, the first requirement for a really convincing presentation. As in the "Jeu de Paume," however, David could never have encompassed these grand scenes without a mastery of space composition, of group arrangement, and of balanced movement which were the fruit of many years' study and effort within the limits of the classical style. This is true of the whole as well as the parts. The influence of tradition is so far-reaching that David employs figures from Raphael's Stanze for certain motifs, and resurrects Giovanni da Bologna's "Mercury" for the first color bearer. He is not to be reproached for this. Many painters of the nineteenth century — Delacroix, even Manet and Van Gogh — from time to time consciously borrowed classical and Renaissance figures. In these pictures the most important problem for David was to create a unity out of many and various details. He succeeded in the "Sacre" even better than in the "Distribution of the Eagles" by an articulation of composition and a control of space, and no less by painterly qualities and the distribution of light on colored planes. It is significant that an artist like Géricault, who was a painter to his fingertips, should have declared that the whole right side of the "Sacre" was as beautiful "as if Rubens had painted it."

Looking at the drawing for the third Napoleonic picture — "The Reception of the Emperor and Empress at the Hôtel de Ville" — with its state coach, its rejoicing crowds, its balconies filled with people, one understands what Géricault, who took the trouble to visit the exiled old man in Brussels, admired in David. Beneath his technical mastery there is often, though not always, that stormy and exciting movement which the French call *fougue.* A passage such as that on the left side of the drawing, with its rearing horses and hurrying people with wreaths, could have been sketched by Géricault from first to last. How many similar official ceremonies have been painted since then in France and elsewhere! How often they have remained cold and prosaic, or become confused and declamatory! The fusion of reality and majestic movement that David partly achieves in the "Sacre" and in the "Reception" has hardly ever been attained since.

Considered externally the two great works, the "Sacre" (begun 1805, finished 1808) and the "Distribution of the Eagles" (also called "Serment des Drapeaux," exhibited 1810), were the climax of David's artistic career. The Emperor himself, in a famous preview of the "Sacre" after a long scrutiny took off his hat to David and said: *C'est bien, M. David, c'est très bien.* The master was surrounded by a crowd of students. Many among them, like Gros, were already famous in their own right, but they were still true to him. His influence extended throughout Europe.

Now again we encounter the characteristic phenomenon of

David's curiously and tragically split personality. His honors and his dictatorial position did not suffice. Nor were his powerful grasp of the realities of the Revolution and the Empire, or his enthusiastic devotion to their heroic accomplishments enough for him. His ideals remained to be fulfilled, and these lay along that course which he had begun to pursue (or at least believed he had) in the "Sabines." He sought emancipation from the older and outworn classicism which still contained so much of the seventeenth and eighteenth centuries. He wished to lead painting back to a greater simplicity, and to this end he sacrificed the dramatic effect (peinture d'expression) so beloved of him and the earlier classicists. The figures were no longer tied into excited groups but left isolated and rendered more carefully in order to fix attention upon each individual person. Along these and similar lines he often liked to theorize to his students. He believed he had found this ideal of calm, equal, and consistent execution in the Greeks (and thereby approached Winckelmann's ideas more closely than he had formerly). He also found it in the Italian primitives — Giotto, Masaccio, Fra Angelico, Perugino — whose paintings he greatly admired, confined as they were within one plane.

With these ideas he moved, about 1800, into that pan-European archaizing movement to which the German early romantics and Nazarenes belonged shortly afterward. This movement evoked in David's own atelier most peculiar eccentricities but led also to significant developments. It was tragic that these ideas and theories, with which David tormented himself for years, did not revitalize his own ideal art. The paradigm of this new doctrine was the tremendous canvas of "Leonidas at Thermopylae." He worked on this from 1800 to 1814, his students collaborating both on the composition and the theory. But the picture has much less vitality even than the "Sabines" and clearly shows the weaknesses of too much meditation.

Archaizing effort is less evident in other pictures of the period, but these, on the other hand, exhibit a porcelain, Canova-like smoothness, as in "Sappho and Phaon" (painted 1809 for Duke Youssoupoff; now in the Hermitage). Here the exaggerated mannerism in the posing of the tender central group far exceeds the earlier "Paris and

Helen." Surely this painting is connected with David's preference for the mannerist predecessors of Rubens. It is remarkable that such a thoroughly artificial picture should have been painted by the same artist and at the same period as the "Sacre," which, despite its ceremony, is so healthy and so living.

In the works executed after David's banishment, the glassy over-all tone and the hard colors become constantly more disagreeable. His themes and compositions (Mars disarmed by Venus, and the like) grow ever more conventional and empty. Unlike most great artists, David did not develop a style of old age. He lacked those large inner "ideas" with which such geniuses as Titian, Rembrandt, and Poussin overcame the natural physical decline and rose to the sublime. David's "grand manner" was from the first too theoretical, and it faded more and more as the possibility of its exerting moral influence was withdrawn. For such influence the ground had long been cut from under him; in his old age the contact with contemporary events which had formerly supplied so much of his vitality was lacking also. Consequently — for internal as well as for external reasons — it was impossible for the aging David to rise above himself.

How much David needed this contact with life, how much strength he drew from it, is shown by his altogether preëminent portraits. Here he was dealing directly with life, and the power of reality that was so deep in him is expressed with full force. To be sure the portraits of his pupil Ingres are much more popular; refinement and sureness of line and delicate harmony of color nuances make them captivating, and these qualities the master's works generally lack. But they have a nobility and a virility, a strength of characterization occasionally reminiscent even of Daumier (especially in the portrait drawings of the Revolutionary period), which give David the portraitist an independent and an exceptional personality. As in the "Jeu de Paume," the "Marat," the "Sacre," and the other representations of contemporary happenings, so too in the portraits the realism natural to David could break through the stylized neoclassic sentiment and form which long training had made his own.

David's equestrian portrait of Count Potocki (1781; Poland, Branicki Collection) still shows the original "Rubenist"; it is a painted parade piece — Van Dyck plus the rococo. Likewise, the portraits of his parents-in-law, the Pécoul couple (1784; Fig. 20), still have a warmth of tonality and for all their freshness and life do not surpass the general style of their time.

Only at the period when he was painting the "Jeu de Paume" did David's portraits become more firm, more solid, and more compact. There are altogether surprising charcoal sketches and paintings of Danton, Bailly, and many others. "Gérard and His Family" (Le Mans Museum) may serve as an example of the group portrait. The heavy-set man in a light blouse sits with his legs widespread, his youngest boy between his knees, the little girl beside him at the spinet, the grown sons behind; everything is simple and unaffected and yet held together by warmth of sentiment. The eighteenth century in France can offer no such forthright presentation of middle-class humanity. In England Hogarth and Raeburn come most readily to mind, but neither achieved such simple grandeur.

Such portraits by David as the well-known pair of M. and Mme. Sériziat (1795; Fig. 19) are of another sort. Here the element of linear decoration comes once more to the fore. The manner of stylization is that with which David treated the "Paris and Helen," or the "Sappho and Phaon." This is evident both in the elegant outline of the young woman (who was Mme. David's sister), and in the great refinement of color with which the white dress and green hat are handled. It is equally evident in the whole attitude and bearing of the young man, with his crossed legs in yellow stockings, his brown jacket, the riding whip in his hand, and the way in which he is posed against the bright, cloud-filled sky. For this manner, as for the previous one, there was little comparable in England.

There is a whole series of portraits in this same style. The best known is that of Mme. Récamier, who is shown reclining on her sofa in a simple but elegant white dress, and barefooted (1800, not completely finished; Fig. 22). At her side, as a vertical counterpoise, stands a classic candelabrum. The whole is a tour de force of overrefined simplicity. The portrait of Pope Pius VII (1805; Fig. 21), on the other hand, has a freedom from artificiality which David never equaled. Despite the detailed execution of the accessories such as the gold embroidery on the robe, the spirit of the expression dominates. The countenance is half-embarrassed, half-cunning, superior and yet humble. The ruler of Christendom is held in the grip of the new Imperator. All this is rendered with such masterly and restrained power that, like Reynolds when he saw the "Socrates," one can only compare it to the greatest examples in the history of portraiture.

At the close of his life, in Brussels, David painted one of his most impressive portraits. The old master was touched once again by the living present and did not fail; in fact, here one can almost speak of a sublimation of his art through a style of old age. The portrait is that of the "Trois Dames de Gand" (Louvre; perhaps done with the help of his pupil, Navez), showing an old woman sitting full face to the camera eye, and her two daughters behind her. Nothing remains of the prettiness and flattery of line that characterized the two Sériziats. Apart from the quaint details of the costumes, which, in so many pictures of this period claim too much attention, it is amazing to see the extent to which David, even in his old age, has kept his courageous sense of reality. At the same time he retains his ability to grasp the outline of a stylized form (as in the young woman with the comb in her hair). The color too has more body and warmth, since the Rubenist element which emerges from time to time throughout his work seems to have reappeared once more in Rubens' own country.

David's portraits supplement the body of his other works in a very valuable way. They confirm our impression of the great power residing in the painter, a power only occasionally exhibited in his program pictures. A landscape (Fig. 23) which David painted from the window of his prison, a view of the Luxembourg done in a realistic, dashing manner, and a still life like Chardin (Brussels) should also be mentioned here. To David's mind, of course, things of this sort were only amusing bypaths. It is his heroic vision and the tenseness of his moral drive that give him historical importance. He is the heroic and ethical painter of an heroic and ethical period — the Revolution. Although many large and generous impulses were reported of him, his character has been much censured. It may have been ambitious, vacillating, even cowardly, as the character of his period was more than necessarily brutal, petty, and disagreeable in its details. This no more affects David's artistic purpose than it invalidates the tremendous ideas of the time. Of all those who strove and aspired with him, of the many who subscribed to pseudoclassical ethical points of view similar to his, he alone was borne above the crowd. This is because in him alone a sense of reality was to a significant degree combined with an imperative craving for an ethical form. When only his ideals were dominant, his art froze (*qu'importe la vérité si les attitudes sont nobles?*), because he then lacked that clarity of vision which only the greatest artists possess. The proof of this is to be seen in his many sterile idealistic pictures, a sterility already evident in the "Sabines" and the "Leonidas." But, like Antaeus, as soon as his feet touched the earth his strength flowed back. Only then could his strong convictions and great forms find expression. The "Horatii," the "Socrates," and the "Brutus," each was a grand gesture, an ethical demand for the Revolution; but only the works drawn directly from immediate contemporary happenings, like the "Marat," transcended the artistic tendencies then current. Almost against David's will, the "Jeu de Paume" and the "Sacre" beat new paths. Through the medium of his art, and without allegory, the immediate even becomes the symbol of a new world. It was no less an artist than Delacroix who called David *le père de toute l'école moderne.*

CHAPTER TWO

ULTRACLASSICISTS AND ANTICLASSICISTS IN THE DAVID FOLLOWING

Gérard, Girodet, Guérin, Les Primitifs

For a long time David's own production and artistic achievement were compromised and overshadowed by the *Davidiens.* David himself, when he followed his preconceived notions of the *beau idéal plastique et intellectuel* too closely, had painted a whole series of lifeless pictures. But for a time David's entire production was seen only through the medium of an endless crowd of untalented imitators. Unlike David, they had never come to close grips with reality and could only reiterate the heroizing schemes. This Davidian epidemic spread throughout Europe. Every museum in every country is filled with spiritless representations carried out in identical pseudoheroic formulas of content and composition.

It was only natural that David's reputation should have declined during the period of Courbet and fallen off even more sharply during the ascendancy of the Impressionists, artists whose ideals were so opposed to his. But the work of his second- and third-rate followers, intermingled with his own, considerably prolonged the misjudgment of David's art. Their productions had first to be set aside before a proper estimate of David's achievement could be reached. Delécluze covers whole pages of the memoirs of David with lists of the names of David's pupils, names of the most various nationalities. Many of them must have carved out at least temporary reputations. Several certainly continued or in some way modified one of the orientations of the David atelier; two or three show a more or less clear-cut personal character. Only one can be compared with David as a whole, and this, of course, is Ingres, who perhaps even surpassed his teacher.

David, as we have seen, had a highly complex nature. There could be various points of departure from the different facets of his personality and his art. David's heroically ethical creations, the "Horatii," the "Brutus," etc., could be continued, and this was, in fact, done in a variety of ways. His experiments in abstraction and coördination, pictures like the "Sabines" and the "Leonidas," done in what he believed to be the Greek manner, could be carried to their logical conclusion. The grandiose conception of his contemporary representations, the "Jeu de Paume," the "Sacre," etc., which are realistic and yet composed in terms of space — these might be imitated or transformed. Finally, one might be moved by his portrait style. David offered both linear and purely painterly possibilities to be studied and followed.

These different tendencies were not exclusively David's. Although represented during his lifetime only by weaker artists (Regnault, Vincent, etc.), they were an integral part of the general artistic development of the period. It is rare for a period to have but a single orientation, to be only classicist, only romantic, or only realistic. And even when one ideal dominates, as did heroizing classicism during the Revolution and the Empire, many other possibilities of an essentially different kind are hidden beneath the surface.

Classiques and *Ultra-Classiques* were the names given to those artists who allied themselves with David (or his school) insofar as they tried to carry on his linear tendencies. But inasmuch as they altered this manner, softening, sharpening, or exaggerating it, they were carried away from the classical, that is to say from the normative. The current also bore them away from the classicistic. By this term we refer to that dramatic and didactic, sculptural and paradigmatic art which derived spiritually and formally from the Roman antique. David, in continuing the Poussinist effort, was the chief classicistic protagonist.

Modifications of the Davidian could lead to various results. For instance, through an imitation of David's linear propensities, which involved at the same time a weakening and a smoothing down of his art, a certain "manner" (or even various "manners") could develop. A similar phenomenon took place in Italy during the late sixteenth century and in the School of Fontainebleau. The die once cast, it untiringly restamps the same coin, introducing only inconsequential variations; so arose a mannered style, purely decorative, occasionally quite graceful, usually insipid and banal. Such were the works of that band of David's untalented pupils, who discredited his name even during his lifetime. Apart from them, many paintings by Gérard, one of David's favorite pupils, belong in this category.

The development of these same propensities into a real "mannerism" of form must however be more positively evaluated. The evolution here was similar to that in Florence and Parma when, out of the preceding classic style, an art grew up sharply opposed to its balanced and normative principles. It is hardly an accident that Girodet's "Danaë" and indeed many of his female nudes recall the first school of Fontainebleau and remind us of Primaticcio's soft and sensuous play of line. This in its turn stemmed from Parmigianino and the Italian mannerists.

Finally there was one more possibility: to take the still very moderate ideal of purified form which David admired about 1800, and to drive it so far toward abstraction that, theoretically at least, a new art or a new artistic point of view would arise. Pushed to the limit, as it was by Maurice Quaï and the "Barbus," this approach could not live. It exerted, nevertheless, a significant influence, above all on the youthful Ingres.

The best known of that great crowd who continued and vulgarized David's classicistic manner is Francois Gérard (1770–1837). Born in Rome and half Italian, Gérard came to Paris when he was twelve and entered David's atelier at sixteen. His master was particularly fond of him and came to his support when he was in distress during the Revolution. David called on the young painter to help with the execution of the "Lepeletier" of 1793, and obtained him a prize for the sketch of a Revolutionary subject similar to the "Jeu de Paume." This lively sketch of an excited convention session was not carried out any more than was David's great project, whose energy Gérard could certainly not have equaled.

The likable, gracious, and elegant character of Gérard's art had no connection either with the political or the heroic, and he could not, like David, attain his full stature in those fields. He was primarily active as the designer of the illustrations for the lovely Didot editions of Virgil's *Georgics*, Longus' *Pastorals*, and Racine. Here he could work in a graceful, rather idyllic manner, somewhat in the spirit of earlier decades of the eighteenth century. The brutal gestures demanded by his own time were alien to him. Even his large pictures such as the "Belisarius" (1795) contain soft and sentimental features. Gérard's general is a blind old graybeard who has come upon his young emperor wounded by a snakebite, has taken him upon his arm, and, with his staff before him, is tapping his way along. The whole is set in a broad landscape. The theme is compelling, but complicated and vague. This could be any blind man. David's "Belisarius" was a simple and virile representation of the begging hero and set forth a universally valid epigram.

Gérard's best-known work is his "Cupid and Psyche" (Fig. 24). Although much praised when shown at the Salon of 1798, it was even then criticized by many as being too affected and *métaphysique*. The figures, again, are placed in a receding landscape and are partly silhouetted against the sky, an arrangement directly opposed to the classical tradition because it makes impossible a composition in layers of space. David's "Paris and Helen" of ten years before, if somewhat affected, is nevertheless physically solid. By comparison this group of figures is effeminate and precious. Cupid, naked and winged, kisses most tenderly on the brow, a foolish, staring Psyche. Here the *volupté décente* familiar in Vien's Athenian women and in Greuze still plays a part. While the figures of David may suggest marble, or occasionally wax, these smooth, soft groups of Gérard remind us of the *biscuit* which for a time was in such favor for salon statuettes.

In spite of his classicist education, Gérard's later compositions, as for example his "Daphnis and Chloe" (Salon of 1824), are conceived in the same soft and regressive spirit. Even his historical pictures lack energy; "Corinna with her Harp on Cape Misenus" and the "Wounded Greeks" (1822, Lyon), typically romantic subjects such as Delacroix might have treated, fail completely in their coloring. The most striking element in all of them is a clear feeling for landscape.

Gérard's reputation in his own time was not based upon things of this sort, but upon his portraits. The early ones are perhaps his best, as that of his Maecenas and friend, the fashionable miniaturist, Isabey, with his daughter (1795; Fig. 25). Here his work is still free and graceful, though obviously without David's additional strength and directness. For this very reason, however, Gérard retained the favor of "society." Mme. Récamier, for example, was not pleased with David's portrait of her; she found it too severe. When Gérard painted her for Prince Augustus of Prussia, he made her much more feminine and sentimental, leaning back in an armchair; and though he employed the fashionable antique *décor* of colonnades, etc., it was all so much more conventional that the classicism was reduced to a mannered style, with none of the intensity of David's conception.

Under the Empire Gérard became the court painter. The whole iconography of Napoleon's family can be composed from Gérard's paintings and studies. Among them there are some very good pieces, as for example his portrait of Napoleon's mother, Laetitia Bonaparte, in a colonnaded court with Napoleon's bust beside her. The clever and superior expression of the old Corsican woman has been rendered very observantly and even endowed with meaning. The portrait of Josephine, posed in a fashion similar to that of Mme. Récamier, is also good. Here, too, the backdrops of columns and a park are not forgotten, elements that are altogether un-Davidian and lend a somewhat sentimental and romantic touch. His many portraits of contemporary dukes and kings gained Gérard the title of *peintre des rois;* and the lavish scale of his social life — he had the most elegant salon in Paris — earned him the ironic appellation, *roi des peintres.*

But Gérard was not a sovereign painter, even in his own domain of portraiture. In his pictures he plays with a kind of "naturalness" which is supposed to loosen the constraint of the tight Davidian form. Often they sink into mere elegance and triviality; they are mannered, understandably, in view of Gérard's mass production. Nevertheless, there are a few really splendid male portraits, such as the half-length rendering of Murat which in bold and bright fashion sets down the black locks and colored epaulets and braid of the marshal-prince. But Gérard could not master a Napoleon; his well-known gala portrait of the Emperor suffers badly from an overabundance of drapery and is almost reminiscent of the manner of Lawrence. In his whole style and feeling Gérard is much more a painter of women.

Girodet's work, even though not approaching Gérard's in quantitative output or influence, is in many ways more interesting. Anne-Louis Girodet de Roussy *dit* de Trioson (1757–1824) was eighteen when he entered David's atelier. In 1789 he won the Prix de Rome and lived for the next five years in Italy, part of the time under difficult circumstances because of the anti-French feeling in Rome.

One of his early pictures, a "Hippocrates" who returns the gifts of the Persian king, is in its moralizing subject, the simplicity of its space, and its dramatic gestures, still within the bounds of the Davidian tendency. But it already betrays individual gifts, and these are still clearer in his completely successful "Endymion" (1793, Louvre). This painting shows a decidedly romantic feeling and attitude. In earlier representations of the popular scene Luna was personified. Girodet lets the rays of the moon play full upon his lovely sleeper and casts over the whole a dreamlike, mystical, magic light. This use of irrational lighting to establish a mood deviates from the classic or classicistic tradition, and the abnormal elongation and abstraction of the lines of the body are mannerist in tendency.

Girodet was entirely conscious both of his subjectivism and of his departure from the usual Davidian ideals and norms. *Ce qui m'a surtout fait plaisir*, he once wrote to his adoptive father, de Trioson, *c'est qu'il n'est qu'une voix pour dire que je ne ressemble en rien à David.*

There was a spirit of contradiction in Girodet, a sort of rebellious self-consciousness which kept him from any pure imitation of David. On the other hand he was too vacillating a character, too little sure of himself, to be able to pursue his own direction; nor was he one-sided enough to fall into the anti-Davidian circle of those rebellious hyper-sensitives called *les primitifs*. However, he was wholeheartedly opposed to the academic, surpassing even David in his hatred of the Academy. "The Academy of France in Rome," he was quoted as saying, "is only a great royal sheepfold with place for a dozen bell-wethers." Later in life he collected pictures of all sorts: Clouet, Bourdon, Tintoretto, the Carracci, Goyen, Terborch, and others. He was probably, above all, an aesthete; a man of spirit, he labored slowly and with difficulty: "Painting is a job for a galley slave," he said. His literary leanings cost him a great deal of time; prompted by his friend the Abbé Delille, who was spreading *la poésie descriptive* in France and who was admired for his extraordinary recitations, he wrote "Le Peintre," a didactic poem in six cantos concerning the study of nature.

Girodet demonstrated a similar talent in many pictures that display a sort of sharpened and refined mannerism. In contrast to David he always insisted on being imaginatively intellectual. *Girodet est trop savant pour nous*, David said of him; and to him (as Girodet himself informs us) he said: *L'esprit, M. Girodet, est l'ennemi du génie, l'esprit vous jouera quelque mauvais tour, il vous égarera.*

L'esprit led him to very intricate themes, often with strongly romantic overtones. Ossian was the great vogue in France at the turn of the century as he had been in Germany at the time of *Werther*. Napoleon read and liked him. Macpherson's inventions and forgeries were widely known in France through poetic translations. Ossianism served as a sort of fantastic and irrational opposition to the cult of antiquity and the worship of things Greek during the Napoleonic era. Ossian was accounted more soulful than Homer; he was in any case more confused and romantic. Bards, Celtic-Germanic gods, mist-obscured hills, Fingal's caves, and other such dark and "gothic" images were allowed to cloud classicism's clearly presented world. Thus, in his "Apotheosis of the Fallen Heroes" (which Napoleon ordered in

1801 for Malmaison) Girodet hit upon the idea of introducing lyre-brandishing maidens and harp-playing bards who welcome the shades of the Napoleonic generals to the Elysian Fields. In many respects Girodet recalls Fuseli, who was equally mannerist and romantically inclined and fond of gloomy scenes, though much more fanciful. While almost twenty years older than Girodet, Fuseli died three years after him in 1828.

Girodet's "Entombment of Atala" (1808; Fig. 26), taken from Chateaubriand's story, is typical of this new attitude. It embodies the kind of Rousseauesque sentiment continued in Bernardin de Saint-Pierre's *Paul et Virginie*. In the painting however, the chaste and naïve spirit of the novel, bathed in fresh, clear air, has been supplanted by an atmosphere that is gloomy, Catholic, and romantic. The scene shows a dark grotto from which one looks out upon a cross placed high in the forest. The maiden Atala who has died for her beliefs, swathed in a white robe and illuminated by a sharp beam of light, is being carried to her grave by a brown-cowled monk and a youth, her playmate in the wilderness. There is no trace of any of the colorism that Delacroix would have employed — only smooth, dead surfaces of local color.

A sensation was caused by Girodet's immense canvas, "Scenes from the Deluge" (Louvre). Painted in 1806, it was awarded a prize as one of the best pictures of the whole decade (within the category *peintures d'histoire*) at the *concours décennal* of 1810. It must have been the overinvolved subject — the family acrobatically trying to save itself from the flood on a tree already breaking — which made such an impression on both the jury and public. (How far removed it is from the simple and unified sentiment of the late picture by Poussin which may have given Girodet his idea!)

In other pictures of a lighter vein the mannerist element is evident in the exquisite rendering of form, as for example the figures in the "Abduction of Helen" (formerly Rouart Collection); *personnages de crystal*, David called them. It is even clearer in his female nudes, particularly the various Danaë. Among these is a small oval picture showing Danaë seated, naked, with a band of egret feathers in her hair, looking at herself in a hand mirror (Fig. 27). This little picture has all the linear sensuousness and elongated proportion of the body found in Primaticcio and the school of Fontainebleau. Painted in 1900, it was a satire on a well-known actress. The striking face of the bird at the side is a portrait, so that when the picture was shown it created a great scandal. In its minute execution and in its whole mental and formal approach the painting is very typical of Girodet. With just a few changes it might have been created in the sixteenth century.

Though Pierre-Narcisse Guérin (1774–1833) was not one of David's pupils, he did, as David once remarked, "listen at the door of the atelier," and learned so much from the Davidian circle that he cannot be easily separated from it. He was the youngest of the generation of Girodet, Gérard, and Gros, but in his use of elegant line, particularly as he employed it in his later pictures, he has much in common with Girodet, who was the oldest. To Guérin the term "manneristic" can be even more appropriately applied than to the restless and much more romantically conditioned Girodet. Guérin was far from romanticism, and he was neither as sophisticated and acute as Girodet nor as banal as Gérard. His real teacher was J.-B. Regnault. This clever, elegant, and coloristically not untalented artist, as his well-known "Three Graces" in the Louvre shows, struck no fundamentally personal note.

Guérin began with the typically Roman and virile themes of the Revolution: "The Corpse of Brutus," etc. He won the Prix de Rome in 1797 but because of the suspension of the school during Bonaparte's Italian campaign he stayed in Paris. There in 1799 his "Return of Marius Sextus" (Fig. 28) had the sort of success characteristically won by sensational themes. Neither its composition, which follows the Poussin scheme traditionally prescribed for such subjects, nor its expression, which remains stiff and lifeless, nor its coloring, which is somber and unaccented, could by themselves have won the public's favor. The approval was due to the theme, the return of the patriot who, driven out by Sulla's tyranny, arrives home at the very instant his wife succumbs to her sufferings. The allusion is to those emigrants who, forced to flee from the terrorism of the Revolution, found themselves upon their return in wretched circumstances. The reasons for this applause were similar to those which, a decade before, had won approval for David's political scenes of the Revolution, but the values are reversed; now it was not the unthankfulness of the ruling classes that was castigated, but the tyranny of the people. The attempt of the Regnault atelier to play the picture off artistically against David failed. Its artistic means — statuesque poses, constructed space, simplicity of composition — were taken in their essentials from the master's revolutionary and classical storehouse without, however, approaching him in artistic power. Indeed, contemporary criticism was in part opposed to the picture, censuring the contradiction between the desired *sagesse* and *tranquillité* and the actual theatrical pretentiousness.

This inconsistency is also found in Guérin's "Phaedra and Hippolytus" (1803; Fig. 29) which was painted in direct imitation of a scene from Racine's *Phèdre* as performed at the Théâtre-Français. This *goût de la scène*, joined as it was with a certain *grâce sentimentale* procured a great following for him as a *peintre de l'âme* and of *coeurs sensibles.* Others on the contrary (particularly those of David's faction) saw in Guérin an *homme de pure réflexion.* In point of fact he united both elements, sentimental grace and disciplined form. When the latter tendency predominated, as it so often did in his later pictures, it produced cold compositions such as his often repeated "Aeneas Telling Dido of the Misfortunes of Troy" (Louvre; another copy formerly in the Youssoupoff Collection, Leningrad). Here Dido lies in a Mme. Récamier pose on an Empire chaise longue against a rose-daubed sky, while Aeneas is a dandy in a great helmet. It abounds in marble and luxury props. These are used as Ingres himself did not disdain to use them, and as they were still echoed at the end of the century in those marble floors and walls beloved of the English academic painters. A chromolike smoothness and finish characterize even such scenes of "horror" as "Clytemnestra Killing Agamemnon" (1817).

There are, however, other pictures, such as the "Aurora and Cephalus" (1810, Louvre; another example 1811, formerly Youssoupoff Collection), which display more gracefully (perhaps after the model of Girodet) that *exquise sensibilité* for which Guérin was famous. Aurora strews flowers upon the youth whose slumbers are couched in the clouds; the preciously drawn group is lit in bright violet and surrounded by the dark night. The colors are quite smooth, the lilac lacquer tones much too sugary. (This kind of coloring is to be found elsewhere in Europe during this period, for instance, often in Turner and in C. D. Friedrich.)

The "Morpheus and Iris" of 1811, now in the Hermitage, was probably conceived as a pendant to the "Aurora." The graceful nudes posed in strong chiaroscuro recall Correggio or, even more, Parmigianino or Schidone, and show how easily any classicism based upon a concept of form can be transformed into mannerism. Here, too, the painting is extremely smooth; if the facture had been looser, the road to the new painterly style which was to be developed by Guérin's pupils would have been easier to find.

Guérin did not lack external honors (he became member of the Institute, director of the Academy in Rome, and a baron), and as a teacher he achieved a well-founded fame. Even more than David he knew how to bring out the real abilities of his pupils without forcing his own manner upon them. For this reason such diverse talents as Ary Scheffer and Delaroche could both emerge from his atelier. It was his particular merit to have been, and more than in name alone, the teacher of the pioneers of the new movement, Géricault and Delacroix.

The strangest and most radically exaggerated continuation of David's leanings towards abstraction was to be found in a small group, "Les Primitifs," whose significance has never been fully appreciated. The reason (and it is a good one) for this neglect lay in the group's pictorial impotence. Its artistic production hardly got out in public and is today altogether lost. Yet the small band cannot be overlooked; in demanding that the ideal style of the period be stretched until it snapped they were symptomatic of a movement which entirely altered the character of France's classicism. Its influence upon Ingres' early evolution is clear. We know of the group through the enthusiastic effusions of the early romantic writer Charles Nodier and through the soberer recordings of David's own pupil Delécluze, who at the turn of the century had a chance to observe at close range the sect's rise and fall.

Most of the members of this sect of "Primitifs" or "Penseurs" or "Barbus" were Delécluze's fellow students in David's atelier. As early as the end of the nineties David had begun to draw away from that didactic classicism which was Roman and sculptural, French and dramatic. We have seen how he turned toward the "primitives" of the *quattrocento*, how he sought to become "Greek," and how, both in the "Sabines" and in the more advanced "Leonidas," his attempt failed. But these new ideas came to David's pupils not only from their master; they were in the air. Even though confused, they were extremely exciting as is always the case when a new style is in the process of formation. They were embodied most purely and directly in those newly discovered monuments, the Greek or "Etruscan" vases. To certain of these pupils these ideas gave an entirely new understanding of life, amounting to a sort of religion. This explains the utter disappointment these youths must have felt before such a painting as the "Sabines." The more the regular Davidians praised the picture as something "Greek" and altogether new, a climax in fact, the more disillusioned were the "Barbus." Though superficially, with such elements as the nude figures, it conformed to the "Greek" ideal which they forthwith had made their own, they felt that this painting was a betrayal because it satisfied none of their longing for a new and purified "Greek style." Their disappointment grew to contempt, nearly to hatred. Among these radicals David and his work were abusively accounted *vieux jeu*, rococo, Pompadour, Van Loo (after the sensuous mythological painter of the eighteenth century). Naturally these heretics could not be allowed to stay in the master's school. David forbade them to disturb the work of the others by their talk or by their presence. So there arose a kind of "secession" which, as is so often true of secessions, was right because it was the road to the future.

Essentially it was a small sect which was joined by writers and poets of the *avant garde* (as they would be called today). All were mere youths, hardly twenty years old, and among them was the fiery and imaginative Charles Nodier. The spiritual leader of the band was Maurice Quaï. Nodier described him as a prophet filled with his heavenly mission, and admired him as the handsomest, the most lovable, and the purest human being he had ever seen. Quaï and certain of his closest disciples wore only Greek mantles, and in a fashion extraordinary for the time they let their beards grow (whence their nickname, "Barbus").

These were merely the externals. What Quaï and his followers strove for in holy earnest was a real and unrestricted return to the "primitive." No doubt this was still one of the echoes of Rousseau's maxims; but they did not wish to return to original "nature," to the noble savage described at about the same time by Chateaubriand in his *Atala* and *René*. Rather they sought deliverance and salvation in a culture handed down by the most ancient tradition, unspoiled by civilization, and its naïveté still close to nature. Their holy books were Homer, Ossian (who for them was as old and as naïve), and characteristically, the Bible. In this they sharply opposed the heathen, ancient Roman, morally active cult of the preceding generation. It was natural that the youth of the generation which immediately followed the excitement of the Revolution should seek a contrast to its movement and its heroic dramatics in an inwardness, a peace of soul, almost a quietism. All show was distasteful to them. The time of Pericles, which the majority of their contemporaries simply accepted as the golden age of mankind, they saw as a *siècle de Louis Quatorze* and despised it accordingly.

They had a similar point of view toward the representational arts which, since most of them were artists, lay particularly close to their hearts. All that until then had been revered as classic perfection they found false, theatrical, unworthy, and mannered. They had a particular antipathy to the Renaissance as a symbol of the downfall and degradation of all art. They wanted to have nothing more to do with the eternally repeated movements and poses borrowed from the storehouses of art: the Hellenistic or Roman antique, the late Raphael, or the *seicento.* Only to the "archaic," the art which they thought preceded Phidias, did they grant any value; only this could be pure and simple, yet capable of arousing great emotion. With the possible exception of a few pre-Raphaelite or some older naïve and primitive works, all the rest, in their opinion, could be destroyed without injury or inconvenience to anyone. Their positive artistic ideal was embodied above all in the painting of the Greek vases, or as they were at that time called, the "Etruscan" vases. These had been newly revealed through magnificent publications, especially those of Sir William Hamilton's collections. This archaic vase painting, stylized linear design reduced to its simpliest elements, created a deep impression by its very contrast to the classical. *Etruscisme* became the password of the Primitifs. They wished to work as "naïvely" as had those masters of vase decoration. So they sought for a pure abstract line, as far as possible without any disturbing chiaroscuro; Delécluze tells us that their figures, nearly six feet high, were conceived in pure line. Since unfortunately Maurice Quaï died very young and nothing is known of his work, one can best form an idea of their general tendencies from Ingres' early work which will be dealt with below.

The sect of the Barbus or Primitifs is interesting historically because it was one of the earliest expressions of a pan-European tendency toward an anticlassical, linear abstraction. It is in many ways reminiscent of the "Lukasbrueder" or Nazarenes in Germany. They, however, came together only in 1808, at a time when the Primitifs (after the death of their leader Maurice) had already suffered a mute, inglorious end. But, though filled with a sincere faith, the French group entirely lacked the catholicizing, "monasticizing," and reactionary tendencies of Overbeck and his circle. Parallels were closer in England, where the "gothic revival" had already begun in the eighteenth century and where the discovery of the primitives, or of the primitive, first became evident. The abstract line of Flaxman's drawings for Homer and Dante, the mystic visions of Blake's art were manifestations of the same spirit that animated Maurice Quaï and his group. (We will presently observe a direct influence of Flaxman upon the young Ingres.) The Primitifs symbolized the appearance of a new artistic wave, European in character, archaistic, abstract, and romantic, that arose within the declining classicism represented by David's "Sabines." It gave this classicism its death blow, but by introducing its opposite — romantic anticlassicism — breathed into it a new and different life.

CHAPTER THREE

PROTOBAROQUE TENDENCIES IN THE PERIOD OF CLASSICISM

Prudhon, Gros

David may be considered, as he was by Delacroix, the beginning of the evolution of nineteenth-century painting, or, on the contrary, his work may be seen as the final resolution of forces that preceded him. For Pierre-Paul Prudhon (1758–1823) the decision is even more difficult. He was ten years younger than David, but the Louvre for a long time classified his work as belonging to the eighteenth century. Like the Revolution, whose painter he was, David gave full expression to longings that were clearly rooted in the eighteenth century, and precisely for this reason wished to be free of the rococo spirit of that century. But Prudhon from the very first, and during most of his career, had a much closer connection with the very things that constitute the charm of the *dixhuitième;* he could not and did not wish to free himself. He was anything but a revolutionary. If he served the Revolution and its heir, the Empire, zealously and with conviction, he put his gift of poetry and his lyrical imagination at the service of a movement which was opposed to his very being. What these movements demanded was a moral, heroic, and activist art, primarily political in both feeling and effect. A nature as soft, as moody, as lyrical as Prudhon's could not breast this stream. It is a tribute to his natural talent that instead of succumbing he managed to keep his style going as a gentle but persistent undercurrent. Little by little this gradually came to the surface and from a historical standpoint was not without importance for the following generation.

PRUDHON

Prudhon was born in Cluny and was early protected and patronized by members of its famous monastery. At the same time a rich and aristocratic landowner of liberal, masonic tendencies took the talented youth under his wing, so that he acquired simultaneously religious and freethinking ideas. The effects of this dual education show in his later works. Many of them produce a pious and religious, although not a decidedly churchly, impression — for instance, not only in such pictures as the "Assumption," or in his very moving last work, the "Crucifixion," but also in many of his sketches and fantasies on the "Soul," "Virtue and Vice," and similar subjects. Along with this, the sensibility and sentimentality of the Rousseau tradition made a great impression upon Prudhon and his art. This is evident in his whole enthusiasm for nature, for simplicity, and for idyllic scenes, in his passionate sensibility (he is of Werther's generation), and in his feeling for right and justice.

Prudhon studied at the academy in Dijon under Devosge, an altogether competent painter. From there in 1784 he won the Prix de Rome, whereupon new horizons opened for him. He left his Burgundian home carrying a heavy load. He had been forced to marry the nineteen-year-old daughter of a Dijon notary because she was expecting a child by him. It turned out to be an extremely unhappy marriage; his wife was emotionally unstable, and there were eventually five children, for whom he had to earn a living. After his years in Rome, he returned to Paris where during the difficult years of the Revolution (as later in Franche-Comté) he was burdened with the grievous task of feeding a large family through his efforts as a painter.

Nevertheless, things never became really desperate and he always found patrons and friends. The minor work that he did, vignettes, letterheads, illustrations, lay within the direction of his artistic bent and of his talent. Nor was he forced to endure an artistic martyrdom because he stood alone against the dominant Davidian style. David himself, with certain reservations, accepted him and his art. He called him the Watteau or the Boucher of his time, and though this could certainly not be construed as flattery, since the period had an entirely different ideal, it was a recognition of the quality of his talent. *Il se trompe*, said David of Prudhon in a fine and generous phrase, *mais il n'est pas donné à tous de se tromper comme lui. Il a un talent sûr.* Prudhon was especially reproached for his "manner," by which was meant the similarity of his gestures and the expressions of his women, and also for his incorrect drawing and his enamel-like tones.

By way of compensation, however, particularly after the turn of the century, Prudhon had a number of enthusiastic adherents who, like the Dane, Brunn-Neegaard in 1804, admired him above all other artists. He was called the magician of *clair-obscur*, the Correggio of France. His paintings and his drawings were in great demand; "Love as Seducer," for example, already had three buyers in 1791. Under the Consulate, after the worst of the social crisis was over, Prudhon was given many commissions, some of an official nature; and under the Empire, aided by his close relations with Napoleon's all-powerful Minister of Art, Vivant Denon (whom Ingres so hated), he was even more in demand. He painted Denon's portrait and that of the Empress Josephine; in 1808, he was given the Cross of the Legion of Honor; later he gave drawing lessons to the Empress Marie-Louise, who took him under her wing. In this way he was protected externally against attacks from the official Davidian school. When he exhibited his great composition of "Vengeance and Justice" (done for the Palais de Justice) in the famous 1810 Prix-décennal Salon, even they had to recognize him as *confrère* and could no longer refuse him the title of *peintre d'histoire*, though he was never made a member of the Institute.

And finally, when in 1803 he obtained a separation from his wife (who was later committed to an asylum), even his domestic and private life achieved some tranquillity. Soon afterwards he met Mlle. Constance Mayer-Lemartinière, a former pupil of Greuze, who at thirty-five became Prudhon's pupil, friend, and mistress, and who for fifteen years gave this impractical man the love and domestic care he so needed. Prudhon was over sixty when this ideal period ended in a catastrophe. Following a clash over their marriage, made possible by the death of Mme. Prudhon, Mlle. Mayer killed herself in Prudhon's atelier. Desperate and torn with self-reproach, Prudhon did not long survive this blow. He finished the picture, "La Famille Malheureuse"

(Wallace Collection), upon which his mistress had been working, painted the "Crucifixion" and the "Ame délivrée" as a final tragic effort, and died twenty months later in 1823.

Naturally Prudhon's early works were in the main consistent with the character of the eighteenth century. They remain essentially within the tradition of pseudoclassicism, that is to say, within that mixture of the rococo and the antique which we have described. He was not altogether enchanted with the one-sided admiration for antique statuary common in the Rome of the eighties. Raphael and Roman, or Hellenistic, antiquity did not attract him, but rather the subjective half-light of Leonardo and, above all, Correggio.

In the eighteenth century Correggio was neither a discovery nor a rediscovery; the French were particularly faithful to the Correggio-Barocci tradition. From the historical point of view an artistic vogue for Correggio can have one of two meanings: either a tendency to a mannerism in the spirit of Correggio's chief pupil Parmigianino, or a leaning towards the early baroque. The development of this style is unthinkable without the participation of Correggiesque art, as can be seen in the works of the Carracci of Bologna.

In Prudhon something of both tendencies may be observed, a softened mannerism, not linear, as with most classicists, but painterly, a mannerism expressed in the elongation of the figures. There is, in addition, a baroque loosening of light and shade, of form and contour, which is most evident in his later works. Prudhon became intimately acquainted with the more advanced and painterly baroque through a commission given him by the Dijon academy. He was to copy (with some variation in detail) the famous ceiling of the Palazzo Barberini by Pietro da Cortona, the chief master of the Roman high baroque. Altogether compatible with Correggism is that Anacreontic style (an antique rococo) which appears in a stiffer and more awkward fashion in Vien's popular works. Vien was the head of the Académie de France during Prudhon's stay in Rome.

The two pictures, "Love Mocks his Victim" and "Love Brought to Reason," that Prudhon painted shortly after his return from Rome are charming, playful, minor works. They are still essentially in the spirit of the *genre Pompadour*, bitterly fought and despised though that was. This is the more astonishing when one remembers that they were painted during the worst period of the Revolution (1791–1792), and that the author of these trifles was a Jacobin sympathizer — a *Robespierre avec grâce.*

Prudhon's third and finest composition of this period has a facetious, mythological character, the "Vengeance of Ceres," a theme which Elsheimer had painted. It shows the droll adventure of the wandering goddess as it is described in Ovid's *Metamorphoses.* There is a masterly sketch for this picture (Fig. 30) which is somewhat reminiscent of Fragonard. The brush strokes are broad and painterly, the chiaroscuro soft and without contours, the modeling fine, and the humorous characterization of the three main figures is excellent, particularly the nude youth who is already taking on a froglike physiognomy. It is hard to imagine a sharper contrast, either in form or in content, to Davidian ideas of art. The only classicist element is the narrow stagelike space which forces all the figures into one plane, but instead of being cold and geometric, this space is filled with warmth and atmosphere.

Under Prudhon's touch even heroic themes taken from the *Iliad* become lovable family idyls — such subjects as the "Departure of Hector" who is shown bidding his young son a tender farewell. Of Biblical material Prudhon chose "Joseph and Potiphar" and by various alterations gave this infamous subject a graceful character. Even his revolutionary sketches, such things as "The Glorification of the Constitution," have a free lyricism. His many small illustrative sketches, some of them for the *éditions de luxe* of the publisher Didot, are particularly charming. The small erotica such as the "Grille" from *Daphnis and Chloe*, or "Sylvia and the Satyr" from Tasso's *Aminta*, remind one on occasion of Gessner's idyls. But how much more lively, powerful, and broadly conceived they are than the Swiss' somewhat petty engravings. Even these unimportant works bear the mark of the born painter.

It is no wonder, then, that possessing this painterly technique Prudhon could also work without effort in a monumental fashion.

This quality is particularly striking in a small work, a triumph of Bonaparte known as "La Paix" (1801, Chantilly and Lyons). It is a *trionfo* in strict formation, of the sort that had often been painted since Giulio Romano in imitation of the antique. But how much painterly strength and warmth there is in this monumentality. How different these antique horses are from the archaic ones of the young Ingres in his contemporary "Wounded Venus." This is the clear road to Géricault's Roman steeds. How softly fall the draperies of the women surrounding the triumphal chariot, and those of the genii flanking the upright figure of the First Consul. The bare hills of the background glow with light and yet are solidly constructed in relief. Nothing remains of the *petite manière* of the *dixhuitième*. Rather, the picture might be compared to a Poussin whose chiaroscuro had been accentuated. Such work as this is on the highroad to the painterly monumentality of the nineteenth century.

A like monumental grandeur characterizes the "Three Fates" (1804), destined for the pediment of the Paris hospital, but never carried out. If these drawings are compared with earlier ones (for example, the feminine allegories of 1796, now in Montpellier), one can see that in the space composition especially there is clearly an effort by Prudhon to attain a stronger style — perhaps under the influence of Davidian tendencies. But in this process the seated forms of Lachesis and Clotho lose nothing of their loose, soft, painterly charm. Even the Fates are essentially genre figures who wind yarn or pull threads, enchanting young women whose fateful action is yet revealed in a seriousness of tone produced through a surprising stylization.

Only after his fortieth year, in 1799, did Prudhon undertake any really large allegories. In this year he painted "Wisdom and Truth Come to Earth, and At Their Approach the Shadows Disperse" (Louvre). Not to mention earlier attempts, French painters of the seventeenth century (Vouet, Poussin, and others) had a liking for such subjects but rarely with happy results, nor was Prudhon more fortunate. Both of the female allegorical figures (the nude Sagesse extremely elongated) are lost in the surrounding atmosphere and appear affected and somewhat helpless.

"Vengeance and Justice" (Fig. 31) Prudhon's most famous picture of this sort, is much more significant. Prudhon was at dinner in the home of the Prefect of the Seine when Horace's sentence, *Raro antecedentem scelestum deservit poena*, was quoted. The visual image it contains, the flight of the criminal whom punishment relentlessly pursues, appealed to Prudhon, oriented as he was toward illustration. He immediately sketched two different compositions. Later these were replaced by a version emphasizing allegory: Nemesis draws Crime and Vice before the throne of Justice who, assisted by similar allegorical figures, pronounces the judgment of death. A woman with a dagger in her breast, still holding her child in her arms, lies bleeding on the ground. The conception was not new; similar scenes appeared in the sixteenth century. But the sketch is admirable for its strength of expression, the painterly quality of the broad charcoal lines, and the baroque liveliness and movement of the figure of Nemesis dragging the criminal after her. In a detailed sketch of this group (with some variations) the effect is even more monumental than in the large composition.

In the finished picture, however, Prudhon returned to his original theme: "Divine Vengeance and Justice Pursuing Crime" is the full title of the painting, now in the Louvre. Prudhon himself has left us this notation: "In a wild and distant spot, covered by the veil of night, the greedy criminal strangles his victim, takes the gold, and looks once more to see if there remains any spark of life which might uncover his crime. The thoughtless one! He did not see that Nemesis, that terrible handmaiden of Justice, follows, and, like a vulture dropping on its prey, soon will catch him and hand him over to her unyielding companion." In the Salon of 1808, the picture had a justifiable success. In it Prudhon demonstrated that he could be more than merely graceful and charming.

As is so often the case, the finished canvas is not as immediately convincing as the sketches, and it is disturbing that the colors now are partly spoiled; but the message, the moral content of the representation, is impressive and convincing. We must not forget that this painting, destined for the hall of judgment of the Palais de Justice, was meant to have an "active" purpose. The preponderance of the allegorical in the composition is reminiscent of an earlier epoch, but compared to the stylization and the cold pathos of such contemporaries of Prudhon as Gérard or Guérin this is a step towards living warmth, towards communication of mood and a human sensibility.

In style the picture approximates the early baroque. The artist had assimilated the ideas of Correggio, and to them he added a strong and somewhat ponderous classical flavor — an interpretation of antiquity like that of the Roman Renaissance. This is comparable to the work of Annibale Carracci, who also began with Correggio and ended with Rome. The next decisive step, the acceptance and assimilation of Rubens, was to be achieved in the art of Delacroix. Prudhon's "Assumption," ordered in 1816 for the Chapel in the Tuileries (Salon of 1819), shows a distinct affinity to Annibale's late "Assunta" in Santa Maria del Popolo. But Prudhon's "Assumption" is closer to the French spirit of the seventeenth century, particularly in its elongated proportions, and the expression of his faces is more modern.

More dependent on Correggio are pictures such as the "Rape of Psyche" (1808) and, almost directly so, the charming "Zephyr," the figure of a boy who, hanging from a bough, swings over a brook. Other canvases are less interesting, as for example the "Venus and Adonis" (1812, Wallace Collection). In these years Prudhon frequently used, for pictures, themes he had originally executed only as fine, small illustrations — and the enlargement was in no way to their advantage. Then, too, the works that Prudhon did in collaboration with his mistress, Constance Mayer, though poetic in theme and likable in their fairy-tale quality (for example, the "Slumber of Psyche," Wallace Collection, or the "Torch of Venus"), never achieve any power of effect.

The period of the Bourbon Restoration called for little from Prudhon's brush. That he had been one of the intimates of the Bonaparte family was not easily amended or forgotten. His "Assumption," mentioned above, was changed and spoiled: the mandorla of angels which he intended to surround the form of the Virgin was suppressed because it was too "heathen." He was awarded two decorative commissions but never carried them out. And then came the tragedy of Mlle. Mayer's suicide which completely shattered him. His last work, the "Crucifixion" (1822, Louvre), was a composition conceived on a grand scale, with a soft, flowing light that falls full on the oblique body of the beardless Saviour. Here, too, the bitumen ground has come through, largely ruining the effect of the picture. It remains a powerful work, but almost more so is a sketch done under the immediate influence of the death of his mistress: "*L'Ame brisant les liens qui l'attachent à la terre.*" Here a nude woman with outstretched arms rises from the mire of the earth towards a better world.

We must say a word concerning Prudhon as a portrait painter. He never attained the level of David or Ingres, and both Gros and Gérard occasionally produced more brilliant portraits. Prudhon's lyrical talent did not lend itself to characterization nor to pitiless psychological record. In his portraits, he is at his best when he can lyricize, when he portrays a mother and child, as in his picture of "Madame Antony et ses enfants" (1796, Lyons); or when he paints the "Empress Josephine" (Fig. 32) sitting upon a rock in the forest in a mood of melancholy reverie.

"Charm and grace will always be the special hallmarks of his talent"—these were the words with which Delacroix closed his eulogy of Prudhon (*Revue des Deux Mondes*, 1846). It is unjust to look at Prudhon merely from the point of view of his place in a development of style. Yet this place, which we have determined, was important, because what Prudhon achieved in the style of his pictures was a stimulus to others. It was not for nothing that Géricault copied "Vengeance and Justice." But even more than in the case of other artists we can and must consider him apart from any idea of "progress." We must admire the lovable, pure, and naïve spirit that he revealed in many of his smaller works, as in his sketches and drawings, which are half playful and yet always have a certain largeness of feeling. And almost to our surprise we must acknowledge that in at least one of his large pictures he was able to surpass himself and achieve monumentality.

GROS

It has already been suggested that David, in spite of his tendency towards abstraction, was no enemy of color. This was true to the extent that he called his students' attention to Rubens and even traveled to Flanders in order to study him. One of David's favorite pupils, Antoine Jean Gros (1771–1835), particularly pursued and developed this coloristic trend. Gros was born in Paris of a Toulouse family. Raised to the peerage by Louis Philippe, he has since been known as Baron Gros. It was through the Rubenist element in his art that he attained — almost against his will — fame and significance for the future. His fundamental artistic ideal was quite opposite, wholly dedicated to the classical and abstract art of David. Yet, all that Gros created of lofty subject and in heroizing style, whether Sappho throwing herself from the cliff, or Oedipus and Antigone, or other similar themes (like his paintings for the cupola of the Pantheon) was empty and ineffective, and has long since been buried and forgotten. Fate made up for this, however, by bringing him into direct contact with the heroic events of the early Napoleonic era. Gros was forced, as David was from the "Jeu de Paume" through the Revolutionary period, into the service of crucial historical events. In a much more intimate way than David, Gros became the painter of Napoleon and his deeds and his art rose to the stature of the history in the making around him.

Gros was in Italy during the Revolution and, in contrast to David and Prudhon, he took no positive stand toward it. Through the good offices of Josephine he met Bonaparte in Milan in 1796, when the consul was in the first flush of success and victory, and this encounter was decisive for the young artist. Napoleon gave him a role in the French army's widespread confiscatory raiding of Italian art for the benefit of what later became the Musée Central or the Musée Napoléon. For this purpose Gros had to travel all through Italy. Even more important, Napoleon took Gros into his immediate entourage, so that the painter was an actual participant in military events. As a result, Gros was able directly to observe reality in an urgently active world, far removed from everything aesthetic; this explains the freshness and the life that in color, form, and movement he knew how to give to the heroic, almost legendary deeds of Napoleon and his paladins. Naturally he was not a realist in the modern sense, but on the other hand, he was no dreary delineator of battles like Van der Meulen in the seventeenth century. He might rather be compared with such painters of dramatic and coloristic battle pieces as Salvator Rosa and Il Borgognone. Gros would not have been a pupil of David, nor the child of an heroic period, had he not, in his paintings of contemporary events, tried to render the ideal of heroism. It was not without reason that a critic of the time compared Gros' battle pictures with Giulio Romano's "Battle of Constantine," even though Gros himself disliked the darkish tones of this great work. Gros' temperament attracted him to Rubens. In Genoa he paid a daily visit to the master's splendid painting of "St. Ignatius" and in his letters to David set down his unstinted admiration. The colorism, the violent movement, the fire and spirit which individual figures and groups in many of Gros' pictures at least suggest, come from Rubens. This is particularly true of the prancing and excited horses that appear in Gros' battle pictures as well as in separate studies. Géricault builds directly upon such scenes as Gros' saber-swinging hussar on a rearing steed, and Delacroix, in his essay of 1840, talks of them at length:

In character and execution, Gros' horses are altogether different from what painters had done in this genre until then. Rubens, it is true, had preceded him with his audacity in giving life and fury to his noble animals . . . but they lack the nobility, I might even say the passion of those of Gros. These, like their riders, seem to breathe a love of danger and glorious adventure. In these poetic melees they are seen to rear, to bite, to neigh, their breasts clashing; their manes, glistening and intertwined, shine under the brightest of suns through the dust of battle and still one admires the knowledge with which the painter has drawn them and the beauty of their proportions. This rare mixture of force and elegance is without a doubt the pinnacle of art.

A prelude to Gros' heroic pictures is his sketch of the young General Bonaparte, flag in hand, leading his troops forward on the bridge of Arcole (Fig. 33). It is interesting to compare this with

David's "Napoleon at St. Bernard" which, though it strives for monumentality, remains somewhat cold and thin. Here in Gros' rendering everything is concentrated on the human being, the finely cut face with the wind-blown hair, the movement of turning, all set down as in a direct impression. What for the time was an innovation in coloring was immediately noticed when the picture was shown at the Salon of 1798. An official commission from the First Consul to paint the battle of Nazareth followed immediately, but the picture was never executed, and only the large sketch in color in the Nantes museum has come down to us. In Delacroix's judgment, Gros here showed himself a finished master; his gift of pictorial invention, his surprising facility in the depiction of a variety of light, moving forms (particularly [illegible]e groups of riders), and their effective translation into color, are all to be found already in what Delacroix called this *admirable esquisse* of the cavalry battle at Nazareth.

To compensate Gros for losing the opportunity to execute this picture Napoleon gave him an important new commission, for a work which was destined to become his most famous painting and perhaps the only one of which the reputation still persists. This is the "Plague of Jaffa" (1804; Fig. 34), showing Napoleon visiting the plague-stricken in the hospital at Jaffa, and touching the sores of one of the victims of the epidemic. As Gros first planned it the scene was laid in a bare hospital room and presented in a terse and factual manner. But this did not suffice — Gros felt the need for a more theatrically effective presentation in a more romantic setting. The scene was therefore shifted to a pointed arcade in the court of a gothic cloister, through which one looks towards battlements and portions of a city half veiled in mist. It is probable that for these details Gros had before him fairly exact written descriptions, but even so, this "gothic revival" was remarkable for a pupil of David, and was symptomatic of romanticism. Thus conceived, the space permitted the disposition of impressive scenes and groups containing all manner of action. The simplicity and frugality of the classicist doctrine, as David had exemplified it in his "Horatii," is softened by a certain fullness of space and abundance of figures that is altogether natural for an artist who, like Gros, was a colorist and a moderate Rubenist. The ghastly subject and its gothic setting both correspond to a certain kind of emotional tone that had already become prominent in the literature and art of France and of England; such elements were to become even more pronounced in the painterly romanticism of Géricault and Delacroix.

The representation of the plague was an old motive of which there were innumerable examples: St. Roch, the patron of the plague-stricken, and San Carlo Borromeo in the Milan plague had often been painted. From the Raphael–Marc Antonio "Morbetto," through Poussin's "Plague of Azdoth," to David's painting of the plague in Marseilles, there was an unbroken series. In Gros' representation, instead of St. Roch or San Carlo Borromeo there now appears a modern hero: Napoleon. Immovable and invulnerable, in a gesture comparable to that of the doubting Thomas of many an Italian picture, he touches the sore on the breast of the sick man. Other figures too, such as the elongated kneeling man with the black beard, are reminiscent of pictures in Italian museums — half Michelangelo, half Domenichino. Gros replaced the dying mother who so often fills the corner of older plague pictures by the figure of the young doctor who, himself stricken by the disease, holds the body of a dying man in his lap.

Out of all this grew a picture which, though based on an old tradition must, through its orientalisms, its exotic gothic setting, and its dreadfulness of subject, have had a strange and exciting effect. The introduction of a modern hero into a world so alien to him in theme and milieu was entirely new. In the Louvre today the picture's coloristic effect can no longer be appreciated; originally, however, it was very striking and served to remove the whole concept even further from classicist formulas, bringing it near that movement of color which was the ideal of the later, so-called romantic painters. The composition alone has such grandeur that, when the "Plague of Jaffa" was shown at the Salon of 1804, David himself, with pleasure and without envy, could join in the chorus of triumph for his pupil. The younger artists of the time wreathed the picture with laurel. A festival banquet, presided over by the hoary Vien and by David, the *maître illustre*, was given in honor of the painter. Gros, barely thirty-three, stood at the peak of his fame.

The first great battle piece which Gros actually executed was the "Battle of Aboukir" (1806). It contains much that is Rubens and much that is Giulio Romano. In the center (like Constantine and Maxentius) are Murat on horseback and a young Arab chieftain who surrenders his curved saber. On both sides there is the wildest disorder of people, horses, and corpses, all rendered in a broad colorism with no attempt at restraint or stylization. *On ne fait pas de peinture à la Spartiate*, Gros was in the habit of saying. The "Battle of Eylau" (Fig. 35), however, is more in the manner of the "Plague of Jaffa"; although instead of a heroic deed of Napoleon — the result of the battle was rather doubtful — it depicts a quasi-humanitarian gesture. The emperor is shown not as a conqueror, but in the role of the magnanimous leader, made melancholy by the horrors of war, come out to comfort the wounded and captured who crowd around him. The picture takes on a new and distinctly unclassicistic, psychological character that is still further accented by the greater realism of the battlefield — the utter confusion after the battle, made gloomier still in the dark light of the desolate, snow-covered landscape. The whole scene appears as an entirely new concept, emphasizing its feeling and its mood by frankly painterly means. It contrast to earlier works it seems something altogether modern. Both in form and ethics the concept of the heroic has here taken on a different complexion, and it was probably this, as much as any artistic merit, which accounted for the picture's extraordinary acclaim: here Napoleon, the symbol of the glory of France, was shown as mightier still in stature through his yielding, in his might, to the impulse of human sympathy.

This and a few similar pictures contain the positive contribution in the work of Gros. He was the painter of Napoleon and his deeds. Though during the Restoration he wished or perhaps had to perform a similar service for Louis XVIII, it was not the same thing; he could not call forth glory from "stories" which contained none. When he portrayed Louis XVIII leaving the Tuileries upon Napoleon's return from Elba, the result was actually "antiheroic"; and the same is true of the "Embarkation of the Duchess of Angoulême" (she whom Napoleon called the only man in the family) — though this picture (1819, Bordeaux Museum) has many good qualities of painting and composition.

In spite of a superabundance of honors which now came to Baron Gros his later life ran anything but a happy course. Those works which placed him among the *avant-garde* and brought him into contact with the younger school of "romantics" were, as we have already indicated, just those which did not satisfy the ideals of his Davidian academicism. For it was David, and strangely enough David the theorizing classicist, not the painter of the "Sacre" to whom Gros was more akin, who remained his idol; he looked upon himself as viceroy for his exiled lord. And from Brussels David, who towards the end became completely ossified, kept goading him on towards an art of *grand goût: Vite, vite mon ami,* he wrote him, *feuilletez votre Plutarque et choisissez un sujet connu par tout le monde* — as if for Gros the "Battle of Eylau" and the "Plague of Jaffa" had not been subjects a hundredfold more living and fruitful than all the great men in Plutarch. Strangely enough Gros himself regarded everything new — that whole romantic, coloristic school which he himself had begun — as *impertinence et vagabondage* (letter of 1822 to David apropos of the famous Salon). He went even farther in 1824 when, in a speech on the occasion of Girodet's funeral, he complained that he had been one of the first to set the bad example, that he had not been rigid enough in his choice of subjects or their execution, and that it was he who had brought on the downfall of the "School," that is, the school of David. So Gros developed an outspoken opposition to everything modern and the rigor of his views brought him into serious conflict with those who thought differently. As President of the Academy and of the jury, he was discredited both among artists of the neoclassic tendency, such as Ingres, and among the true romantics (in spite of Delacroix's correct judgment of him). Though unpleasant personal circumstances were contributory, it was above all a feeling of inner insecurity which drove him to a sort of old-age melancholia and finally to suicide.

Doubtless Baron Gros did not have the natural talent of his teacher

David. In the judgment of posterity David, after understandable fluctuations, has always returned to a respectable level of esteem, but even Gros' contemporaries already found his works either very good or very bad. For us this last hard predicate must often stand, and we can assent to the superlative only for a few of his best works, successful though many of them are. Gros was a transitional master and so must be evaluated mainly from the point of view of his place in the historical development. In the narrow historical sense, his significance lies in his representation of the Napoleonic epic, though Delacroix overreached himself when he compared him to a Homer who depicted "Napoleon's character as made of epic traits, and like Achilles, grander than all other heroes who ever sprang from poets' heads." In the history of art Gros is important because, in spite of his close connection with the Davidian ideals, he led (in much more energetic fashion than the Correggist Prudhon) from the classic school to the baroque, painterly, Rubenist tendency in nineteenth-century art, and because Géricault and Delacroix were inspired by his style. To grasp Gros' art and personality correctly we must see him through the eyes of Delacroix: we must not forget that in 1840 Delacroix wrote one of his finest essays, full of splendid words, moving praise, and many historical insights, on Baron Gros — once his artistic enemy.

CHAPTER FOUR

THE TRANSFORMATION OF CLASSICISM IN THE ART OF INGRES

Of the two main tendencies in French art — the rational or Poussinist and the irrational or Rubenist — the first, the so-called classicistic current, certainly had the preponderance at the beginning of the nineteenth century. However, in spite of the jealously guarded dominance of the academic school, the opposing baroque and coloristic tendencies were by no means dead. We saw elements of this in David himself, and still more clearly in his disciple Gros, whose works seemed to prepare the way for a neo-Rubenism or a neobaroque, and independent of the school of David we saw a sort of protobaroque developed by Prudhon. Moreover, there were still irrational elements of a quite different nature, which stemmed from Rousseau and the eighteenth century but which must be called romantic because they were related to the ideas and whims of the romantic writers. Of these elements the most important were the following: an emphasis on sentiment and emotion; a newly awakened interest in nature and landscape; a historicizing tendency, especially evident in the revived interest in the gothic, which until then had been considered barbarous; a taste for the ghastly, even for the cruel; a new wave of spiritual interest in Catholicism, and finally the inclination toward the primitive and the archaic which resulted in the abstraction and reduction of art forms. By the penetration of these foreign elements into the fabric of its ideals, rational classicism in the old sense was strongly shaken. David himself and much more so his school were affected by the new ideas and feelings though these did not yet lead to an immediate and decisive change in their general style.

Gradually the reappearance of the two old currents, the linear and the coloristic, became clearly discernible again although they now took on an entirely new meaning as a result of the penetration of both currents with romantic and sentimental elements. At the same time these two currents became more sharply opposed to each other than ever because of the accentuation in each of its specific formal character. Both currents emerged positively only towards the end of the second decade of the century; only in the third decade were they fully developed. The strongly coloristic and high-baroque development, first represented incompletely in Géricault, was then gloriously embodied by Delacroix. This movement is generally called the French romantic school in the proper sense, partly because of its connections with the late romanticism of Victor Hugo, Berlioz, and others.

The contrasting development was the neoclassicistic current, with its strong concentration on line and structure. This new classicism was quite different from that of David because of its absorption of new romantic elements, especially that of archaizing abstraction. There was further, a shifting of the classical ideal from Roman antiquity toward the High Renaissance of Raphael. The leader of this movement was Ingres. The fundamental contrast between the two new directions in style is vast, and far more embittered than the battle of the Rubenists and Poussinists in the seventeenth century. To the historical spectator these two implacable antagonisms seem to dominate French painting of the maturing nineteenth century.

Jean Auguste Dominique Ingres (1780–1867) came from the town of Montauban in Gascony. His father, a versatile artisan and entrepreneur in the arts, had moved there from Toulouse. Entering the academy of cultured and conservative Toulouse when he was only twelve, Ingres received a solid training which, though it included drawing from medieval monuments and gothic choir stalls, naturally had the Latin ideal of form as its constant focus. For the young Ingres the *divino Raffaello*, chief sun of the academic heaven, shone even brighter than the antique; a copy of the "Madonna della Sedia" was his great revelation and the *réligion de Raphael* stayed with him throughout his life, as did his early discovered passion for music and the violin. He said once of himself that he had remained essentially *ce que le petit Ingres était à douze ans.*

When he was seventeen or eighteen he had the great good fortune — as he said himself — to enter David's Paris atelier, escaping thereby from the provinces and coming into the main artistic current of his time. For David's art, as well as his atelier, had become a European phenomenon. Yet David's teaching represented no break for Ingres, because its main tendency moved within that Latin tradition upon which Ingres had been brought up at home. David quickly recognized the extraordinary formal talent of his young pupil, and gave him the opportunity to aid in the execution of his pictures, as, for example, with his "Mme. Récamier." But Ingres was too independent to become a regular "Davidian" and soon, towards 1800, a certain estrangement seems to have come between the master and his twenty-year-old pupil. To be sure, David was broad-minded enough to permit his pupils to pursue aims at variance with his own, but only within certain definite limits, and Ingres seems to have been sympathetic with the Primitifs who, as we have seen, struck David at his weakest point by their pitiless criticism of his "Sabines" — at this time his latest and, he hoped, his most advanced work. To be sure Ingres did not belong to the inner circle of Maurice Quaï — he was not the man for that sort of idealistic eccentricity, not even when he was young. But for a while the strong demands of this sect for primitivism and archaism became so far his own that they resulted in a split between his point of view and that of David and the "School."

Ingres' close connection with this archaistic movement comes out most clearly in a very early work: "Venus Wounded by Diomedes" (Fig. 36). Venus, wounded in the hand by Diomedes, mounts Mars' chariot, in which, led by Iris, she is to hurry back to Olympus. The choice of a subject out of Homer, the favorite author of the Primitifs, immediately characterizes the work. Even more indicative is its formal relationship to "Etruscan" vase painting, attributable to examples in the Louvre which Ingres must have known. But there was another and more direct influence, that of the famous English sculptor John Flaxman, who was known on the continent less for his sculpture than for his illustrations of Homer, Hesiod, Aeschylus, and Dante. In the form of outline engravings, these attained an extraordinary diffusion. Flaxman was in Paris in 1802 and there saw Ingres' Prix de Rome picture, "Achilles Receives the Ambassadors of Agamemnon" (Fig. 37), which much to David's irritation he held to be the finest picture in Paris. Flaxman looked upon David not only as an "atheist and regicide" but also, after the manner of the Barbus, as a *retardataire* artist. A small drawing by Flaxman for the *Iliad*, showing the scene in which Iris brings Venus to Mars, and illustrating the passage immediately preceding that chosen by Ingres, certainly gave the latter his inspiration for the "Wounded Venus." In Flaxman, Ingres found and realized that for which, in essence, the Barbus were striving: linear abstraction on a primitive foundation, that is, based upon vase painting and *quattrocento* drawings. In his picture, likewise, Ingres sought an abstraction which departed from that convention of plastic bodily mass which had until then been the classical ideal. In archaic painting with its lack of space alleviated by linear overlappings, with its head turned in profile and so bound into the same plane as the bodies, with its somewhat wooden proportions and stiffly articulated movements (particularly evident in the horses), Ingres and his like-minded contemporaries found an unsurpassed prototype. In this Flaxman had definitely preceded them; and we must recognize that there was an international movement which emphasized "linear abstraction" and "freedom from the classical."

Ingres' picture, however, is at once richer and more subtle than anything Flaxman had done. What set Ingres apart was his strong feeling for the finest nuances of movement, for the most delicate and lifelike rise and fall of bodily outline, a feeling which breaks through all his archaism to produce living form. The way in which Venus, her head thrown back in pain, mounts the chariot while her wounded hand droops from her outstreched arm — there, already, we have the whole of Ingres. When later he paints Thetis coming to the aid of Jupiter the movement and the form of the body, though fuller and more refined, is that of the Venus of this early picture. Nearly all his women, whether Francesca or Angelica, retain something of this archaistic and at the same time sensuously graceful character. That David, in spite of his coquetting with the "Greek" style, could not be sympathetic with gold-maned horses so evidently derived from vases, with the profiled head of Mars, or with the forward-bent pose of the chariot-driver (which likewise comes from a Greek vase), in short, with this strongly antirealistic and anticlassical stylization, must be obvious. The delicate and tender rhythm, the soft tone of the rose background, the abstraction which is yet alive, are the most characteristic expression of Ingres — and more clearly visible in his early works than in many of his later productions. We can now understand why Ingres' contemporaries, insofar as they did not share a similar "modern" point of view, should at first have found his works, even those less extreme than the "Wounded Venus," strange and at times repellent. They considered them too "gothic," and gothic meant anything primitive or anticlassical, whether found in the Middle Ages or in the *quattrocento*, in Giotto and Fra Angelico or in the archaic Greek.

But side by side with this penchant for the archaic and abstract linear design, Ingres from the very beginning had (though it was overlooked at first) a much stronger passion which inevitably went far to paralyze the first: his lasting love, rooted in him from childhood, for the ripe and self-contained art of Raphael. The imitation of the archaic Greek style, of the primitive in general, could easily have turned into a merely playful and decorative manner. Among the Barbus the exaggerated desire for abstraction and primitiveness turned into a kind of meaningless game, as to a certain extent it did among the German school of Nazarenes. Ingres escaped falling into this sort of loose and playful formal mannerism because of his innate desire for living form, for the kind of idealized realism that was embodied in Raphael and those who shared his approach. For Ingres the work of Raphael was not a ghostlike academic dogma, but the individual, the natural, and the living lifted into the realm of ideas. He had such unbounded admiration for Raphael's art that he made it his declared ideal. On the other hand, his youthful "revolution" into linear abstraction and the primitive kept him from becoming a mere follower of the Raphaelite tradition.

In the light of all this, it may be asked whether Ingres can properly be called a classicist. (Terms such as gothic, baroque, classicistic, etc., are in themselves somewhat ambiguous and unprecise, but for the purposes of demarcation and summary they cannot be lightly abolished.) Nevertheless this question must be answered in the affirmative. To be sure the classical ideal had now changed; it was no longer the Roman antique as it had been for the second half of the eighteenth century and for David; it was Raphael, but surely Raphael's is the most preeminent position in the classical canon. And to the degree that this is true every retrospective follower of Raphael is a classicist. But there we must not overlook the fact that every clearly distinguishable main current is influenced and colored by differing countercurrents and tributary streams. The archaic, the primitive, the linear-abstract, these are all attributes of a romantic tendency. Ingres' work fell within a period in which romantic sentiment and romantic art were preponderant and basic throughout Europe — in Germany and England as well as in France. And so Ingres' classicism was necessarily influenced in an essential way by the romantic point of view of his time. The result was a romantic classicism — in which romantic, irrational, and anticlassical elements (revealed in his subjects as well as his form) penetrate and modify in a particular way the general tone of rational classicism. As a linear classicist Ingres was a deadly enemy of the coloristic, baroque romanticism of Delacroix; as an archaistic romantic he was opposed to the classicism of David and his adherents.

It was in this spirit that during the first years of the new century Ingres and two like-minded artists set up an academy of their own within the walls of the old Capuchin monastery off the present Rue de la Paix, proudly setting themselves apart from David's school. Completing the academy were Lorenzo Bartolini, a young Italian sculptor who was trying to escape from Canova's frozen classicistic schemes by studying nature, François-Josephe Fétis, a Belgian musical theoretician who (historicizing in the romantic manner) was one of the first of his time to study early music seriously. We know nothing definite about Ingres' large compositions of this period, though there must have been sketches enough. Delécluze dates the first version of "Jupiter and Thetis" as early as 1805, though the finished painting (Fig. 38) was not exhibited until 1811. This picture still has close affinities with Flaxman, as in the concept of the enthroned Zeus, and its "Etruscanism" is stronger than that which the later, Roman, Raphaelized Ingres ever permitted himself. However, it is Ingres' portraits that give us our chief information of his activity during this period of the "Atelier des Capucins" and many of these are as ripe, as sure, and as accomplished as those of his later years.

An artist is attracted to the "primitives" and to "Etruscan" vase paintings because they present the possibility of producing a direct impression by line alone. The "pure contour," because it omits unimportant interior forms, allows a clarification of the essentials. This holds good, above all, for the rendering of character; it is in his outstanding achievement in portraiture that Ingres is closest to us today. Here, too, are fused those two characteristics which are proper to his art: his feeling for linear abstraction and his strongly "classical" feeling for bodily form. By the union of these two he attains both an extreme refinement of contour and a surprisingly precise characterization of the living individual. Perhaps only Bronzino can compete with Ingres in the apparently simple and primitive and yet unsurpassedly refined grasp of the portrait form. It is historically noteworthy that the middle of the sixteen century, when Bronzino worked in Florence, was a period in which a primitive, archaizing, and what may be called a "gothic" style superseded the classicism of the High Renaissance, though still thoroughly impregnated with classicism's formal language. Thus Bronzino and Ingres worked under artistically similar conditions.

Two very early portraits, those of Bernier and of Ingres' father, still show a dependence upon David in their modeling and light arrangement, and even the portrait of Napoleon as First Consul (Liège) contains nothing exceptional; official and ceremonial paintings were not the forte of Ingres. On the other hand, his self-portrait of 1804 (Fig. 39; also an earlier, even more forceful version) is altogether remarkable in its maturity and individuality. It is a sharp silhouette, the head turned in three-quarter profile above the high-pointed triangle of the body; the highly charged expression, with the black curly hair and the stubbornly pushed out mouth, reveals something of the zealot.

Stylization and quasi-archaizing are pushed even further in the pictures of the Rivière family, among which that of Mme. Rivière (1805; Fig. 40) is a magnificent example of Ingres' portrait style. In contrast to a Davidian portrait such as the famous "Mme. Récamier," in whose execution Ingres had participated five years earlier, Ingres' "Mme. Rivière" has undergone a tremendous refinement in two ways: first, towards a formal abstraction and, secondly, towards individual expression and reality of characterization.

David set his figures in an imaginary, bare, artificially emptied space. Ingres destroys the space and puts bodies, heads, garments, and drapery all in one almost uniform plane; in this there is, again, an approach to an "archaic" style. David replaced the pomp of the typical eighteenth-century portrait with a laconic simplicity; Ingres again complicates his portraits, reasserting the ideal of elegance; he almost revels in luxuriant stuffs and in embroidery. But how delicate, how sensitive are his folds, in contrast to the rougher, more conventional draperies of David; with what extraordinary simplicity he renders the full oval of the face, the eyes, the mouth, the elongated surface of the hand, and the broad fingers. And yet the portrait of Mme. Rivière is no schematic arrangement, and it is no anemic Nazarene ideal that sits before us. The cheeks are rounded, the black locks turn and curl coquettishly on the brow; the large eyes are lively and, like the forceful mouth, somewhat mocking; the white cloth (emphasized by the reddish tones of the cashmere shawl and by the ornamentation of the sofa) spreads out, showy and expensive, like a still life. Behind all this external refinement lies a sensuousness such as David, whose innate ideal was much more robust, never attained, nor ever attempted.

One must not evaluate Ingres exclusively as a draftsman — not even in these protraits. He built his art upon his drawing as upon a solid rock. He drew continually, everything, everywhere. He said to one of his pupils: "*Voyez-vous, mon enfant*, drawing is the first of the virtues for a painter, it is the foundation, it is everything; a thing well drawn is always well enough painted. So, we shall start drawing, we shall go on drawing, and then we shall draw some more." But in addition to his altogether unusual feeling for the most delicate modulation of line, still further sharpened by incessant practice, he had a clear sense for sensitive gradations of color value, which in the Rivière portrait he pushed to the utmost refinement. Ingres never became a Rubenist, that is, a colorist who paints color as the fusion and dissolution of tones in light. Though David, in spite of his classicism, could make certain concessions in this direction, such a practice would have been contrary to Ingres' whole nature. For this reason alone Delacroix, whose whole art was built on this (in the narrow sense) coloristic foundation, necessarily became Ingres' hated antipode.

On the other hand, the constructive method of Poussinism, the building up of strongly emphasized surfaces of local color against and behind one another, did not entirely satisfy Ingres' color feeling either. Refinement of line and surface demanded refinement of color values in order to bind the surfaces more closely together. Here, too, one is reminded most of the way in which Parmigianino and Bronzino, the so-called Mannerists of the sixteenth century, employed their colors. Ingres' sensitive feeling for tonalities helped correct any excessive effect of linear abstraction and helped him to give convincing existence to the material and sensuous charm of things. This is true of his masterly portrait of the "Belle Zélie" (1806; Fig. 41). Her hair, falling in dark ringlets over a white brow, sharpens the clean, clear oval of the face. The material over her breast is handled somewhat more simply than in the "Mme. Rivière," but still is emphasized enough to make a contrast to the barely modeled, yet expressive countenance.

Even Ingres' pure pencil sketches suggest his special feeling for color. His stroke is never really abstract, but retains a feeling of warmth that needs only be touched with the suggestion of atmospheric effects of color and light to come alive. In the "Forestier Family" (1816), which as a group drawing is unsurpassed in Ingres' work, every stroke lives and vibrates. In spite of the extreme restriction of the space, an interesting grouping and movement among the four figures is achieved by the subtle modification of their placement within what is almost a single plane. And in the same way, through the delicate handling of light and shade the details of the modeling become rounded, alive, and individual. Instead of the "pure contour" favored by the German Nazarenes and romantics, there is here a movement of line so nearly glittering that it is almost a substitute for color.

In 1806 Ingres finally received the Prix de Rome stipend for which, because of international conditions, he had had to wait for years, and so at the age of twenty-six arrived in the promised land of Italy. He belonged there — he was a "southerner," like Poussin or Claude. He could hardly live outside this atmosphere; he was much more Roman (even if completely French in nationality) than his teacher David. "How they deceived me," Ingres is supposed to have said, as he finally stood before the originals — perhaps in the Brancacci chapel, perhaps in front of Raphael. He must have meant that the classic ideal as expressed by Raphael and also by Masaccio looks different in reality from the form in which it was handed down by the Davidian school. But in the last analysis he had not let himself be so badly deceived. Had not the ideal of the Renaissance, melodious and harmoniously balanced, which now surrounded and took possession of him, always been his natural artistic habitat? In Florence as in Rome he found only confirmation and justification of what had been — at least in the essence of his artistic nature — his being and his striving ever since childhood. It was only natural that his instinct for Raphaelism should become further intensified here on classic soil. His many — perhaps too many — years of residence in Italy pushed the gothic, northern, romantic side of his art farther and farther into the background, and he turned away from the extreme archaizing of the Barbus and from the influence of Flaxman which had culminated in the "Wounded Venus."

Ingres himself, always highly sensitive to criticism, had been embittered by the appellation "gothic" with which for a considerable period both critics and public contemptuously dismissed his work. "It is not possible," he wrote at the beginning of 1807, "that one day I suddenly became gothic; it is only the comparison with the sloppy and cowardly sort of painting which makes even connoisseurs misjudge my paintings, so that they call gothic *ce qui est sévère et noble.*" What critics characterized as "barbaric," or as a "return to the childhood of nature," was in Ingres' eyes a "strong and noble" stylization. One could imagine an artist who, starting with the outlook of the Primitifs, would develop the chords which he struck in the "Wounded Venus" into greater harmony and strength. But Ingres did not go any farther in this direction. On the country, under Italian influence the classic and Renaissance component of his style, the static balance which appears in Raphaelesque designs, emerges into greater prominence, especially — and often most disadvantageously — in larger compositions. Still, Ingres retained enough of his abstracting, gothic quality to prevent his pictures from becoming copies or pastiches of the beloved masters of the Renaissance. Ingres himself objected violently to being counted simply as a slavish imitator even of his idolized Raphael. He once said that he had taken in the art of the great masters like mother's milk, that he had tried to make their sublime qualities his own, and from them had first learned to draw properly; nevertheless, every work of his had his own personal stamp: *J'y ai mis ma griffe.* But it so happens that one feels the impress of this "lion's-claw" most strongly and significantly when the primitive, stylizing element appears below the classical surface. And it is the works of this sort that — subject matter aside — at first really attracted the romantic writers who had been reproached with their desire to cast their poems in the language of Ronsard, in much the same way as Ingres was reproached for returning to gothic in his paintings. On the other hand, it is understandable that when the classic element in Ingres' style gained the upper hand and made his work at once cold and sweet, that Ingres should then have encountered an uncompromising, even if unjustified, opposition from the romantics of his time.

As Gautier said, Ingres lived in Rome *seul*, *fier*, *et triste*, and admired Raphael. After his five-year Prix de Rome stipend had run out he earned his living chiefly through small, delicate portrait drawings ordered from him mainly by English travelers; drawings which he himself despised and which today are especially admired. In 1813 he married (there is a charming picture of his young wife in a blue shawl, in the Reinhart Collection, Winterthur); in 1820 he moved to Florence where he again came into intimate contact with his friend Bartolini. Not until 1824 did the "Vow of Louis XIII" bring the desired recognition from home; and not until then, after fourteen years of untiring labor, did he return to Paris.

Apart from certain copies (among others, that of Raphael's "Fornarina" — whose traits are clearly borne by some of his female nudes — and, also, copies of Titian), the Roman years produced a large number of original works. Ingres worked slowly, continually reworking certain themes, and carried some of them through more than a decade. He made an endless number of preparatory drawings, often needing nearly a hundred different studies of movement for the placing of an arm. But he was so thoroughly trained by his ceaseless practice in drawing that he could complete extremely fine portrait drawings such as those mentioned above in about four hours and did not need much longer for a painted portrait. It was in this vein that he produced really splendid works. Among these, early in the Roman period, is the portrait of the painter Granet (Fig. 42), built up in a pyramid similar to Ingres' youthful self-portrait and with a wonderful view of Rome in the background. The city landscape here is painted as beautifully and in as simple and cubic a fashion as an early Corot; this is all the more remarkable since Ingres, like David, very rarely painted pure landscapes. In reply to the question of a German landscapist as to how one could best learn to paint a landscape, he answered: *étudiez Phidias, Raphael, et Beethoven, et vous serez le premier paysagiste du monde.*

The portrait of Mme. Devauçay (Fig. 43) is clean and tender. The modest liveliness of the frontal oval of the face is inimitably drawn, the nose, the mouth, and the eyes with their gently curved brows simply indicated; yet, by means of the slightest nuances the characteristic and unique qualities of the personality are made to emerge. The flat, dark hair, parted down the middle, emphasizes the spherical form of the head, and without resorting to any evident contrast of light and dark the backward and forward movement of the plastic forms has been seized and held. In the same way that the head is almost inperceptibly fixed into its place in the design, the bust is brought into the structure of the picture by the arch of the chair, which seems to be insolubly joined to the line of the shoulder and arm. This pure construction is broken only by the fine wool shawl, wonderfully set off by its color, which introduces an unexpectedly luxuriant note. A sketch at Montauban clearly shows Ingres' consideration of the construction and how it developed from an abstract to a living form. Several of Raphael's portraits, such as the "Donna Velata" with its pure figure outline and the nearly Venetian materiality of its sleeve puffs, could have served as models, or even Bronzino's still more sharply set off portrait forms. Ingres perhaps surpassed them both in the subtlety of his feeling line.

Ingres went still farther in the portrait of Mme. de Senonnes (1814, Nantes) in which the painterly richness of the foreground plane, a still life made up of a Turkish shawl, a brilliant damask, and the ring-covered hands is set in subtle contrast to the emphasized simplicity of the facial modeling. But occasionally Ingres could strike a much stronger note. In his portrait of the Countess of Tournon (1812; Fig. 44), with her broad mouth and little moustache, her fleshy, drooping nose, her great sly eyes, and her fat arms and hands, he achieved a pitiless description of a forceful and witty ugliness that is reminiscent of Goya's gruesome portraits. Of a similarly powerful character are certain of his line portraits, sometimes richly elaborated (for example, "Lady Lytton"), sometimes rendered with a minimum of strokes, as in the astounding drawing of Mme. Rhode (Groult Collection), in which the least is said, and yet the essence of a personality is given.

In these portrait oils and drawings Ingres was free of his historical and classical constraint, and of any exaggerated pretensions. Thus, for all their realism, they continued the linear abstraction and primitiveness of his early works longer and more intensively than most of his other productions. It is not surprising that for us today Ingres' portraits put everything else he did in the shade (with the possible exception of some of his loveliest drawings of nudes). Naturally he himself held a different opinion. He felt himself to be first and foremost a creator of epic compositions, not a painter of accidental faces. *Je suis peintre d'histoire, je ne suis pas portraitiste*, he was accustomed to say, when, during those financially difficult years in Rome, a customer asked for *M. Ingres le portraitiste.*

But those large compositions containing many figures, which for Ingres represented the essence of his art, today demand considerable effort to understand. Least comprehensible are the subjects drawn from French history. In David's atelier there was a whole group of aristocrats and returned emigrants, the so-called *muscadins*, who favored such historical-patriotic themes. Before this time such subjects had been treated only occasionally (for instance, Vincent's "Murder of the President Molé"). Now, however, they became a fashion which the ruling powers — including Napoleon — understandably encouraged. It was a reaction, and since like everything retrospective it was romantic, Ingres' compositions in this genre drew the romantics' approval. Ingres, who had been in David's studio with the *muscadins*, had also been infected with this plague, which created such havoc in the romantic camp. With his excessive conscientiousness, Ingres worried over every detail of *couleur locale*, that is, the exactitude of his antiquarian properties; with dogged zeal he drew halberds, period costumes, and so forth, producing pictures such as "Pedro of Toledo Kissing the Sword of Henry IV," or "Henry IV Playing with his Children Receives the Spanish Ambassadors," which we can enjoy today only as we would enjoy a masquerade.

The religious pictures, such as "St. Peter Delivering the Keys" (1820, for Trinità de' Monti), are not much better. The "Vow of Louis XIII" (1824, for the cathedral of Montauban), the large picture which helped him to fame and changed his whole position in the social and artistic worlds, is a cross between the historical and the religious genres. In it Ingres' Raphaelism borders upon imitation (even though it was precisely concerning this picture that Ingres protested such a criticism). The Madonna to whom the kneeling king hands his crown and scepter is taken directly, with certain changes, from the "Madonna of Foligno," and the angels with their tablets are essentially Raphaelesque. It is true that the larger winged angels above are somewhat livelier, but on the whole they are academic, and the kneeling king with his purple robe and ruff is in the traditional French style of Vouet and Lebrun. After all this there is little left that is Ingres' own, and one does not quite understand why just this particular picture should have had such a tremendous success. Perhaps it was because in this same Salon of 1824 Delacroix exhibited his "Massacre of Chios" and, needing an upholder of tradition to oppose this revolutionary innovator, the public was happy to find an artist who brought to the conservative point of view such great technical skill and such an irreproachably worthy style.

During this period Ingres painted some other, more original, pictures in which he gave a better demonstration of his powers of conception and composition. At the very beginning of his Italian sojourn he produced the well-known "Oedipus and the Sphinx" (Louvre), a picture whose combination of archaism and three-dimensional materiality is reminiscent of the "Jupiter and Thetis" in Aix. The youth with his foot set high upon the rocks is executed with surpassing skill. The pure profile position of the Oedipus and the containment of his three-dimensional body within a single plane are at once archaic and modern. An ancient statue of an athlete from Tivoli served as a model for the Oedipus, but unlike a painted prototype the statue had a contrary effect of lively movement. As for the subject matter, it is typically romantic — a somewhat terrifying fairy tale from antiquity.

The effect of the picture suffers because of its pretentious size. This is true of other pictures of the same kind: there are large empty surfaces, and passages that are altogether dead. Only particular figures, strongly and finely modeled, enable us to overlook Ingres' inability to subordinate details to a powerfully unified whole. The precious form of the "Thetis" is attractive in the same way as is that of the

"Angelica" whom Roger (in accordance with Ariosto's story) saves from the dragon. The perfect execution of this female nude, with the pure line of the contour, her turning motion, and sensually bent-back throat (a motive already found in Flaxman, and much favored by Ingres), her obvious terror; all this is excellent in and for itself, but not as part of the composition. A "Virgil Reading from His Aeneid" (Toulouse; see Fig. 45) is rather dull and empty, but the preparatory study for the group of listeners with the swooning Octavia in the lap of Augustus (Brussels) has a monumental stylization and is very impressive. Dramatic subjects were for the most part outside the range of Ingres' talent. The group of "Paolo and Francesca," done after the words of Dante, "on this day we read no more," is in spite of the youth's stormy pose, half moving, half comic, and certainly not tragic.

But when Ingres paints single figures the effect is entirely different. To this group belong above all his variously seated and reclining female nudes, as for example, the "Bather" of the Louvre (1808). Here we see a nude, with a turbanlike cloth wound around her slightly turned head, sitting back to us on the edge of a couch. (The half-length version of 1807, in the Musée Bonnat, Bayonne, is perhaps even finer.) Particularly lovely in color is the "Grande Odalisque" (1814; Fig. 47), a beautiful figure which in the Salon of 1819 was called "Gothic" and "primitive." The pose of this nude has a much more complicated contrapposto than Titian's "Venus" by which it was inspired; the back and hip are turned toward the spectator, but the head is turned nearly forward, and the left leg is crossed over the right. In spite of these interior movements and twistings, the whole figure is gathered within one plane and, for all their fullness, the uncommonly elongated forms of the body are rendered with strength and cold restraint. A kind of frozen sensuousness, which emerges in Ingres as in many classicists, permeates the whole. Here again, as in the portraits, a contrast occurs between the cool reserve of the face and the richness (in color as well) of the accessories. Manet's "Olympia," which used to hang in the Louvre almost as a pendant to Ingres' "Odalisque," makes an interesting comparison. One sees that the gap between Ingres' classicistic "gothicizing" and Manet's knife-sharp reduction of planes is basically not impassable.

Unique in Ingres' *oeuvre* is the "Interior of the Sistine Chapel" (various versions: 1814, sketch in Montauban; 1820, Louvre; Fig. 46). Like David in the "Jeu de Paume" Ingres here mastered an interior, except that all the agitation and conflict of masses for which David strove were foreign to Ingres' temperament. On the contrary, Ingres tried to render the restrained pomp of a pontifical mass — celebrated in a spot made solemn by Michelangelo's art — through an emphasis on the measured movements of the celebrants, the pope and the cardinals, and by colors heavier than usual. Here Ingres put by all that was anecdotal in his historical pictures and created something essential and lasting in its color and largeness of spatial composition. One regrets that Ingres did not more often employ the great art that he displayed here in the service of similar problems.

Through the triumph, in the Salon of 1824, of the "Vow of Louis XIII," Ingres was for the first time on solid ground. His art was no longer written off with offensive epithets such as "gothic," or even (as had happened) "Chinese"; he no longer, as in his youth, counted as a revolutionary, an opponent of the school of David — a role in which he had fancied himself. Now he became the recognized leader of the conservative tendency, in his own phrase, a *conservateur des bonnes doctrines*. It is not too much to say that in this capacity he felt himself to be the God-given defender of the pure ideal, a kind of pope of classical Raphaelism. This is the explanation of his obstinate, narrow-minded hate of all dissenters — quite in contrast to David. He even forbade his pupils to look at the Rubens in the Louvre, and if any one of them dared to make some slight concession to colorism, he was counted a deserter and an apostate. For Ingres there was no one more terrible than he who seduced others into the way of such sin; the real Lucifer, the embodiment of all evil, was Delacroix. And because he had to admit Delacroix's great talent as an artist, he was that much more fearful that that baneful influence would spoil or destroy the seed he had sown. Nothing pained Ingres more than that at the World Exposition of 1855, where he had a retrospective showing of his work, he had finally to share top honors with Delacroix, who was given similar space; or that in 1856 Delacroix was at last elected to the Academy, of which Ingres had been a member since 1825. At the base of all this hate lay the insecurity of a by no means outstanding intelligence, a fear of everything that was modern and hence revolutionary. As Baudelaire pointed out, the new romantic school felt itself to be the progressive school, yet Delacroix, who was regarded as its leader, was not nearly so fanatically opposed to Ingres as the latter was to him. Even Baudelaire, the defender of the romantics, accompanied his sharp, just criticisms of Ingres with a dispassionate recognition of Ingres' real merits and talent, and other late romantic critics such as Théophile Gautier were occasionally more enthusiastic about Ingres than were his own followers. This was perhaps because even in his later works Ingres' classicism remained in many ways essentially romantic: religious themes ("St. Symphorien," "Madonna of the Host"); themes of historical sentiment ("Francis I at the Deathbed of Leonardo da Vinci"); exotic themes ("Odalisques," "The Turkish Bath"); on occasion even neo-gothic themes ("Saints" for the Chapel of Sablonville); all these were attractive to the romantic temperament by their subject matter alone. Ingres' fear was not occasioned so much by romanticism itself, or by the attacks on him of the so-called romantics, as by the new colorism and the freer manner of execution which went with it. This fear, and the consciousness that in the last resort he could do nothing against the rising new school, led him to emphatic, nearly hysterical exaggerations of his classical doctrine. At the same time he continually tried to multiply the external props of his artistic power, not so much because he wished to enhance his personal position as because he wanted to further the true doctrine of the "School." He became Professor at the Ecole des Beaux Arts; in 1834 he had himself named Horace Vernet's successor as director of the French Academy in Rome, whence he returned six years later to Paris with his reputation further enhanced; he became a member of the Institute, Senator, Grand Officer of the Legion of Honor, and maintained a famous school (of which Amaury-Duval has left an amusing account). In short, Ingres had a position such as even David had hardly occupied, and of which the enjoyment was marred only by Delacroix's increasing fame.

When one examines the many works large and small produced during these long years, it becomes apparent that the only really worthwhile ones (with certain exceptions from his last years) are those which still show traces of his youthful style. Most often they simply continue the early themes which occupied him recurrently throughout his life. In all such cases that archaistic and abstracting element, which in his youth Ingres had adopted and made his own, has not altogether disappeared. Naturally Ingres no longer wished to have anything to do with his youthful ideals or with his anti-Davidian revolt. When the charming little work of his Etruscan-Flaxman period, the "Wounded Venus," was later shown him in Paris, he laughed in confusion and said, *O cela . . . c'est un péché de jeunesse.* And more and more he detested the gothic-primitive. When he had first arrived in Italy he had made sketches from the Campo Santo frescoes in Pisa and from Giotto and was extremely enthusiastic about this early period of art: *c'est à genoux qu'il faudrait copier ces hommes-là.* But when, thirty years or more later, in Rome, he heard that two of his favorite pupils were copying Fra Angelico and the like in Florence and working in a primitive-Christian manner, he was greatly angered: *Ces messieurs sont à Florence; moi je suis à Rome . . . Vous entendez, je suis à Rome. Ils étudient le gothique . . . je le connais aussi . . . je le déteste . . . Il n'y a que les Grecs.* The Greeks now no longer meant "Etruscan" vases, but an ideal seen in the light of the Roman High Renaissance, and in the manner of Raphael. The result was that in many of his more important pictures Ingres became what has been called "a self-conscious classicist." This category includes his most famous composition, the "Apotheosis of Homer" (Salon of 1827), originally designed as a ceiling decoration for a room in the Louvre, but painted as an immense easel picture without regard to its destined position — an altogether classicistic approach. Worse than this, however, was the fact that in this picture Ingres set his sights much too high. His aim was to show a kind of "School of Athens" containing all the famous men of ancient and modern times. But a period such as the Restoration in France could not set itself problems similar to those of the High Renaissance, with whose humanistic ideal it no longer had anything in common; nor was Ingres a creator like Raphael who could find the solution of such a problem. In spite of one or two fine single figures (such as the Muses at the base of the throne), and in spite of the clear, brilliant color scheme, the large canvas is stilted and unconvincing. In comparison with Raphael, or even David, Ingres lacked the imagination necessary for such a project; as Baudelaire said, *l'imagination, cette reine des facultés, a disparu.*

This is also true of other pictures, such as the "Martyrdom of St. Symphorien" done for the cathedral of Autun (finished 1834), a canvas on which Ingres worked for many years and in which, in contrast to his usual calm, he wished to create powerful forms, *en mangeant du Michelange* (with whom it has however nothing to do); it lacks throughout the creative imagination required by such a large undertaking. Sometimes this imagination seems to be almost frozen or crystallized. The painting of "Stratonice" (1840, Chantilly; replica of 1866 in Montauban) suggests such a hardening process, particularly if one compares it with the original drawing of 1807 (Louvre) which is still built up in Ingres' early relieflike and practically spaceless archaism. In the finished picture, begun almost thirty years later and developed in nearly three hundred sketches and studies, the marble floor, marble columns, marble bed canopy, marble walls, and so forth so exaggerate the *couleur locale* that nothing remains but the cold, false splendor of an archaelogical restoration. The effect of the theme, which is impressive even if it is sentimental, is almost entirely swallowed by its setting — in spite of the fact that Ingres was originally so taken with the story that when he read Plutarch's tale of the sick king's son to his pupils at the Villa Medici, he broke into tears. But this marble splendor and the equally marble figures aroused tremendous enthusiasm among Ingres' public, so that his reputation, somewhat injured by the "St. Symphorien," was now further consolidated. Admired much more for their virtuosity than for their art, these show pictures answered in every detail to the artistic ideal of the bourgeoisie (of whom Ingres himself essentially remained one). With such pictures Ingres created the precedent for a kind of imitation-marble classicism, which at times took on altogether grotesque forms. Ingres' later historical canvases, such as "Francis I at the Deathbed of Leonardo da Vinci" (1848), only reinforce this kind of pompous and sentimentally deceitful painting, a style which does no honor to the nineteenth century.

In comparison with what is perhaps the purest work of art in Ingres' *oeuvre*—the nearly Far Eastern delicacy of the Louvre "Odalisque"—the single female figures of his later period are less successful. An enlargement of the same theme, the "Odalisque and Slave" (1839, Fogg Museum) is still very fine, even though the accessories occupy somewhat too much space and the former archaic chastity and severity have been replaced by a fuller, warmer, more voluptous conception. (Thematically, this invited comparison with Delacroix's "Moroccan Women," but the differences between them are nevertheless significant.) The "Venus Anadyomene" (1848, Chantilly) is also the revision of an early work. The figure rising from the sea spray and the charming *putti* about her feet are indeed lovely, and underneath this surface one can still feel the early tenderness and abstraction; but as Amaury-Duval (who saw the composition in its first state in Ingres' atelier) remarked, all its original *naïveté* has been lost. This is even more true for Ingres' most famous picture, "La Source" (1856, Louvre), which in its earlier stages may well also have been appealing. The finished work. however, charmed even such a critic as Theophile Gautier: *chef d'oeuvre inimitable, merveille de grâce et de fraîcheur, fleur d'un printemps de Grèce, pur marbre de Paros rosé de vie.* But for our taste today this figure contains both too much "marble" and too much "rosy life"; it is too like a statue and, in spite of some deliberate elongations and stylizations, somewhat painfully too like its lovely model. The lack of that artistic "distance" which the element of "gothicism" had formerly provided here results in an oversweetness which in earlier works had been avoided. The road to Bouguereau has now been opened.

In his later years Ingres did continue to produce many excellent portraits. Examples are the famous "M. Bertin," of the newspaper magnate (1832, Louvre); "The Duke of Orleans" (1842); "Mme. d'Haussonville" (Frick), which still has much of the tenderness and grace of the early portraits; the elegant likeness of Mme. Moitessier; his self-portraits, among them the clear and simple one of the Uffizi; the fine portrait of his second wife whom he married in 1856 at the age of seventy-six; and many others. They are still more masterful and accomplished than the earlier portraits, and they do not, as do many of his other paintings, become cheap and trivial. Yet, most of them lack that characteristic charm and that abstraction which makes the pictures of the early period so extraordinarily lovely. There are portrait drawings of the very last period which demonstrate, as surprisingly as those of his youth, Ingres' virtuosity in the handling of a delicate and yet not petty line; an example is that showing his godchild holding a candle in church (1856, Bayonne).

Ingres did, in his late years, produce some pictures which were frighteningly bad (such as the Apotheosis of Napoleon, 1853, for the Hôtel de Ville in Paris). Yet, we must insist that Ingres in his old age did not decay as completely as the old David had in Brussels. There are at least two works which transcend the late decay; works which, even though their conception dated back decades, and though they were based on youthful memories, received their final form only during Ingres' later years. The first is a mural decoration: "The Golden Age" in the Chateau of Dampierre. Begun in fresco in 1841, it was abandoned unfinished in 1850; the composition was fully executed only in an oil painting of 1860 (Fig. 48). A commission for such a mural scheme, in fresco, must have been very welcome to an artist of Ingres' disposition, because of the opportunity it offered to translate his strong and classic style into an appropriate medium. From Ingres, or rather from his atelier (Mottez, Flandrin, Amaury, etc.) there had already stemmed a kind of renaissance of fresco painting. Most of it employed an archaizing note which derived from the youthful, "gothic" Ingres, and dealt with Christian themes; in contrast to this, Ingres himself in this one fresco wished to produce something altogether heathen, something "Greek."

The theme of the Golden Age (which, according to the project, was to have been placed opposite a fresco of the Bronze Age) had long given artists of Ingres' tendencies the opportunity to represent a great group of nudes in the open, resting or moving about in gentle play, in an atmosphere of a serene, law-abiding *dolce far niente*. Poussin, in that lovely work of his old age, "Apollo and Echo," simply strove to represent an *âge d'or*. In fact, the landscape of the background and some figure groups in Ingres' fresco derive directly from Poussin's picture, and the atmosphere and sentiment are more dependent still. Poussin once defined the final aim of any art as "delectation." In such a picture Ingres could give wide play to his delight in the human form and could create groups nobly posed and arranged which, in their intertwining and overlapping, remind one of some works of the antique. No monumental painting by his successors — not Flandrin nor Puvis de Chavannes — surpassed this. Perhaps Chassériau in France and in Germany Hans von Marées (whom the right, unfinished side of the fresco brings to mind) could measure up to this standard. It may be fortunate that the fresco was never completed: for once Ingres could not indulge that zeal for finish and perfection which so often drove him to pettiness in detail.

"The Turkish Bath" (Fig. 49) was even more original. It was first painted, in 1859, as a rectangle, then revised to its present circular form in 1863 — the small, out-of-scale figure in the pool was added at that time. In this painting the theme of the early "Bather" (1808, Louvre) is taken up again. Here, with some changes in the pose of her legs and with the addition of a guitar, she is used as a *repoussoir* figure, but she still retains the essence of her original simplicity and chaste naïveté. But around this figure, and far beyond her into the background, there lie, sit, or wallow the forms of naked women, almost a tangle of them. The sensuality of the "Odalisque and Slave" (Fogg Museum) here recurs, much intensified by the sense of compression among the female forms. The immediate source for the theme of this picture was certainly the amusing description by Lady Mary Wortley Montagu, in her Turkish letters of the previous century, of a woman's bath in Adrianople. But, in a more general sense, what we see here is a reflection, even in the "Greek" and Raphaelesque Ingres, of the romantic taste for the exotic and the oriental — a taste already remarked in Gros, expressed most vividly in Delacroix, and present in Ingres' own earlier "Odalisques." Actually, Ingres had always shown in his art his fascination by this particular type of sensuous, sleepy, animal-like woman. In the fullness of her young but phlegmatic flesh and the naturalness of her expression, the "Belle Zélie" of Ingres' youth has much in common with Renoir's women. In contrast to Delacroix, Ingres looked upon his odalisque not as an object full of colorful charm, nor simply as an exoticism, but rather as a type of female. The harem woman lying back upon her cushions, her thick, supple limbs apathetically stretched out to any gaze is the perfect expression of this type. Here too was the beginning of a kind of abstraction, a reduction to an essential core which, even though its form was different, was still related to the archaism of Ingres' youth.

It is amazing that a man eighty years old should have been able to create a work that had both the living warmth and the artistic distance of the "Bain Turc." With all his calculated and stubbornly held limitations Ingres still possessed a tremendous vitality. To appreciate how living Ingres was and still is, one must compare him with his contemporary Cornelius, who played a similar role within the same period in Germany. Both possessed only mediocre intelligence, neither realized the limitations of his talent and so picked out high-flown, literary subjects which he could not master; both harnessed themselves to a rigid system from which escape was difficult, and through their Olympian poses both produced their artistic worst: the *genre ennuyeux*. But while, with some youthful exceptions, Cornelius' every stroke remained wooden, stiff, and lifeless, whenever Ingres stepped down from his self-imagined throne to work more or less for himself he showed an artistic power, an expression of a new creative vision, which has enriched his own world and posterity. This new style had in it both the "classical" and its contrast, the gothic-archaic; it united the "classicistic" and the "romantic." We have described at length and in detail the elements that throughout Ingres' long life went into the formation of this style, where and why it failed, and where it led to pure works of art. Ingres' historical role lay in his purifying the art of his time by ridding it of the worn-out formulas and gestures of an old, stale classicism. Out of all Ingres produced during a long and arduous life, posterity could get artistic nourishment only from the drawings and a few pictures: those few works that were impregnated by the "gothic" and the "archaic," which thus took on that clear and abstract character which is also found in the Japanese drawings which the great draftsmen-painters of the nineteen century loved so much. "A Chinese or a Japanese artist who has strayed into Greece" was the description given of Ingres by one of his contemporaries. And in this sense it was not the weak and pious frescoists nor the stilted neoclassicists, more or less directly connected with his school, who were really Ingres' followers, but Manet, Seurat, and above all Degas.

CHAPTER FIVE

EARLY BAROQUE AND REALISM IN THE ART OF GERICAULT

Théodore Géricault (1791–1824) was eleven years younger than Ingres, and seven years older than Delacroix. His work bore no relation — unless it was that of decided contrast — either to the Davidian tendency as it was established in the "school" or to its most important offshoot, the romantic-archaic classicism of Ingres. Géricault's roots lay not in any preconceived moral or artistic ideal, but in the very real impressions of his early youth, primarily those of the heavy Norman horses that he could see, ride, and study in the fields around his native town of Rouen. Had he not possessed the gift of artistic observation he might just as well have become a professional breeder of horses, or a gentleman jockey. Throughout Géricault's life horses and art went inseparably together, though never, thanks to his violent temperament, was he even for a moment a mere portraitist of horses or an animal painter after the tedious Dutch fashion. Because great emotional excitement was inherent in his character, he developed naturally as a dynamic, baroque painter. Just as naturally he developed a leaning toward Gros, the only painter of the Davidian school who, especially in his horses and riders, sought for coloristic movement and baroque excitement.

Certainly Géricault's innate talent was far above that of David's distraught and self-tortured pupil. But further, the gap between the generations was also important. Among the men who had helped to prepare and had lived through the tremendous moral and social upheaval of the Revolution and who then, as active or bemused spectators of Napoleon's world-shaking deeds, took part in France's most glorious epoch, there was a different feeling about life than in the men of the next generation, who were but being born during this period. Géricault was born in the third year of the Revolution, and Delacroix during the Directory. Both these younger men retained a strong measure of feeling for the heroic; both were still children of a heroic period of history. But their impulse toward heroic deeds could no longer be directly translated into the description of real actions, as had been possible for David or Gros. Under the Bourbon reaction conditions were not in the least favorable to such temperaments. Heroism became a memory of childhood, something retrospective, and so one of the typical signs of romantic feeling.

Of course, this romanticism took on its particular shape and coloring through the special traits of genius that were mixed with it. In David and Ingres there was nothing particularly inspired, nothing intentionally spirited, much less any atmosphere of genius — nothing exuberant, sparkling, energetic, or extravagant. But Byron's work and personality helped to spread these qualities throughout France toward the end of the second decade of the century and they became fashionable. The general attitude toward life of an artist such as Géricault contrasted sharply with that of the whole preceding generation of the Revolution and differed as much from David's principle-studded morality as from Prudhon's dreaming. Plutarch's manly and virtuous biographies, which Ingres still loved, the Anacreontics, Ossian, Homer, the books of an earlier period, no longer matched the spirit of the times. Géricault read Byron and Walter Scott and, with somewhat less zeal, Tasso, Milton, and Schiller. But he was not essentially literary in any case; almost more than anything else, what interested him was riding and the circus. Franconi, the famous circus rider, was as dear to his heart as Rubens; both were his ideals and by ceaseless copying he tried to emulate the one, by physical training and exercises to imitate the other. He dressed with the greatest care, like a dandy. In Guérin's atelier he played the maddest practical jokes which no one, not even Guérin himself, held against him. His pranks were excused because of his likeableness and, above all, his overflowing talent — Guérin said he had enough to supply three or four painters. Altogether, Géricault perfectly represented a worldly type of inspired romantic. He had a brief political activity during the famous Hundred Days as a sort of *camelot du roi* guarding the Bourbons; compared to what David and Gros had risked, this was only a playful gesture on a much less heroic occasion. But, restless and passionate as he was, he later turned violently anti-Bourbon and was part of a group of extremists who during the worst period of reaction continued to be inspired by freedom and justice.

After a short apprenticeship with Carle Vernet, that fairly dry painter of battles and genre scenes — to whom he was in all probability drawn by his predilection for horses — Géricault moved to the studio of Guérin. Guérin had the reputation of being a good teacher; he allowed his pupils to preserve their own personalities and did not force them into the "Spanish boot" of an academic method. There Géricault could peacefully continue to follow his inclination for applying color in a Rubens-like impasto; in the atelier he was given the nickname of *le pâtissier*, or *le cuisinier de Rubens*. "Your studies from the nude," Guérin said to his pupil, "have as much resemblance to nature as a violin case has to a violin" — meaning that Géricault's natural bent was towards a painterly expansion of forms and space, in contrast to Guérin's manneristic, linear conception of the bodily contour.

It would have been altogether fitting had Géricault gone to study under Gros who, artistically speaking, was his closest kin. But he never became his pupil, even if his first pictures did follow Gros' turbulent equestrian portraits so closely that some of Géricault's early drawings have until recently been considered as works of Gros. Among the paintings of this early period, one which had a great success in the Salon of 1812, the "Officer of the Imperial Guard" (Fig. 50), is still strongly under Gros' influence. It shows a guardsman on a leaping horse with a leopard-skin saddle, turning fiercely with saber bared in an attacking gesture. A small reversed study of the rider with upraised sword (also in the Louvre) is looser, more painterly in atmosphere, and more natural in movement than the finished painting, which is too ambitious in size and not completely controlled. Altogether it is a picture of fine passion and lovely color, showing the greatest talent, but nothing more. *Pour les portraits équestres un bon peintre de plus*, said a critic. It contained no suggestion of anything revolutionary; it was simply an emphatic continuation of the Rubenist current which, as we have seen, had not entirely disappeared in David, and had risen to the surface again in Gros.

More personal and mature was the "Wounded Cuirassier" (Salon of 1814; Fig. 51), which mirrored the tragic end of the superhuman wave of Napoleonic victories, and so is more gloomy in its color. The panting, worried horse and the wounded man, who leans resting on his saber and quietly turns to look back toward the battle, fuse together into one daringly compounded group. The shoulder-length figure of the "Carabinier" (Fig. 52), with his breastplate and his military moustache and sideburns, is striking in the quality of the paint as well as in expression. Here is heroism, but with a melancholy note, transforming it into romanticism. One can also understand from this Géricault's interest in wild animals, which he studied and painted in the Paris Jardin des Plantes; he saw in them intense passion, hemmed in by fate.

In the fall of 1816, Géricault went to Rome. But he did not go to breathe deeply of the classical air, to satisfy a great, longfelt desire, as did nearly all the winners of the Prix de Rome — Ingres above all. In typical romantic fashion, Géricault was passionately in love with a married woman. His trip to Italy was a kind of flight, in which he was so restless that he soon broke off his stay in Rome and went to Florence in order to lose himself (his action is reminiscent of Stendhal) in an extravagant and elegant society life. Despite all this he was greatly influenced by the new, southern forms around him, by the manners of the people, by the natural environment, and by the art — influenced much more than Prudhon, and very differently from Ingres, for whom Italy merely confirmed a preconceived ideal. To Géricault a closer acquaintance with the antique and with the artists of the *cinquecento*, particularly Michelangelo, meant an accentuation and strengthening of his romantically fired, impulsive nature. This is particularly clear in his representation of horses, which he continued to favor in Rome. They were no longer the race-horse portraits of Vernet, which he had tried to imitate during his very first period in Paris, nor the prancing, biting baroque steeds of Rubens which Gros had again brought to life. The stylization of the horses on the Parthenon frieze, casts of which Géricault saw in Rome, enchanted him. The instantaneousness of movement, the swift twist or turn which occurs so often in his early equestrian portraits, now disappears almost completely in an arresting and monumentalizing of the motion itself. Often the formal conception takes on a sculpturesque character; indeed, it was in Rome that Géricault developed his liking for sculpture, which he occasionally practiced.

The most important problem Géricault set himself in Italy lay altogether within his province; it was limited neither by history nor by tradition, and was inspired by an actual impression. He was attracted by a piece of Roman popular life, the so-called *corso dei barberi*, the race of stallions along the Corso during the Carnival. Twelve or more studies and innumerable drawings of them still exist; for, though he was haphazard and unconcentrated in his external life, Géricault prepared his artistic work with extreme exactitude and stubbornness. He was one of the first artists to study anatomy again in a fundamental way in order to learn the structure of the body (even of horses' bodies); Ingres, on the other hand, had a pronounced antipathy for this sort of analysis. Géricault's "Corso dei barberi" was unfortunately never finished. We must content ourselves with the broadly sketched-in studies in the Louvre and elsewhere (Fig. 53) — some of them magnificent — of which certain ones show the beginnings of the compositional idea: the excited horses held back from the starting line by half-naked youths, and in the background there an idealized antique architecture. In Rouen there are other studies of single groups, finer and more complete in their stylization. In these, against a lovely wide landscape and a light-filled sky, naked youths with large and measured movements restrain a powerful steed. Deep but muted colors alternate in light and dark. The coloristic technique and the body modeling are reminiscent of Poussin, the soft tones somewhat recall Prudhon (whose "Justice" Géricault had copied), and the sculpturelike conception of space is classicistic. But the whole is shot through with a new painterly baroque impulse, which one can consider, if one likes, as romantic. During this Roman year, 1817, Géricault also did a series of handsome drawings of classical subjects that carry on the eighteenth-century tradition of Fragonard, as well as of Prudhon: "The Triumph of Silenus," "Mars and Hercules," "Centaur Abducting a Woman," "Leda and the Swan," and so on. "Hercules and the Bull" (Louvre; like many others of this series, also executed in lithograph), one of the finest of this genre, goes back in its general conception to classical reliefs, though the nude Hercules, seen from the back, derives from Michelangelo's cartoon of the bathing soldiers.

For Géricault, the Michelangelo of the Sistine Chapel, and particularly of the "Last Judgment," was the great experience which overshadowed even the antique. The influence was not immediately perceptible, but it lived on in Géricault and became apparent in his most important work, the "Raft of the *Medusa*." Baudelaire (in his *Salon* of 1846) spoke of *Michelange, qui est à un certain point de vue l'inventeur de l'idéal chez les modernes*. And his judgment was correct, for Michelangelo, the father of baroque movement, could be associated with the painterly tendency of Rubens; while Raphael, though not despised (even Géricault copied him), remained the ideal and model of the Ingres tendency. Ingres, as a typical Raphaelite, always spoke of Michelangelo with a certain constraint. A kind of early baroque revival was beginning to appear in the painting of the nineteenth century. We have seen how Correggio, who contributed so much to the formation of the protobaroque of about 1580 became the model of Prudhon's protoromanticism. More decisive is Géricault's strong interest in Caravaggio and his movement — of which David had already taken a short-lived notice. As it had affected a significant stream of seventeenth-century painting in Italy and Spain, Caravaggio's so-called "naturalistic" movement exercised a strong influence, direct or indirect, upon the realistic painting of the nineteenth century. On the corpses of the "Raft of the *Medusa*" Géricault used Caravaggio's black shadows and his manner of handling the nude heavily and honestly and without artificial poses for the sake of modeling.

When, after more than a year in Italy, Géricault impatiently went back to Paris, he was filled with impressions and the desire to create. But the idea that could fuse these impulses was still missing. Military subjects, carabiniers, and chasseurs with or without their horses no longer meant anything to him; and the mythologic drawings of Leda or Hercules that he had done in Rome were only a pastime, finger exercises which he was not inspired to execute in painting. He needed something at once contemporary and monumental. At first he tried to monumentalize another popular scene like the *corso dei barberi*—the Paris cattle market (*marché aux boeufs*; Fig. 54). But soon a subject came to him which overrode all the others; it was at once contemporary and monumental, political and artistic, gruesomely sublime and fantastically adventurous. The *Medusa*, an official frigate bound for Senegal, foundered. A raft was made, which the lifeboats of the frigate were supposed to tow. But for some reason the sailors in the boats cut the towropes, and the raft, with about one hundred and fifty people on it, was left to the mercy of the sea. There were terrible scenes: sailors revolted against their officers; torn by hunger and thirst half-mad people fought each other bestially, until finally after twelve days at sea the survivors were picked up by a brig. Back in Paris this terrible event caused a tremendous sensation, which was heightened by a brochure published in 1817 by two of the survivors. Politics played its part as well. The ministry was accused of negligence and favoritism which, it was charged, had caused or at least aggravated the catastrophe. At this period Géricault belonged to a group of political malcontents at the head of which was his friend Horace Vernet. But it was not merely a desire for political criticism or his passionate human sympathy for all victims of injustice that aroused his interest in the tragedy; it was rather that in his artistic imagination there at once emerged plastic images of the striking, tremendously impressive episodes of this marine disaster.

With the unbelievable energy and enthusiasm that possessed him when he was gripped by an exciting problem, Géricault went to work. It was characteristic of him that, combining a feverish desire for creation with an almost pedantic scientific study of his material, he should need a tremendous amount of study and preparation in order to bring forth his work. The basic elements had to be historically accurate. The two eye witnesses — authors of the accusing pamphlet (for which Géricault later did five lithographs) — were questioned concerning every detail and their portraits painted for insertion in important positions in the picture. Each individual figure was studied in great detail, partly using the painter's friends — among them the young Delacroix — as models. Because a Negro played an important role in the event (the emancipation of Negroes was already being discussed), he applied himself to drawing and painting Negroes (Fig. 55). Some of these studies have the grandiose plastic modeling of bronze casts. His old love of anatomy and the study of cadavers was now intensified: he examined heads and the twisted arms and legs of executed persons in every conceivable position and light (Fig. 56). In the hospitals of Paris, where his interests had made him friends, he studied the sick and the dying (Fig. 57). He made a trip to the seaside, where he took notes on the light and the cloud shapes, and had a raft built in order to observe its motion on the waves. He worried about the choice of the best episodes out of all this epic material. Should he pick the moment when the towropes were cut and the raft with its human cargo left behind or, what certainly attracted him, the episode of the revolt; should he paint the final rescue, or the moment just before it when the appearance of the brig on the horizon awakened hope in those few who still survived? After an enormous number of sketches (unfortunately now scattered in various places, and to my knowledge never all exhibited together; Figs. 58–60), he finally decided on the last episode, because it afforded him the most varied expressive possibilities (Fig. 61).

The picture grew so big (15 × 21 feet) that Géricault had to rent a specially large studio to paint it. It represents the storm-driven raft with its tilted makeshift mast and wind-filled sail. The raft is placed on a diagonal, one corner at the bottom of the picture, and so leads the eye obliquely into space. (In an earlier version the angle is even stronger and more violent, and the resulting crescendo still livelier and more moving.) Not only do the waves lift the raft diagonally into the picture space, but the figures are pyramided in a tremendously impressive fashion to follow and to emphasize this movement. Where the waves play over the raft at its lowest point are grouped the passive figures — made passive by death or by fatigue and despairing resignation, among them the statuesque group of the father with his dead son in his lap. Towards the center a rising, mounting movement begins. Here some of the shipwrecked (among them an Arab), have awakened from their apathy, and with lifted hands push excitedly towards the horizon, where the rescue ship appears. Then the single stream of the composition broadens out towards the sides, like the short arms of a Latin cross, though all the movement still points forward, and the central axis moves straight on to its triumphant summit, the slim, nude back of the Negro. Mounted on a barrel and supported by his comrades, waving a white cloth into the air, he is the final peak of a pyramid of moving and excited bodies.

In the picture as finally executed this accentuated, impressive stream of movement is opposed by a very evident countercurrent, whose importance to the composition may be judged by comparison with the sketch, where the whole design is weakened by its absence. In the study the planks of the lower edge of the raft in the right corner of the picture are covered with waves and so invisible; now they are clearly outlined and drawn into the general movement, and close to the edge the body of a dying or a dead man points in the same direction. The group standing near the mast (among them the ship's doctor and engineer, the two authors of the pamphlet) is enlarged and clarified. And finally, in a last-minute revision of his picture after it had been finished, Géricault painted in the naked body that hangs over the side of the raft with its head hidden in the water — in all probability to fill in what would otherwise have been an empty spot. Though the main axis still dominates, the result is now a system of two crossed diagonals such as is often found in the painting of the early baroque. It is perhaps for this reason that the composition, so free and full of movement in the sketches, has, in the painting, become infected by a somewhat stiff and academic atmosphere. At any rate the classical system of constructing space by means of overlapping parallel layers, favored by David and still used by Géricault in his Roman works, has here been decisively broken.

With all its realism and its individual handling of detail, with all its study of the model (which remains somewhat too evident), the echoes of older art are many and clear. Géricault's enthusiasm for Michelangelo's Sistine Chapel, and especially for his "Last Judgment," comes out in many of the poses, particularly those of the more tragic groups. In the plastic form of the corpses and in the sharp chiaroscuro with which they are handled, the influence of Caravaggio is just as strong. Of more recent masters, the most influential was of course Gros, whose "Plague of Jaffa" Géricault greatly admired and for which he wanted the "*Medusa*" to be a pendant. The only reminiscence of Rubens, the master he had at first preferred, occurs in the colorful warm tone of the sketches. The finished picture is not based on a painterly massing of colors, but on the arrangement in a plastic form of figure groups which are carefully differentiated and graded in expression. Here too there is a link with older painting — that of the high baroque, where light contrasts are maintained, while color is purposely made more dusky and restrained.

This definitive version, too large in its format, does not produce the immediate effect, nor does it entirely fulfill the promise of the sketches and studies. Nevertheless, the essential artistic idea remains. Not only do the worn-out formulas of the Davidian school pale before this; so also does Gros' "Jaffa" which, in effect, is only a new version of earlier plague pictures, with Napoleon as the miracle-worker. Géricault does not represent heroes, but heroism, the heroic endurance of the anonymous, suffering at the hands of fate and their fellow men; he lends them a pathos and passion attained neither by his predecessors nor by his contemporaries. How far Ingres and his aestheticism are from everything social and collective! Géricault's "*Medusa*" splits wide open not merely the form of classicism, but its content and its feeling.

But when at length the great work was exhibited in the Salon of 1819 it did not find the recognition it deserved, even if Delacroix and the other younger artists were enthusiastic. It won only an honorable mention and was not, as Géricault had hoped, bought by the government. Angered by this, Géricault decided to accept an English offer to make a sort of traveling exhibition of the picture, as the result of which he earned a handsome sum. This was what prompted Géricault to go to England in 1820 for a brief stay. Here in the classic country of racing he returned to his first love, and it was perhaps here, in a small canvas, that he first attained the full expression of his artistic personality. He was disgusted with large-scale painting, with high tragedy and noble gestures, possibly because of the small success of the "*Medusa.*" So he turned entirely to what was probably most basic in his make-up: the acute observation of immediate reality. He turned over a commission for a religious picture in a provincial church, given him by the government in compensation for its not having bought the "*Medusa,*" to the youthful Delacroix. *J'abdique*, he wrote to a friend from England, *le cothurne et la Sainte Ecriture pour me renfermer dans l'écurie.* He carried out a whole series of lithographs of street scenes and horses which gave inspiration to his companion of the trip, the amusing draftsman and lithographer Charlet. But these lithographs did not have any great success, and did not bring in their hoped-for return in money. (Géricault said that he wanted to come out of the stable *couvert de l'or.*)

Essentially Géricault remained altogether a painter, a colorist, who applied his tones nervously and quickly and knew how to produce a brilliant effect with every brush stroke. His work is, therefore, in sharp contrast to the school of David, and even to Gros, who in comparison seems to employ flat and local tones. The English school made a great impression on him: not only Constable, whose division of color was to carry away Delacroix in the Salon of 1824, but also the English genre and animal painters, Ward, Morland, and Wilkie (see Fig. 62). All the passion for stylization he had had in the "Corso dei barberi," everything Michelangelesque, anything in any way traditional, whether derived from Rubens or from the early baroque, dropped away. He had early learned to grasp movement, but until now he had bent it into a tight and conventional framework. For the first time, in the "Horseracing at Epsom" (1821; Fig. 63), he grasped the whole of a scene in terms of a momentary impression. Here he no longer rendered the beginning or the end of a race, as he had formerly done, nor a picture of immobilized life, but the race and the motion itself. Four horses are stretched out in an exaggerated flying gallop on a wide, flat racecourse, their hoofs hardly touching the ground, jockeys on their backs; there is a gently rolling landscape, a splendid cloud-filled sky; in all the scene only one vertical, the white pole. This is an absolute sensation of the eye, a sudden grasp of the flying and the fleeting. Historical precedents for such a portrayal of the momentary are hardly discoverable; even in English painting there is nothing similar. A new genre had been created, which was to be continued only later in the century by the impressionists and by Degas.

The few years which were left to Géricault after his return from England were unhappy ones. Inner conflict, contrary mischance, bodily infirmity, all came at once. The accident which at length brought on his final suffering and death appears almost as a natural conclusion. Géricault lived on a large scale, kept a carriage and many riding and race horses, frequented society, and all this demanded a large income. He speculated and naturally lost; he founded a factory which just as naturally failed. Finally in jumping a barrier he hurt his spine, did not take care of himself, contracted an abscess, and after awful suffering died at the age of only thirty-three.

During these last three years it was no longer possible for him to paint any large pictures, though he was still planning them on his deathbed. He was conscious of not having spoken his final words, of not having entirely expressed his essential nature. He complained that he had accomplished little if anything. His projects again combined the living and the timely, the ethical and the political: the opening of the Inquisition, the freeing of the slaves, scenes from the Greek war of independence (which Delacroix too was to adopt). He could still carry out smaller works and he did a whole series of lithographs, among them some with handsome painterly effects, suggestive of color. A landscape in oils of this time, "Le Four à plâtre" or "The Limekiln" (1824; Fig. 64), is surprisingly advanced. It shows a kind of factory building with sheds, a road on which are carts and horses, and a cloudy sky. In strong contrast to all composed, ideal landscapes, such a picture (reminiscent of the Dutch, or even more of Louis Le Nain) unites realism with the creation of a mood and leads to the painting of the forties. The "Moulin de la Galette," a water color of the famous Montmartre mill (often painted early in the century by the Montmartre painter, Georges Michel) points in the same direction. Géricault's study of English landscape painting was certainly influential here, but the tone is harsher and more decisive, one might almost say more social.

Géricault's representations of mad people, which he did as a sort of series for a friend who was a doctor of the insane, were altogether new in French painting. (Of ten pictures completed about five are now known; Figs. 65, 66.) The old woman with her wicked glance under her white cap is a masterpiece of realistic characterization (only Hogarth is worthy of comparison), while the profile of a young woman in a great beribboned bonnet on which the light plays in broad strokes is a study that anticipates Courbet.

In Géricault's many-sided, often apparently contradictory art, perhaps the most important of all is this last phase of realism. It is more significant than his beginnings, when he was influenced by Gros and his movement, more so than the soft Prudhon-Poussin-like pictures of his Roman period, with their statuesque stylization, more so even than the great Michelangelesque undertaking of the "Raft of the *Medusa*." It should not be forgotten that Géricault was one of the first artists to go back seriously to Caravaggio, that is, to that realistic stream of Italian seventeenth-century art from which, partly by way of Spain, both French realism and impressionism took their start. Géricault was not, as he is often called, the exclusive forerunner of Delacroix; the latter, though obviously under his influence at the beginning, soon developed, as we shall see, more and more in the direction of the full-blown baroque. It was rather Courbet, the leader of French realism, who continued the vein of Géricault; Géricault was Courbet's prime enthusiasm. Many of Courbet's portraits, in their soft and lyrical realism, remind one of Géricault. There are even paintings of deer by Géricault which are direct precedents for Courbet.

Géricault, after all the variously directed efforts of his short life, represents a particular and an important phase in the history of French painting. His taste — he greatly admired David — was in no way revolutionary. But even when he followed tradition he was always alive, interesting, and filled with an inner ardor — one of the greatest French artists of a rich century.

CHAPTER SIX

ROMANTIC HIGH BAROQUE IN THE ART OF DELACROIX

With Eugène Delacroix (1798–1863) a wave of wholly high-baroque style, sparkling with light and color, swept into French painting with greater force than ever in artistic history before. The old fundamental contrasts, which French art theory of the seventeenth century had divided into opposing camps under the banners of Poussin and of Rubens, and which had led to so much conflict, once more came to life, and more strongly. Ingres and Delacroix were divided by more than a difference of generation. When they showed their pictures at the Salon in 1824, a yawning gulf opened between two absolutely opposed artistic points of view. Ingres was represented by the academic, Raphaelite "Vow of Louis XIII" which brought him his first and most decisive triumph among his fellow countrymen, while Delacroix exhibited his "Massacre of Chios," which even the well disposed, such as Baron Gros, called a *massacre de la peinture*. This picture contained all the essentials of a style that marked Delacroix as the leader of the new painterly, baroque, romantic tendency. Since the battle of the Poussinists and the Rubenists a century and a half earlier the gulf between them had significantly deepened; Ingres' art, in its radical emphasis on draftsmanship and abstraction of form, set up a far more extreme ideal than the Poussinists, while Delacroix went much further in that painterly direction which was associated with the name of Rubens. The often formulated contrasts of classicism and romanticism are worth little in the stylistic definition of the two artists and their adherents. We have seen that at one time Ingres' works contained many romantic elements and that, further, through his "gothic" style, he set himself off from the classicism of a David or a Poussin. On the other hand, Delacroix exhibited all the unmistakable symptoms of romanticism: subjectivism, exoticism, Byronism, etc., but the enumeration of these things, which are part of the general spirit of the time, does not even approximately describe the essential characteristics of his art. Far more important than these qualities was Delacroix's personal temperament and genius which developed an existing baroque trend (in France as elsewhere parallel to the stream of classicism) to its fullest culmination. This importance of Delacroix's genius remains even in comparison with his immediate predecessors of generally similar orientation. As we have tried to make clear, such painters as Prudhon still showed protobaroque characteristics through their dependence on Correggio; others, like Géricault, mixed their baroque tendencies with realistic traits derived from Caravaggio. In Delacroix these protobaroque or early baroque adulterations were completely absent; in particular any approach to the dark-toned realism of Caravaggio was alien to him. His art was altogether dedicated to coloristic, dynamic movement and, considered stylistically, his work must therefore be described as of a purely high-baroque style which had altogether shaken off the insistent static and statuesque demands of neoclassicism, as well as any tendency towards naturalism.

Delacroix was born near Paris toward the turn of the century. Through his mother, a Riesener, he had in him the artistic blood of that famous family of eighteenth century *ébénistes*; the family of his father, a minister and ambassador under the Directory, belonged to the category of high officials. However, an old rumor, recently seriously reconsidered by his biographers, points to no one less than Talleyrand as his real father. Be that as it may, Delacroix grew up the possessor of a distinguished manner and a rich culture, and with a gift for spirited and witty conversation. These outward social graces were matched by a reserve in all personal matters which befitted his inward nature, proud and melancholy. All his works, no matter how colorful their sparkle, or how bold and magnificent their appearance, are imbued with the deep sincerity and melancholy of his being. Nowhere do Delacroix's creations show the sturdy, life-affirming balance of a Rubens. The pessimism of Byronic romanticism played a great part in molding his character. As he grew older, that contempt of mankind natural to such a constrained character increased and he turned away more and more from his own time and surroundings. Though he never allowed his love of society, music, and the theater to die out entirely, his inner spirit, especially since he remained unmarried, became ever more solitary. This meant that he could pour all his undivided passion into the limitless abundance of his artistic creation — though not in the exhibitionist, revolutionary, mystic fashion of a Van Gogh. Perhaps more than anyone else he possessed what the French call *fougue*, a fiery enthusiasm of creative heat and fury, though he detested having this word applied to his painting. He did not want his *plus belles inflammations* taken for *des ardeurs inconscientes*, nor the "holy fire" which consumed him interpreted as "animal" heat. An important part of his self-discipline was *de dissimuler les colères de son coeur, et de n'avoir pas l'air d'un homme de génie*, an attitude fundamentally at variance with the pose of "genius" affected by Géricault and the romantics. Dominating all the rest, mastering his natural impulses and that excitement which left him trembling *comme le serpent dans la main de la Pythonisse* was a methodical discipline, achieved by his clear and inexorable intellect.

Il signor Poussin è un pittore chi lavora di là, said Bernini in Paris on looking at a landscape of Nicolas Poussin, and he pointed to his forehead — a painter who worked with his mind as well as his heart. In this respect Delacroix was a spiritual relation of his great compatriot; though he was a glowing Rubenist and no Poussinist at all, Delacroix was closely related to Poussin as an artistic personality. They possessed the same warmth and the same brilliance of invention — evident above all in Poussin in his wonderful drawings and sketches — and they both relied strongly on theory in order first to clarify their own intentions to themselves, and then to determine the fundamental principles of all art. They also had in common a love of narration; Delacroix, like Poussin, was a great teller of legends and stories, and both possessed a considerable literary culture. Delacroix had a fairly wide range as a writer on art, and even wrote a remarkable essay on Poussin. The three volumes of his *Journal* are famous, especially in artistic circles, containing as they do, particularly from his forties on, an overflowing wealth of technical and theoretical remarks. It is a pity that he never carried to completion the all-embracing work which, like Poussin, he had projected and begun: *Dictionnaire philosophique des beaux arts.* Delacroix was, therefore, a man ready at all times to give an account of himself and his actions. *Passionément amoureux de la passion*, he was coldly determined to realize the most explicit expression of the passions in his paintings. *Delacroix peintre de grande race*, concluded Théophile Silvestre in an article written in 1858, "[he] has a sun in his brain and a hurricane in his heart; for forty years he has sounded the whole scale of human passion; grandiose, terrible, or calm, the brush went from saints to warriors, from warriors to lovers, from lovers to tigers, and from tigers to flowers."

Delacroix became acquainted with Géricault in the atelier of Guérin, and it is important to determine their relationship. Géricault recognized the great talent of the younger artist and as we have seen even turned over to him the important commission for "The Virgin of the Sacred Heart." "The Raft of the *Medusa*" made a deep impression on the young Delacroix. He himself tells how he ran home "mad" with enthusiasm when for the first time he saw the large canvas half completed in Géricault's atelier. It was natural that from that moment on he should have been possessed with the desire to create something just as significant. In spite of this, Géricault's influence on Delacroix was not as great as is sometimes supposed. The difference in their natures was very great, but even more essential was the fact that in spite of their common "romantic" feeling for life and art, their work belonged to two different stages of stylistic evolution. Delacroix himself helps us understand these differences. He was, on the whole, very enthusiastic about Géricault (it was only in 1854 that he formulated certain critical objections, particularly concerning the lithographs). He even compared him (in his late notes as well as earlier) to Michelangelo: *Le genre de mérite* [of Géricault] *a le plus grand rap-*

port avec celui de Michel-Ange. Even the "incorrect" drawing, which in no way injures the whole, is to be found in the one as in the other.

But Michelangelo, "sublime" as he is, and much as Delacroix admired him (it was Michelangelo who inspired the pendentives of the Palais Bourbon), was not his highest "ideal." In Delacroix's eyes Michelangelo did not sufficiently subordinate the parts to the whole, but instead formed his sublime ideas out of a gathering together of realistically studied bodies. The same held true for Géricault (Delacroix always had the "Raft of the *Medusa*" in mind). In him Delacroix perceived the individual detail, the anatomical study, the coördination of statuesque groups, the union of the monumental with the realistic; in him, too, Delacroix felt the "sublime" and recognized it, but saw here neither his own road nor his own goal. He strove for a still higher unity, for a joining of all forces into a single harmony, for a master idea to which every point and line of form and color must be subordinated, not a series of elements placed side by side and not a Renaissance-like formal synthesis achieved through external calm and balance, but a river of force which carries everything with it. This ideal, which the period of the true baroque perhaps also desired, but which it rarely attained, Delacroix tried to approach in practice and in theory. One can follow the stages of his tireless effort to achieve an ever clearer and simpler unity of content, form, and color by increasingly tense control over all these elements at once. It was characteristic of him that he conceived his ideal not in the image of a painter, not even in that of Rubens, from whom he took only a method, but in that of a poet, Dante. In Dante he saw a sublimity which, unlike that of Michelangelo, no longer had anything in common with merely realistic truth. What enchanted him in Dante was this sublimity achieved with the most colorful means of expression, and the ability to use the power of images to strike directly at the heart of the thing imagined and mold it to a single form. Delacroix's highest ambition was to rival, by the means proper to painting, the colorful synthesis and unity of tone of Dante's melancholy pathos.

Delacroix's first large painting, "Dante and Virgil in Hell" ("Dante et Virgile traversant le lac Dité," 1822; Fig. 67), was drawn from a passage of the *Inferno* and is charged with a Dantesque melancholy. The thematic arrangement obviously stems from Géricault's raft — a boat heavily laden with people, moving on the water — and this motive of the boat, in an ever clearer and more daring form, was pursued by Delacroix into his very last period. The large figures moved up close to the beholder are perhaps reminiscent of Géricault in the way in which they fill the surface of the canvas and in their isolated monumentality. But the epic, restrained tragedy which traverses the whole grandiose composition of figures and binds them together is altogether new and personal. The color as well contributes to this unity, and represents a decisive step away from Géricault's plastic, Caravaggiesque chiaroscuro, even though it does not yet have the brilliance that Delacroix later attained. It is astounding how this first work, done at the age of twenty-four, is lifted from the realm of naturalism into the artist's characteristic sphere of grandiose fantasy. Delacroix *fut grand dès sa jeunesse, dès ses premieres productions,* said Baudelaire, referring precisely to this picture; yet it fell far short of the level that the mature and even the ageing Delacroix was to demand of himself.

The new sentiment expressed by the "Dante and Virgil" forced sensitive artists to take notice. Baron Gros was one of these, saying of the picture that it was a *Rubens châtié*, a purified Rubens freed of the physical and lifted towards an ideal. It was the highest praise he could give a young artist, and nothing could have pleased or encouraged Delacroix more. But neither the public nor the critics responded to his second large picture, exhibited in 1824, and even Gros was cold to it. The "Scènes du massacre de Chios" (Fig. 69) in many ways constituted an advance over the "Dante and Virgil." Here for the first time we find a characteristic formulation of Delacroix's special version of the baroque: the figures are pushed forward towards the beholder; they no longer come out of a single monumentalized plane, but issue from a deep three-dimensional space, in which the background landscape of scattered scenes also plays its part in setting the mood of the whole. The sense of movement is increased to the point of restlessness: individual groups tend to fall apart and, instead of a single picture, form diverse incidents that are somewhat anecdotal in effect (the title "Scènes" suggests this). The gap between the group on the left, frozen in its suffering, and the movement of the lofty right side is much too great and is not softened by any transitions. It is apparent that Delacroix had not yet mastered this form of composition (one that he often used later), in spite of the fact that he worked considerably longer over it than on the quickly painted "Dante and Virgil," which is, as it were, more nearly cast from a single mold. A small water-color sketch of the "Massacre," colorful and powerful, is much more compact in effect. In both color and composition it is reminiscent of Persian miniatures of which Delacroix (like Rembrandt before him) was very fond. There are lovely individual scenes in the finished work: the "dying mother with her nurseling" is a brilliant passage showing that Delacroix had mastered the union of color and form. The motive was a favorite one in France and Italy in the sixteenth and seventeenth centuries (when it was often similarly placed in the composition), but it had never been painted as beautifully and as expressively as here. The picture's exotic orientalism and savage cruelty clearly exhibit its connection with the contemporary romantic movement; Gros, in the "Plague of Jaffa" and elsewhere, had shown the way. The "Massacre of Chios" was more topical than the "Dante and Virgil" since its depiction of Greek suffering was part of that great wave of philhellenic sympathy which, heightened by Byron, swept over Europe — and the United States as well — and inspired Delavigne and Victor Hugo and the other romantic poets to pen glowing verses.

The "Sardanapalus" of 1827 (Figs. 70, 71) is another great step towards the full and powerful movement of a high baroque, orgiastic in both content and form. It is a typical romantic subject, inspired by a tragedy of Byron (whom Delacroix would have to thank for a whole series of themes). The satrap, on his bed of state surmounting the funeral pyre, has his eunuchs slay all his fondest possessions — his wives and concubines, his pages, his dogs, and his favorite horse. Here is the complete unfolding of the "molochism" of Delacroix, that inclination towards the representation of cruelty — *les villes incendiées et fumantes, les victimes égorgées, les femmes violées, etc.* — which haunted the romantic generation, that joy in *atrocités et tourments* already documented in Victor Hugo's early *Han d'Islande.* Such a theme as the "Sardanapalus" might not have been wholly foreign among the academic eighteenth-century Prix de Rome, with their then baroque tendencies. In theme alone, even Ingres' "Stratonice" or odalisques are not too unlike. But where Ingres would have striven, in a subject like the "Sardanapalus," for the antiquarian local color of the scene, Delacroix rendered a pandemonium of passions, a whirling mixture of human and animal forms, the brilliant flesh of women, dark Negroes, caparisoned horses, rich stuffs, smoky clouds, and supreme over this turmoil, the black-bearded Assyrian with the loveliest of his wives at his feet. The whole is a tremendous theatrical structure composed upon a diagonal plan, highly coloristic, and altogether baroque. A "*Massacre numéro 2*," it was called by Delacroix himself.

Delacroix entered directly into the revolutionary present with his picture of the July Revolution: "Le 28 Juillet, La Liberté conduisant le peuple aux barricades" (1830; Fig. 68). In the whole manner of his being Delacroix was an aristocrat who poured all his passion into the drama of his works and wished to have nothing to do with the masses. But he was not as far removed from contemporary life as Ingres, and when the July Revolution swept across his vision he could not remain apathetic. He sided with the revolting oppressed, those who storm forward across the corpses in a dusky whirlwind. It was even said that he was himself the young student or artist in the foreground who, sad and introvert, has about him something personal, realistic, and "charged" that already points in the direction of Daumier. And the figure of freedom herself is no allegory, but a *femme du peuple* with bared breast and blowing hair, holding a flintlock and waving the tricolor. *C'est que la liberté n'est pas une comtesse/ du noble Faubourg St. Germain/ . . . c'est une forte femme aux puissantes mamelles/ à la voix rauque, aux durs appas/ . . . c'est cette femme enfin, qui toujours belle et nue/ avec l'écharpe aux trois couleurs/ dans nos murs mitraillés tout à coup reparue/ vient de sécher nos yeux en pleurs.* In such terms had Auguste Barbier described his ideal of the goddess of freedom, and Delacroix, so open to literary inspiration, probably got from them the impulse for his lonely form of the freedom of the people, one of the most active and natural, and at the same time one of the noblest figures that he ever imagined, and one which already seems to foretell the loveliest of all his women, the Medea.

As a composition the "Liberté" has a much greater unity of structure, and there are no such gaps as in the "Massacre," though the movement is considerably greater and the truly baroque asymmetrical arrangement much freer. The picture's effect lies in its extraordinary brilliance of color and chiaroscuro, with the burning city and the towers of Notre Dame in the background, and the radiant female figure beneath the hues of the tricolor. No other revolutionary picture combines such stormy and irresistible *élan* with such great tragic restraint. Of all Delacroix's works, it was the only one in which an imaginative concept and a truly contemporary feeling were forcefully united.

These were the four key pictures of Delacroix's youth, the decade of his twenties. In 1824 and 1832 occurred two events which greatly influenced his art in general and particularly his color: his introduction in Paris to English painting and a resulting three months' trip to England, and his more significant journey to Morocco.

In the famous Salon of 1824, next to the works of Ingres and of Delacroix, the exhibits of the English produced the greatest sensation. Constable's three great landscapes — among them the famous "Haywain" — stood out particularly because of their power of color and the method of its application. Delacroix was altogether carried away, and at the last moment, when the "Massacre" was already in the exhibition halls (such at least is the legend), he tried to rework it in the manner of Constable's color technique. Essentially, it was a relatively simple observation that made a great impression upon Delacroix: the lovely green of the fields in Constable's pictures retained its intensity because it was composed of various different green tones, set down side by side and kept separate from each other. In this way the general or the local color was retained, but was loosened; and what would otherwise have been a monotonous surface was broken and variegated by innumerable brush strokes and became nervous, alive, and vibrating. Géricault had already turned Delacroix's attention to contemporary English painting, which had produced particularly interesting achievements in landscape and portraiture. Even Turner was for a while the object of Delacroix's admiration.

Altogether, borne along by the general current of his time, he had nearly turned into an Anglomaniac. He was passionately fond of Shakespeare, whose plays had a tremendous influence upon him as upon all young romantic Frenchmen, and Byron and Walter Scott played decisive roles in determining his point of view. He was upon intimate terms with many Englishmen. The brothers Fielding, who showed landscapes at every Salon, were his friends; Bonington, whose exceptional talent (particularly in the field of water color, a medium little practiced in France) he highly esteemed, was his companion. *Il y a terriblement à gagner la société de ce luron-là*, he wrote when after his return from England he had lived with Bonington for a while. But Bonington's influence on Delacroix, who was two or three years older and already very mature, should not be overestimated. In the first place Bonington had already come to Paris as a youth and had grown up among French influences, choosing many of his subjects from French history. And then though he was, to be sure, an extraordinarily clever and skillful "rascal" from whom Delacroix, as he wrote, could learn much, this talent was coupled with an altogether external, partly Van Dyckish sort of elegance completely at variance with the essential inner nature of the creator of the "Dante and Virgil," as were Bonington's brilliant but flaring colors with their cleverly added accents and glittering lights. Certainly Bonington and Delacroix mutually influenced each other, though Delacroix was incomparably stronger; where Bonington's influence predominated, as in the obviously emphatic preference for the theatrical and for scenic arrangements, it was not to Delacroix's advantage. A small picture in the Wallace Collection in London, "Faust and Mephistopheles," shows the well-known scene (which Delacroix had seen on the London stage) in an overheightened, theatrically dramatic form, even to its accessories, and is related to the numerous Bonington compositions in the same collection. Such themes are much more effective as illustrations in black and white. Evidence for this may be found in the lithographs for *Faust* (1828; warmly greeted by Goethe) which in their painterly, baroque excitement furnish a remarkable contrast to the respectable bourgeois sterility of the illustrations by the German artist, Cornelius.

Even some of Delacroix's larger pictures of this period, many of them historical subjects, are in the Bonington line. "The Execution of the Doge Marino Faliero" (1826, Wallace Collection) in the power of its artistic conception obviously far surpasses Bonington's often petty pictures of this sort. But in spite of the carefully thought out balance of the composition, which is built around the lighted vacuum of the marble steps, the effect of the picture as a whole is too illustrative (particularly since the color is today far from what it was originally); perhaps it is still too much under the influence of the stage setting of a Byronic drama. Delacroix here appears in a new light, elegant in his arrangements, Venetianizing not only in his subject, and clearer in his construction. Perhaps this is why the later, more constructive Delacroix continued to have a particular fondness for this early picture while, on the other hand, he decisively veered off from the "Sardanapalus."

In 1832, seven years after his trip to England, Delacroix undertook an expedition to Morocco which had a much stronger influence on him and on his art. He went as part of a special French mission and thus was enabled to penetrate into the residence of the Sultan and all sorts of other fantastic places previously inaccessible to Europeans. His illustrated notebooks have not incorrectly been compared in thoroughness and factual exactness with Flaubert's notes for his *Salammbô*. For Delacroix this experience replaced the usual trip to Italy and Rome, a thousand times used and misused; but, despite his romantic and anticlassical bias, even here in exotic Africa he did not abandon his memory of the antique. Here at the edge of the ancient Empire, in the nervous forms of Moroccan warriors and sultans on their Berber steeds, in the age-old marriage ceremonies, in the dances of the *convulsionnaires de*

Tangers, in the strong, colored light of Africa he had a vision of antiquity more alive, more Dionysiac, more really antique than any of the cold and outworn formulas taught in the academies.

Along with studies of topography and costume, which enabled him years later to paint such scenes as the "Jewish Marriage," Delacroix the painter brought home observations on the intense light and brilliant color of Morocco. This was the most worth-while result of his voyage. From English painting he had learned a new method of color application — Constable's division of tones into separate color surfaces; now it was the principle of complementary colors which occupied him. He noted, for example, that a native with yellowish skin showed violet tones in the shadows, and that one with reddish coloring showed greenish shadows. To be sure, he had previously noted this law of complementary colors, and all sorts of characteristic anecdotes concerning it have come down to us. But it was in Morocco, where the contrasts of light and shadow are sharper and more colorful, where in the rugs and pottery he could study the rules of stronger, more systematically harmonized tones, that he first built up his system of colors. Basing his work on these observations, and using a conscious juxtaposition of complementaries (red against green, blue against orange, yellow against violet), he obtained powerful effects.

In that famous picture of the Louvre, "Algerian Women in a Harem," he put a blue-green lining next to the orange-red bodice of the woman in the left corner, and decorated the cupboard with alternating red and green stripes; while in the "Jewish Marriage" the spread of the red carpet is answered by the double green stripe of a wooden molding around the back wall of the house and the jutting balcony. When the complementary colors are placed closely side by side in thin brush strokes, they fuse in the eye, and in accordance with the laws of optics create a gray which is much more effective than that produced by a mechanical mixture on the palette. There is an impressive picture in Toulouse of the Sultan of Morocco, Muley-Abd-el-Rhaman, on horseback surrounded by his guard; *Cette grande coquetterie musicale*, wrote Baudelaire, "is so harmonious that, in spite of the splendor of its tones, it is gray, gray as is nature, as is the atmosphere in summer when the sun spreads a trembling haze of dust over every object." Delacroix greatly admired the over-all silver gray of Velásquez and Zurbarán, and to study it made an excursion from Morocco into Spain. His principal desire was to create a certain "color-atmosphere" which would draw together all the colors of the picture and give them a relationship to each other. (The whole question of the influence of one color on another enters here; Delacroix discussed this difficult problem as late as 1840 with his friend George Sand and her son Maurice.) "In every picture of Delacroix," said Baudelaire, "there is somewhere in the canvas a particular key tone which determines all the rest. All the colors are proportionately influenced by the dominant atmosphere." The observance of these facts and rules created in the finished picture a more thorough union of all the colors than, in spite of all their efforts, the Italians of the sixteenth and seventeenth century had ever obtained. To make his general idea real and effective Delacroix counted more upon color than upon composition, costume, or landscape.

But one must not imagine that the sum of these observations was a rigid scientific system such as the partly scholastic neo-impressionists later founded. In spite of his "regulating intellect," Delacroix had too much temperament for such an approach. He did not have the scientific interest in color theory of a Goethe or the German painter Philip Otto Runge, nor their interest in color symbolism. However, he employed colors that expressed a particular content: in the "Shipwreck of Don Juan" he uses heavy, dark green and black tones with a shrill white; violently contrasting angrily sparkling colors for Oriental battle scenes and hunts; and stately, harmoniously lighted tones for quiet interior scenes. But this regard for the "modes" of feeling proper to a subject (which Poussin discussed at length in one of his letters), as well as the arrangement of color, Delacroix carried out instinctively and the rational confirmation only came afterward. Much of this new attitude toward color had already been prepared by the old masters — Baroccio, for example, employed blue-green shadows in rosy flesh, and Parmigianino had a similar practice — but it had never been as thoroughly or urgently carried out. Delacroix himself did not develop this attitude to its logical conclusion. A good deal in his technique still connected him with an older manner: bituminous underpainting rather than direct painting, use of ocher colors, etc. For this reason one cannot say that a Delacroix painting is in a specific and absolute sense "more modern" in effect than a Rubens, or a Guardi, or a Watteau. Indeed, among French academic work of the late eighteenth century one can find many pieces whose over-all movement of color is reminiscent of Delacroix.

Even in his palette Delacroix was not a real revolutionary, but coloristically and technically he was the extreme exponent of an evolution in the treatment of color which corresponded to the artistic tendency called "baroque": a movement of the particles of color by loosening the elements that bind them, resulting in an emphasis on space filled with light and color in which bodily volumes fuse. Above all, what Delacroix's technique creates is a painterly unity so constituted that each touch of color is dependent on, and reflected in, all the others, so that instead of many separate local tones a synthetic color harmony is achieved. These baroque or high-baroque characteristics are decidedly opposed to the classicist feeling for color and space which begins with undivided color areas and then divides its space into layers of color which contain more or less plastic volumes.

The extraordinary movement of color in Delacroix's painting is intimately connected with the excitement and movement of his forms and their romantic content: lion hunts, fantastic animal battles, crusaders, Oriental dwarfs and dervishes, historical, Greek, or Oriental atrocities, etc. Often, particularly in the pictures of his middle period, the sparkle of the powerful yet harmonious colors practically obscures, or renders unimportant, if not the form at least the content of the picture. One perceives something fiery, brilliant, flashing, and does not ask, at least at first sight, if it is a jaguar biting an alligator, or a Greek woman defended from the Turks; it is of little importance if a boat in danger is filled with the excited people of some terrible Byronic fantasy or with Christ and his apostles. Baudelaire, who wrote about Delacroix with an unequaled penetration and a poetic precision, said that his precise and delicate palette resembled *un bouquet de fleurs savamment assorties*, and was particularly fond of comparing Delacroix's pictures — the "Sultan of Morocco," the "Algerian Women," and many others — to splendidly composed bouquets of flowers. Seen from a distance, said Baudelaire, so that one can judge neither the contours nor the dramatic content, a canvas by Delacroix gives the beholder a *volupté surnaturelle*.

Altogether personal, and therefore more appreciated in later times than in his own, were his "Orientalia fantastica." The taste for the exotic and the Oriental was already widespread in France in the eighteenth century, and Napoleon's expeditions had created great interest in the Near East; the subsequent wave of romanticism enhanced this taste. Delacroix did not discover the Oriental on his trip to Morocco. Rather his voyage was the fulfillment of a long-entertained desire, a desire rooted in his inmost nature. Quite apart from the great Greek and Turkish pictures of freedom, the "Massacre" and "Greece Expiring on the Ruins of Missolonghi" (1827; Fig. 72), Delacroix was preoccupied almost from the first with the stir of Oriental battle scenes, of which the various versions of the fight between the "Giaour and the Pasha" are the most prominent. But only after the experience of his trip to Morocco was Delacroix in a position to create a finished and rounded work on such a theme, most personal in feeling and of tremendous effect. Delacroix never became an "Orient painter" after the manner of his contemporary Decamps, who painted Oriental genre pictures (Turkish schools and the like), in a talented and amusing but thoroughly superficial fashion, or like the later Fromentin and the many others whose works have long since been forgotten. In spite of his exact factual notes he never contented himself with simple descriptions. With the penetrating rendering of color and movement peculiar to him, particularly in the later pictures of this sort, he combined a close-knit, almost classical composition. He achieved fundamental unity not only through a color harmony encompassing the entire picture, not only through formal structure, but also through an entirely personal spirit of wild melancholy which permeates the whole and fuses it into a work of art.

The well-known "Algerian Women" (1834; Fig. 73) attracts the eye by its powerful new harmony of color values, its completely baroque and asymmetrical yet balanced rhythm of bodies and space, and its full loveliness of indolent movement; and it enchants the imagination because it lends its figures an entirely convincing and yet unique existence. These three women, their large forms lolling on the rugs in the foreground, surrounded by the rich harem interior, with the turning Negress as contrast, live and breathe in a remarkable heavy, damp, musical atmosphere. Again, as in the "Dante and Virgil," but in a much richer and riper manner, there is that grasp of reality, *de la chose*, that Delacroix had found in the poet; a grasp not of details and separate parts, but of a whole bound together into an almost dreamlike unity. Here is a *poème d'intérieur plein de repos et de silence.*

Just as serious and dignified and, in spite of the lively subject and the brilliant colors, just as oppressive is the "Jewish Wedding in Morocco" (1839; Fig. 74), painted seven years after his visit. The space composition is entirely different from that of the "Women of Algiers"; instead of obliques and diagonals it is built upon horizontals and verticals placed in depth, and is therefore less complicated. The figures are smaller and more distant and, following the recession of the limiting walls, are arranged in a wonderful way within the space so that the center with its rose-red carpet is almost empty; and the counterpoint of colors is clearer and simpler than in the "Women of Algiers." All anecdote and folklore, the sentiment and symbolism into which the exotic so easily falls (as, for example, in Gauguin), has been avoided. Although underneath there lies that exact, small, and accidental truth derived from the study of nature, Delacroix always lifts this to the higher level of an almost visionary yet precisely captured scene in which color, form, and content are fused into a single unity.

A whole series of paintings, watercolors, studies, and sketches (Figs. 75–78) grew out of his impressions of northern Africa—

nearly all of them enchanting, lovely in color and movement: Moroccan horsemen in wild sham battles; a still and melancholy Arab at a grave, his horse behind him; a sharply silhouetted Arab wrapped in a white burnoose lying on the ground, noble as a figure on an antique tomb; exciting scenes of the "whirling dervishes" the *convulsionnaires de Tanger*), painted with a vigor of brush stroke, a *férocité de brosse, que personne n'a dépassée.* The further the actual experience of the journey receded, the more clearly the artistic vision seemed to crystallize. Even in the forties, when Delacroix's style achieved a new concentration and solidity, we meet these exotic scenes, removed from the familiar and the real, with an ever simpler form and greater unity. The splendid picture in the museum at Tours, the "Bouffons Arabs" (1848) with its wonderful melancholy landscape into which the figures almost fuse, belongs to this period as does that festive and grandiose painting of the Sultan in Toulouse with the "gray" over-all tone, already discussed. In construction and in color the latter is one of the most delightful of the larger pictures that Delacroix ever painted. None of these works recounts an imagined tale, each rests upon a direct experience, yet they all seem fabulous — colorful, lively, yet strangely distant.

The same impression is produced in us by the many animal pictures, the great cats, chiefly lions and tigers, which Delacroix painted with so much pleasure. In spite of their extraordinary vivacity of movement and color they remain unreal. No more than an enraptured child questions the truth of a fairy tale, or a boy the reality of an Indian story, do we for an instant question the possibility of a lion attacking a crocodile. Rubens' lion hunts here set a precedent; but Delacroix's attempt was not only to clarify certain confusions in composition which he believed present in Rubens' work (for example, the "Lion Hunt" of 1854 in Bordeaux, partially burnt), but above all to heighten the fantastic element. In this attempt, too, the baroque and the romantic — form and content — are closely interwoven. Most of these excited and exciting animal picture were painted in the forties and fifties; a few, mostly lithographs, were done in the twenties. Their variations are infinitely rich, and no picture repeats any other. Pose, feeling, and expression, all are differentiated or at least given differing nuances. A pitiful horse lies helpless on its back, body pointing obliquely into the picture space, while a panther clings obstinately to the white belly (1843). A naked Arab lies stretched out to his full length while beasts coming from behind fasten their claws in the corpse (1848); a lion struggles in fierce battle with a wild boar or, stretched out horizontally, quietly and majestically tears apart a rabbit (1856). Racing clouds and bending trees are the lyrical and romantic setting for a young woman trapped by a tiger at a water hole and collapsing almost in the movement of a ballet. Among the grandest is one of his last works, the "Lion" of 1863 in the Louvre; here there is a complete fusion of the bare, terrible landscape and the lion ready to spring upon his prey, and paradoxically out of the tremendous tension in each muscle there emerges a monumental simplicity. Above the unmatched splendor of color which Delacroix unfolds in these pictures hovers the gleam of a wild and dreamlike adventure.

If in the Moroccan scenes and the animal pictures romantic content and neobaroque movement of color and form go splendidly together, there is another category of Delacroix's pictures to which we respond less easily, although the quality of the technique is equally high. If one looks at Delacroix's tremendous production (850 paintings, plus a large number of watercolors and lithographs, nearly 60 sketch books, and many thousands of drawings), not a few of his works seem as far removed from us as is a large part of the work of his greatest rival, Ingres. The indifference that even the cultivated public accords certain of Delacroix's works (such as the monumental pictures) does not mean that it underrates him but is a reaction to the themes themselves.

Even Delacroix did not entirely escape the romantic epidemic of medieval and patriotic historicism which, beginning among the *muscadins* of David's atelier, then engendered those awful historical pictures that flooded France and the rest of Europe as a sort of semi-official art. Even Delacroix fell a partial victim to the historicizing taste of his period, a taste whose original romantic expression had had a certain justification and produced certain significant results, but which in the wake of Walter Scott and others engendered little that was worth while either in literature or in painting. First of all, under the influence of England and particularly of Bonington, he did a series of pictures with subjects such as "Milton and His Daughters" (1824), "The Assassination of the Bishop of Liège (1829), "Cromwell at Windsor" (1830), "The Murder of Jean sans Peur" (*ca.* 1830), "The Duke of Burgundy Shows the Duke of Orleans his Mistress" (*ca.* 1832), or "The Return of Christopher Columbus" (1839). Most of these pictures are too anecdotal, their subjects have undergone too little visual transposition and remain at too short a psychological distance, so that in spite of great beauty of color they cannot hold their own with Delacroix's achievements in the realm of Dantesque fantasy or exotic fairy tale. Much the same is true for the various battle pictures although these include some of the purely optical showpieces from Delacroix's brush.

To most of Delacroix's religious pictures the same kind of objection must be made. From earliest youth to old age Delacroix drew a whole series of subjects from the New Testament, especially the passion of Christ; he painted several versions of "Christ on the Cross." Such pictures (for example, the very empty "Christ on the Mount of Olives" in the church of Saint-Paul, Paris) show that he was too far removed from a living feeling for the Christian-Catholic tradition for it to animate his art. He could derive a traditional picture scheme from the Catholic baroque, but Prudhon, weak though he was, was more able to infuse personal sentiment and so achieve something new. To be sure Delacroix's religious pictures never became as cold and empty nor "as pedantic, mystic, and neo-Christian" as those of Ingres and his school, yet it is not correct to say with Baudelaire that he was the only artist who *dans notre siècle incrédule a conçu des tableaux de réligion*, at least not in the churchly sense. Obviously when, as in the "Apparition of Mary" (*ca.* 1852), he could put two Oriental women in a lovely landscape or, as in "Daniel in the Lions' Den"

(1849), tell an Oriental animal story, he was altogether in his element. And wherever, using his religious material as a romantic painterly pretext, he could allow full play to his Dantesque sentiment of melancholy, as in the different versions of the "Christ on the Sea of Galilee" (Fig. 81), the result is impressive, exalted, and perhaps even religious.

One must not imagine that even in high-baroque art there is a complete loosening of form or an abandoning of stable composition. There may be a significant tendency in this direction, but movement of form, movement of color, and movement of light are all always arranged and ordered, especially in the case of monumental art, within the limits of certain static laws. Among Latin peoples, whose cultural tradition includes a stability of form, this is quite obvious; even Rubens was suffused with it by his years of study in Italy. The order and comprehensibility of Delacroix's art must also be understood in this way, penetrating and regulating his tendency to loosen and liberate color. This classical element is absolutely and indissolubly bound with the kind of art for which Delacroix strove. It is therefore not paradoxical that Delacroix the *rubéniste* should also be an *adorateur de Raphael* (though he never knew Raphael's principal and monumental works in the original). Delacroix's whole nature was such as to enable him, as George Sand said, *par les côtes multiples de son intelligence* to appreciate *les diverses faces du beau.* Moreover, certain Raphaelesque elements went into the making of the strong and constructive side of seventeenth-century high baroque, and Delacroix must have approached Raphael by the same route, without undergoing more than an indirect and passing influence. As his art progressed his preference for the constructive, classical baroque grew, at least when dealing with certain problems. Intimately connected with this is the fact that in later life Delacroix strongly objected to being classified with the baroque school and considered himself much more a "classicist" (even if not altogether in the sense of an Ingres). His large paintings of the early forties were largely built on the basis of *grandes lignes* and were constructed throughout with the greatest care. This is particularly true of that rich composition, "The Justice of Trajan" (1840; Fig. 79). The scheme of more or less crossed diagonals is here quite obvious. Virtuoso fashion, they fill both the surface and the depth of the picture in the manner frequently employed in *seicento* art. The Roman columnar architecture of the background, breaking the diagonal movement by its vertical rise, also belongs to the favorite old baroque compositional scheme. Delacroix, who so often passes merely for a romantic revolutionary, here puts himself within the confines of a tradition which, if not classicistic-academic, is at least baroque-academic. With a masterful grasp of the traditional arrangement, he has developed it into something grandiose, has united a gorgeous surface detail with a clear emphasis on the essential story, and given the whole a new life through color. The result is a finished, artistic, and impressive work, which commands respect though it may leave one cold; it has always been praised as among Delacroix's great achievements.

Even more famous is the "Entrance of the Crusaders into Constantinople" (1840, Louvre). The diagonal scheme is more cleverly concealed than in the "Trajan," and is softened by an emphasis on the verticals. Nevertheless, in this giant picture (*ca.* 13 × 14½ feet), whose color arrangement is a fabulous achievement, there is rather too much emphasis on construction. Some of the groups (such as the suppliant and the despairing, to the right and left) give the effect of stage props which by various artistic means (adaptation into a sharp triangle, turning of the horse's neck, etc.), have been a little too obviously connected with the leader of the central, advancing echelon of horsemen. Many spectators, both now and in the past, have found the picture altogether too "theatrical," though they have not failed to recognize the imaginative power and grandeur of this group of riders against the shimmering white sky, the *beauté shakespearienne* of the composition, and its many wonderful details. The artificiality is felt less in the pathos of the gestures, which are fully justified by the subject, than in a purposefulness of representation that is particularly disturbing on a large scale. For this reason, as is so often the case, the sketches for the "Crusaders," like that at Chantilly, or the small-scale, varied replicas, like the one of 1853 in the Musée des Arts Decoratifs in Paris, have much more immediate impact. In the latter the group of horsemen has been moved into the middle ground and so is less isolated from the whole composition, which in turn is more mature and more unified than in the larger picture.

A third example, among many others, is the "Abduction of Rebecca" of 1858 (Louvre; another version, Fig. 80), in which the diagonal composition still plays a part. But in this late picture (as often with Delacroix, a variation of an earlier composition) the rigid system has become much looser, the atmosphere much more binding. The figures no longer rush out at the spectator but merge harmoniously into the general whole.

Without this concentration and drive towards structure, Delacroix would not have been able to master the great monumental decorative compositions which occupied many years throughout his middle period. These include: the paintings in the Chambre des Députés (Palais Bourbon, Salon du Roi, 1833–1837, and the Library, 1838–1847), and those in the Library of the Luxembourg Palace (1841–1846); a part of the ceiling in the Galerie d'Apollon in the Louvre (1849–1851); and finally three paintings in a chapel of St. Sulpice (*ca.* 1853–1861). In spite of the undoubted importance of this side of Delacroix's art and the light which it can shed upon his inner artistic development, little attention has been paid to it.

Ceiling decoration (seen as pure art and not for its decorative value) is always difficult for the public. Apart from the Sistine Chapel, which is in a class by itself, very few ceiling decorations have become popular. Besides, Delacroix developed no essentially new decorative ideas; and no facet of work surpassed the showpieces of the great fresco painters of the *cinquecento* and the high baroque. This was partly due to the fact that a Veronese in the Villa Maser, an Annibale Carracci in the Palazzo Farnese, a Rubens in the Luxembourg, a Tiepolo in Würzburg could work in rooms which they themselves had more or less helped to create or which were adequate to their particular styles; that a Pietro da Cortona could pour out his stream of fiery baroque color in the state rooms of Roman and Florentine palaces which were conceived with such works in mind and which were awaiting their final completion by them. Delacroix, however — and all monumental painting in the nineteenth century suffers from this — had to decorate rooms that were already historic monuments; it was really a sort of archeology: ceilings in the Palais Bourbon covered with a row of cupolas and niches, the Lebrun showroom of the Louvre where subordination was demanded, chapels in churches such as St. Sulpice. One cannot but admire his effort to overcome these handicaps. By means of his intensive knowledge and experience of color effects he attempted to give life and meaning to those dark, unhappy spots encountered all too often on walls and ceilings. He was able to make a coherent structure out of a row of isolated cupolas and half cupolas by giving them a living ornamental distribution, holding the entire structure together by his colors, and filling the separate parts with the richness of his figured *invenzioni*. However, the whole remains an anachronistic concept, unsolved and unfulfilled, in spite of the spiritual values and the mastery of the color scheme. For this reason the large oil study for his allegorical and symbolic myth of "Apollon vainqueur du serpent Python" (Brussels) is exalted and sublime, but as the centerpiece of the ceiling in the Galerie d'Apollon the executed work does not distinguish itself from the other ceiling decorations by Lebrun.

Yet, obviously, compared with any other monumental decoration of Delacroix's time or after, his works are filled with a much greater vitality. One has only to think of the false monumentality and the anemic, affectedly pious, pre-Raphaelistic stylizations of Ingres' pupils, Flandrin, Amaury-Duval, etc., or the later (though somewhat stronger) Puvis de Chavannes. Here, as elsewhere, Delacroix strove for a truly baroque painterly effect, not in the illusionistic sense, but in a style at once monumental and open in color. He was the last great artist to pursue such ideals and to carry them to completion, however imperfect. There existed no neobaroque architecture to give an adequate setting to Delacroix's new baroque analysis and synthesis of color. In more congenial surroundings his concepts would have produced an entirely different effect — perhaps they would even have altered the backward-looking structure of his sketches.

This restriction applies to nearly all his monumental painting. Surely it is not due merely to a carry-over of the impressionist point of view that we often prefer Delacroix's sketches or studies in color to his finished large-scale pictures. In the increasingly bourgeois nineteenth century the monumental pictures no longer had any proper place. They required great perspectives and decorative surroundings, and the necessary rooms were no longer available. For this reason painting was forced into restrospective concessions. We have already pointed out how in the "Trajan" and other large compositions Delacroix overemphasized his academic construction at the expense of a really effective articulation of his meaning, and so became stylistically retrogressive. His so-called *manière magnifique* did not heighten or broaden the formula of the classic-academic baroque, and it therefore did not parallel the really progressive neobaroque of his color movement. The result was that a great residue of academic (seventeenth- and eighteenth-century) *grand goût* painting remained undissolved in the new imaginative form. This holds equally true for his last monumental works in St. Sulpice (finished 1861): "Heliodorus," "Jacob's Struggle with the Angel," and "St. Michael." Even in fresco (which Delacroix used effectively for the first time here) the colors and their composition are interesting and novel. The shepherds, the camels, the Orientals in the "Jacob," and the colored still life in the corner of the "Heliodorus" are light and relatively modern. But in the latter the monotonous theatrical architecture of the background is altogether obsolete. The isolated group of the two wrestlers is also dated in style; and the pose of Michael on the ceiling is reminiscent of Giovanni Bologna's "Mercury." Even the generally admired composition of the "Expulsion of Heliodorus" is a structure built up out of old props, and although these are masterfully controlled, they are not recast in the heat of a new emotion. Thus, the schemes and formulas of the past break through the new stylistic impulse and disturb that complete harmony of the whole for which Delacroix strove and often attained. Delacroix himself once wrote of Rubens: "When Rubens imitates Michelangelo, as he often does, or Veronese or Titian, then in these various phases he is nearly always a borrower and ill at ease. When he frees himself from his models, *il est le grand Rubens.*" This is even more true of Delacroix: wherever he was too dependent upon the formulas of the past, he is today dead and ineffective; wherever he conquered and freed himself from them, he is *le grand Delacroix.*

Delacroix reached his greatest artistic height in a monumental single figure, the "Medea." It combines clarity of form, psychological penetration, and tragic sentiment with great strength and beauty of color movement. The suggestion of the theatrical is not far distant but here we are not reminded of it by props, ready-made passages, excited gestures, or historical handling. This is theater, but great theater, and Medea is played by a tragedian of genius—outwardly calm amid all the passion of despair, with noble bearing even in the last horrible, dramatic moment. Delacroix's "Medea" is the purest, strongest expression of his conceptual power. As early as the twenties Delacroix had begun the creation of this noble and dramatic woman in the "Liberté" and the "Greece Expiring"; "Medea" is the final, grandiose culmination. The definitive version in the Louvre (Fig. 83) was achieved only after much effort and many studies and variations. The first version (Lille, Museum), like most of the drawings, contains the essentials of pose and movement found in the final painting, but in color (partly due to bad preservation) and in space it is greatly inferior. Another version, done at the end of the fifties (Berlin, Staatsgalerie), is more complete in its painterly integration than the Lille picture, but the form of Medea is less noble and the inclusion of the smaller figures of the pursuers lessens her proud isolation. The painting in the Louvre of 1862 is really a copy of the Lille canvas, but the extension of space which further centralizes Medea's figure and the wonderful harmony of colors create an entirely new feeling, and there is no doubt that this last version is the perfect resolution of the problem Delacroix had set himself. Compare it to the heroically conceived female figures of other artists, such as Feuerbach's Iphigenia or his Medea, and it is astonishing how bloodless they seem next to the color and vitality of this tragic form. The richness of the *contrapposto* movement, the chiaroscuro, the dynamism of color are characteristic elements of a developed baroque; form, bodily volume, light and shadow are almost imperceptibly, yet geometrically, interwoven and harmoniously united within the space. If in the face of this achievement one may still talk of a formula out of the past, then Delacroix has heightened that formula in every respect and has translated it into a personal sensibility. The melancholy of the moment of rest at the edge of the brink, the truly tragic tension, lends this "Medea" of Delacroix its moving expression.

It is obvious that an artist with so great an abundance of invention must inevitably develop an "old-age style." Such a style is characterized by a deepening, a condensation, an increasing harmony of the underlying artistic concept at the expense of those qualities of stability of form and conscious construction which are the product of maturity's strength. Delacroix's progress along this road can always be traced, even if at times his movement seems roundabout and so cannot be described in simple and direct terms. From his youth on his pictures exhibit a great variety: the "Sardanapalus" and the "Marino Faliero" were painted at about the same period, yet in style and construction they are very different. The large canvases of the thirties and forties emphasize and reinforce his structural and classical leanings, but during the same period he executed a whole mass of smaller works which depend essentially upon liveliness of form and movement of color. Or there is the wonderful "Death of Ophelia" (1844; Fig. 82), whose lyrical and intimate manner (already suggesting Courbet) is difficult to reconcile with the baroque pomposity of the "Trajan" done only four years before.

Delacroix's reworkings of apparently long-concluded themes gives us an insight into his general development and the nature of his old-age style. At various stages in his life Delacroix liked to rework old material, and the improvements he made in the construction of form and color clarify his more mature and recently reached point of view. We have already examined the various versions of the "Medea" that appeared between 1838 and 1862; there is said also to be a late, altered replica of the "Trajan." The lovely rendering of the "Women of Algiers" (Montpellier) done in 1849, fifteen years after the first large version in the Louvre, is well known. Though the arrangement and movement of the figures are very similar in the two, the feeling for space and mass is entirely different. In the Montpellier painting, the picture space of the earlier painting is increased, and as a result the large figures of the foreground are pushed back and so are much more intimately fused with the space into whose depth they sink. Atmosphere and mood replace monumentality. Here, much more properly than in the case of the earlier canvas, one may adduce Rembrandt as a comparison; the Rembrandt who, as Baudelaire again remarked, was the only painter who had made excursions into the realm of a *drame naturel et vivant, terrible et melancholique*. Delacroix himself wrote of Rembrandt towards 1850 (he was one of the earliest to do so): "Perhaps one will discover that Rembrandt was a much greater painter than Raphael." It is the achievement of a bodily and at the same time spiritual union with space that gives Delacroix's old-age style a certain likeness to that of Rembrandt. The similarity has its obvious limits because Delacroix's romantic feeling for form could not tolerate its concealment in that Rembrandt-like chiaroscuro which is the *commencement de la sauce*. So he remains at a certain distance. And yet this loosening up of atmosphere, this sinking of bodies into space, this new harmony indicates that Delacroix was taking at least some steps toward the Rembrandtesque baroque and the dissolution of the voluminous, large-figured, structural and constructed style that we have called the "classical baroque."

The goal Delacroix envisaged in his later work becomes even clearer if one follows that "boat" theme which had haunted him from the period of Géricault's "Raft of the Medusa" and his own "Bark of Dante." The isolated, scenically arranged group of the early work, with its effect of a "theatrical machine" produced by the large proscenium figures, disappeared entirely in the later versions. This is true for his 1840 painting of the terrible scene from Byron's epic, "The Shipwreck of Don Juan" (Louvre) with the half-starved castaways of the driven bark. It is especially true of the different versions of "Christ on the Sea of Galilee" (*ca.* 1853). In this wonderful composition the obliquely placed boat with its excited people, the waves of the sea, the atmosphere of the air and sky, all constitute one single harmony of color. Variations in the strength and purity of the movement of light and color create a compactness and unity compared with which the figures of the "Dante" seem isolated and sculptural. And yet at the same time the dramatic power is so direct that one can understand how such a composition, trembling with inner excitement and yet controlled in every detail, must have affected an excitable artist like Van Gogh — who was deeply impressed by "the terrible sea of Smaragd that rose and rose, to the height of the frame."

During his lifetime Delacroix was often compared with Victor Hugo. Parallels can certainly be found, those of style and those of generation, Hugo being only four years younger than Delacroix. During the twenties and thirties Hugo was the leader in the battle for the romantic movement in literature: his 1827 preface to *Cromwell* presented the theory of the new romantic drama; the performance of *Hernani* at the beginning of 1830 led to the decisive battle between the conservatives and the adherents of the new free, subjective romanticism; half a year later his *Chants de crépuscule* celebrated the July Revolution which split the reactionary elements from the progressive spirits, politically; and in *Les Orientales* he grew enthusiastic over the Greek war of independence — an event in which all the freedom-loving and romantic spirits of Europe took spiritual part. In a similar way Delacroix was the leader of the romantic revolutionary tendency in painting — indeed, if Géricault is to be considered only a forerunner, Delacroix, from the twenties and early thirties on, was its single real exponent. He too paid his tribute to philhellenism in the "Massacre of Chios," and he too with his "Liberté" celebrated and illuminated the barricades of the July Revolution. Like Victor Hugo he too favored "romantic" subjects whose exoticism, melancholy, and sheer terror gave them excitement and drama; and the theater played an important part in the imaginations of both men. It is, however, above all in their technical effort that they are similar. In sharp opposition to the schematism and rigid rationality of the dominant school, both strove for a free structure and for a colorful, open language. Delacroix's optically loosened colorism corresponds to the pictorial speech of Victor Hugo's verses (Hugo said, "A verse is the optical form of a thought"), but Delacroix's loosening of color goes much farther than Hugo's opening up of verse structure (which does not reach *vers libre*).

On the other hand Hugo, in disregarding the consecrated rules of the classical drama, was much more radical than Delacroix who, as we have seen, put great stress on the structural elements of his compositions and, when they seemed appropriate, willingly adopted traditional forms. At the basis of this lay his persistent desire for a regulated ordering of artistic structure — the same impulse which later made him object so violently to his being labeled, as he expressed it, the *chef patenté du romantisme*. If he was *romantique* at all, he explained, he was so only to the extent that when he was eighteen he preferred Prudhon and Gros to such people as Guérin and Girodet (that is, the coloristic baroque, to the linear classicistic, or the post-classicistic). He disliked both Hugo's romanticism and Hugo himself, and called him a *brouillon d'un homme de talent*. Baudelaire also objected to the comparison; Hugo he characterized as a very clever artisan lacking imagination, *bien plus correct que créateur*, and contrasted him to Delacroix "who is sometimes awkward but whose fundamental nature is creative"; Baudelaire thought that Delacroix was the greater artist.

Apart from the individual differences between the two artists, the direct comparison usually made between Delacroix's place and significance in the history of French painting and Victor Hugo's in the development of literature does not seem justified. The currents of the visual and verbal arts are not always parallel, and the structure of French painting is built up differently from that of poetry. Victor Hugo is or was considered a revolutionary, a liberator who freed French drama from the yoke of fixed rules which had weighed on it for centuries. Though the influence of Rousseau, of the Revolution, of England, and of Germany may have produced a certain loosening which prepared the struggle of the romantics in the twenties and their later victory, it was Hugo alone in 1830 who made the decisive breach. He ushered in a new period, and ended a three-hundred-year-old tradition of classicism and rationalism.

Delacroix's position in the history of art is not the same. He did wage a bitter battle with the classical rationalist school which saw itself as the conservator of tradition and as the exponent of the only truly lofty art. But this battle had lasted, as we explained at the beginning of this book, ever since the seventeenth century; and the free, optic, baroque current had never completely dried up. Delacroix could and did continue this tradition, as he himself never forgot. But even more striking, he never gained the kind of decisive victory over his opponents that Hugo achieved. The classical rational tendency, in the particular variation given it by Ingres, was far from dead; it no longer had the arrogance of earlier times but it remained full of life and energy. However, Delacroix was not as narrow minded as his embittered opponent. With a correct historical insight he saw that the spearhead of the "modern period" — the nineteenth century — was neither himself, nor Gros, nor Géricault, but David, the leader of the classicists. Delacroix was therefore no revolutionary, no liberator, no propagandist like Victor Hugo. That sort of thing was repugnant to his whole nature. He was in any case not a battler — unless within himself. But though it is necessary to emphasize these differences, it is obvious that one cannot separate the early Delacroix from that circle of young *exaltés* — poets, painters, musicians, and writers — of the twenties to whom by age and destiny and by their common battle against the bonds of rationalism he was for a while at least closely bound. In this sense — and he was drawn in this direction by an important part of his artistic nature and preferences — the young Delacroix, despite his protestations, has been correctly classified within that current which in France is called the *école romantique*. But by this appellation, the historical position and meaning of his art are by no means unambiguously defined.

Stendhal — who hardly cared for his painting — has also been compared with Delacroix. Certainly here, too, there are many common characteristics, but Delacroix lacked entirely that penetrating analysis and psychological vivisection which distinguished Stendhal. All in all, one must agree once again with Baudelaire: the passion to discover *à tout prix* parallels and analogies between various arts and artists often leads to singular misconceptions.

Delacroix was *sui generis*, he was above all a painter. He was also a *poète en peinture*, but that does not mean that he yielded too much to the literary movements of his time. His purpose was to conjure up a unified, an inevitable, almost a visonary "atmosphere of human drama" by means of the movement of colored forms; and he strove for this goal by purely visual means and by disciplining his genius. In his most characteristic manifestations he is hardly imitable — and he had no successor. The impressionists followed paths that led away from Delacroix's high baroque sentiment; all they could continue was his technique of color. Only the young Cézanne and a mystic and visionary such as Van Gogh could go beyond impressionism and in part return to him. They were attracted by the baroque excitement and the colored movement because it contrasted with the cool and objective attitude of impressionism. Delacroix never actually achieved a general popularity in France. The linear and rational manner of his great opponent, Ingres, was more inherent in the French character and in some works — for example, "La Source" — is extremely accessible to everyone. Delacroix's work was perhaps too strange and exotic and of a too melancholy mood to be understood immediately. Only his color was always admired — by the neo-impressionists because of the technique and as a source of delight and joy by Baudelaire. With Delacroix the baroque movement of the Rubenists in France reached its highest spiritual peak.

ILLUSTRATIONS

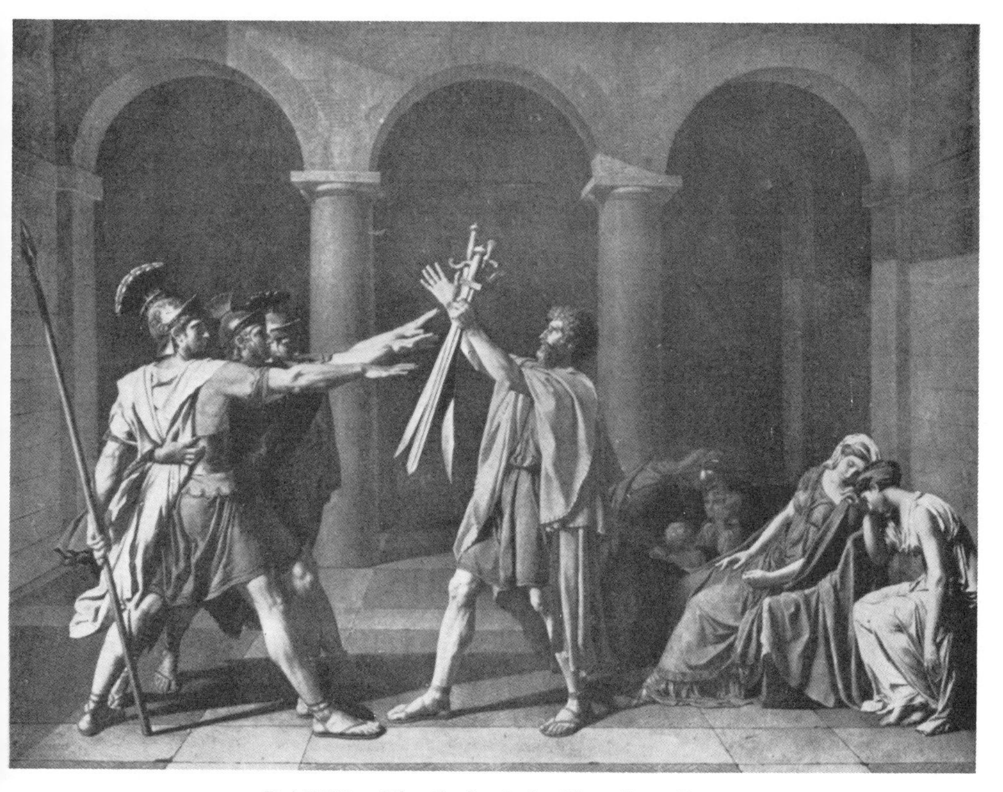

1. DAVID. *The Oath of the Horatii.* *Louvre.*

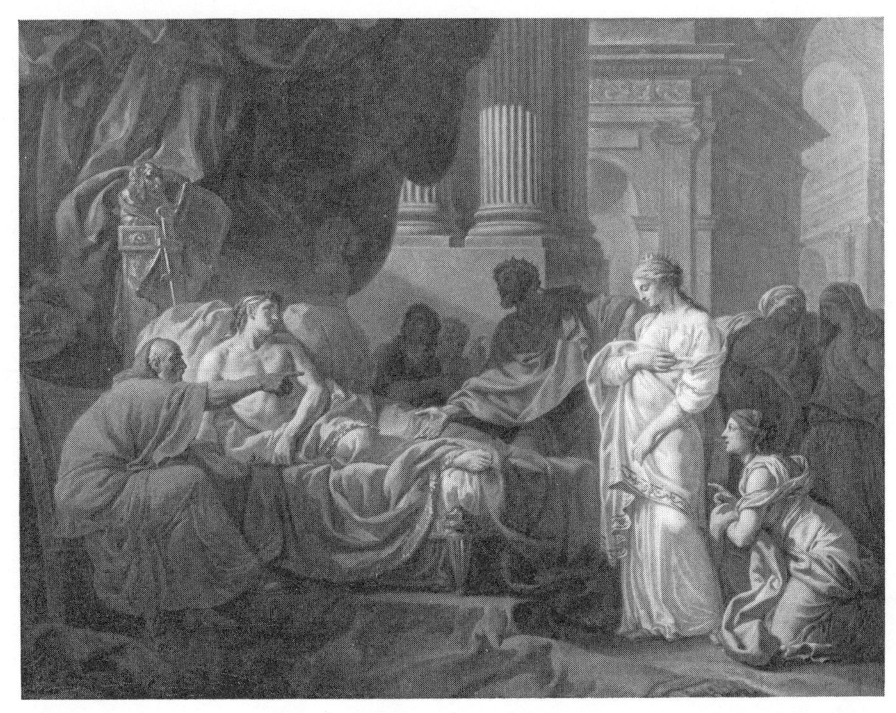

2. DAVID. *Antiochus and Stratonice.* Ecole des Beaux-Arts, Paris.

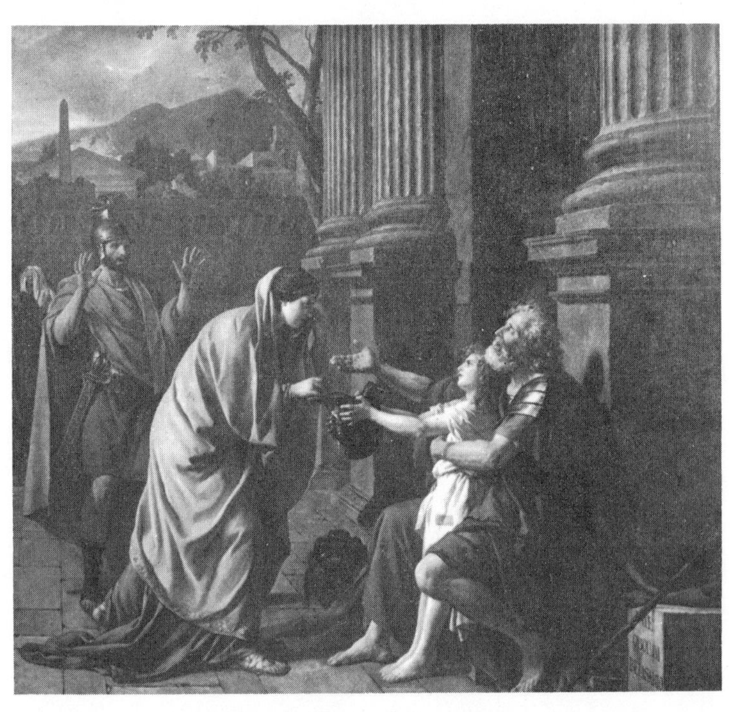

3. DAVID. *Belisarius Asking Alms.* Lille.

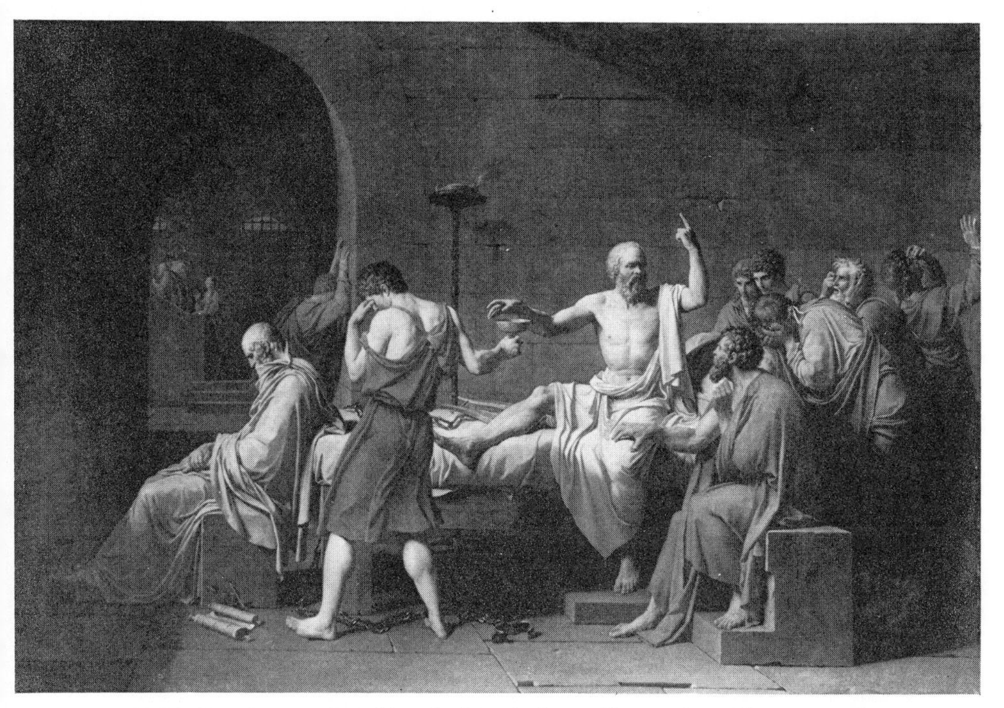

4. DAVID. *Socrates Drinking the Hemlock.* *Metropolitan Museum of Art.*

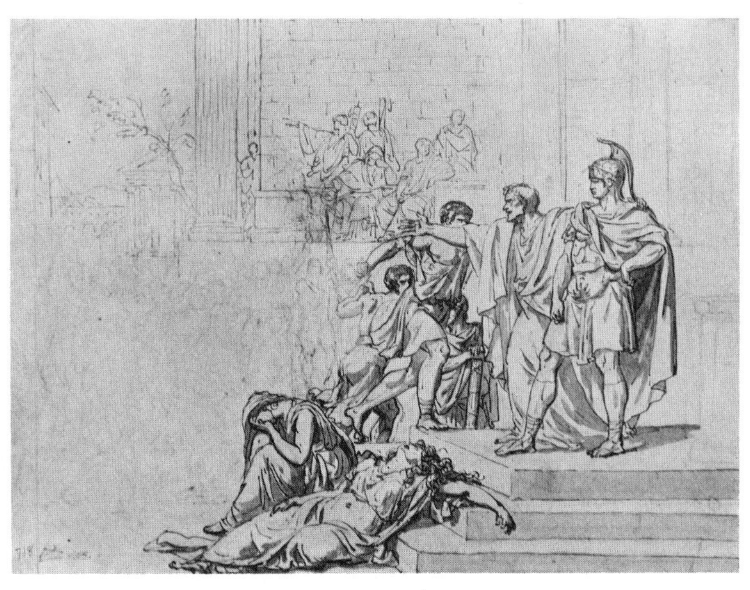

5. DAVID. Study for *The Oath of the Horatii.* *Louvre.*

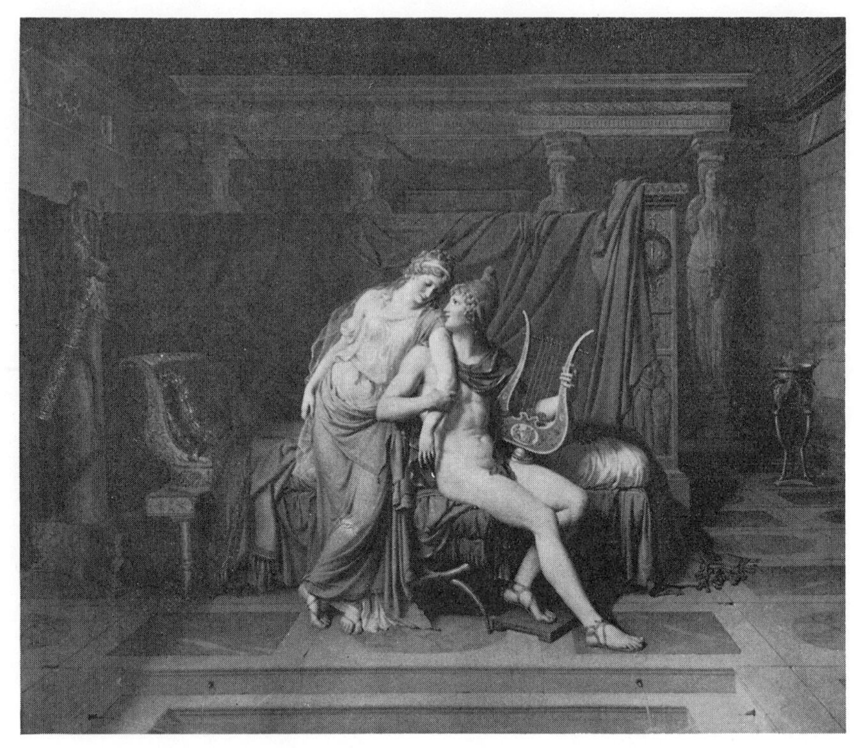

6. DAVID. *Paris and Helen.* *Louvre.*

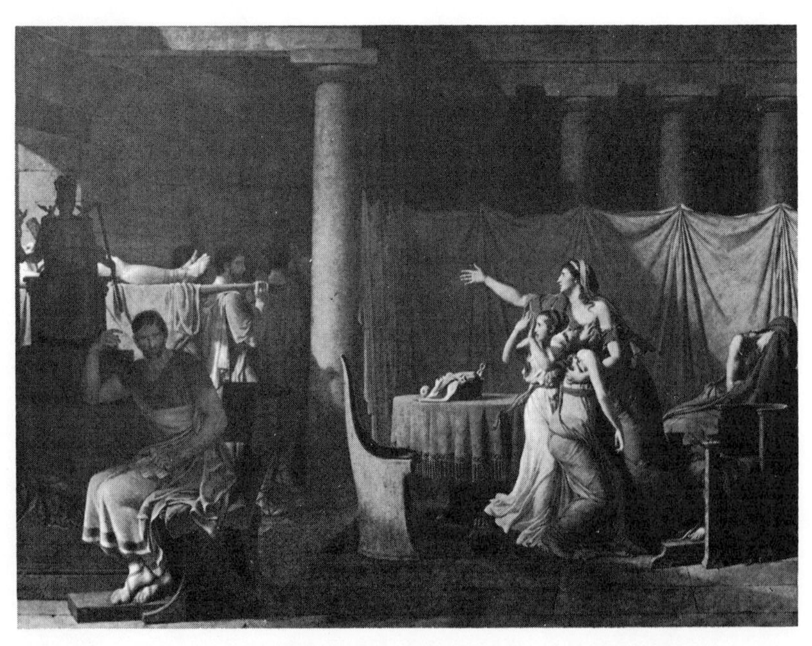

7. DAVID. *Brutus and His Dead Sons.* *Louvre.*

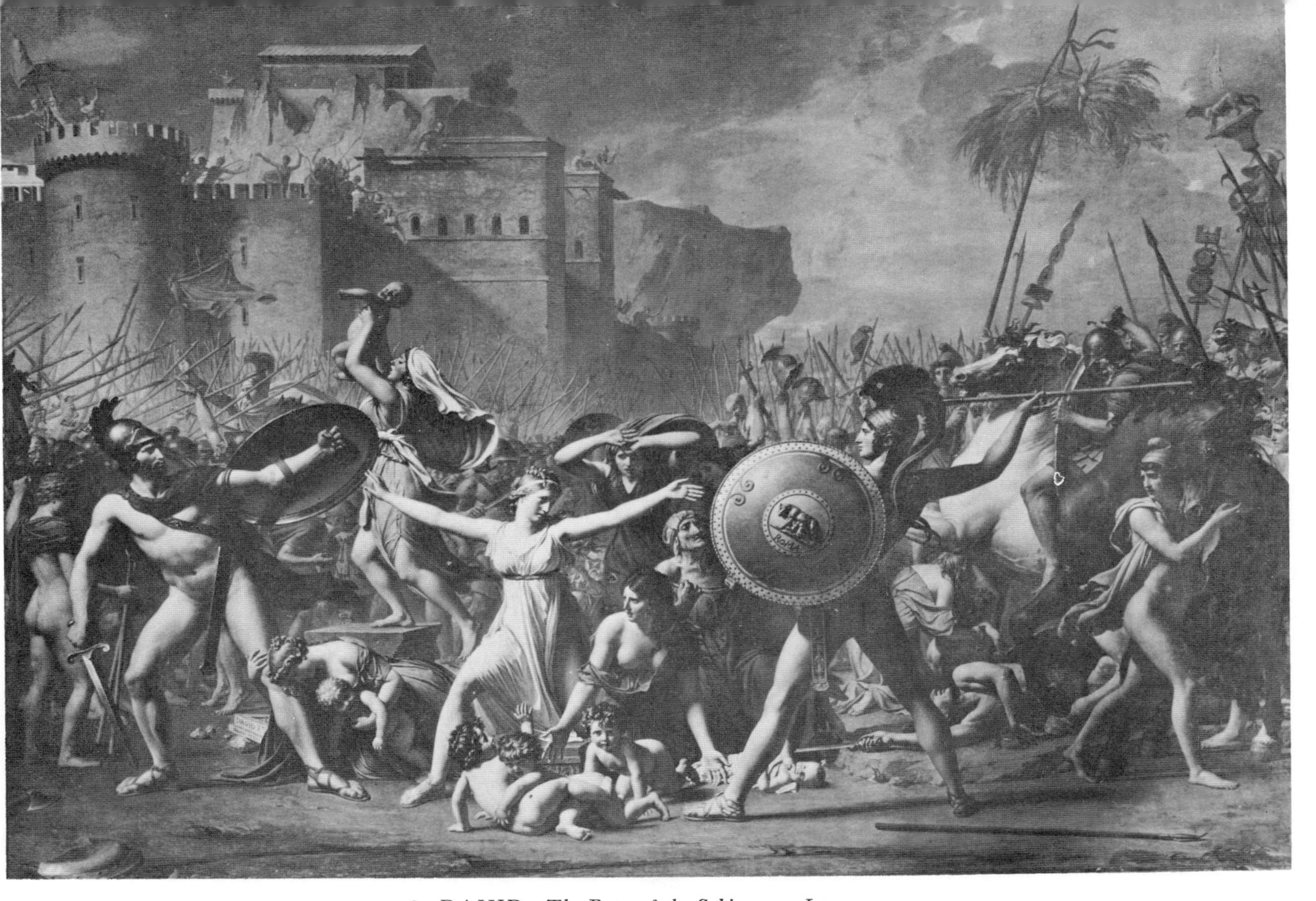

8. DAVID. *The Rape of the Sabines.* Louvre.

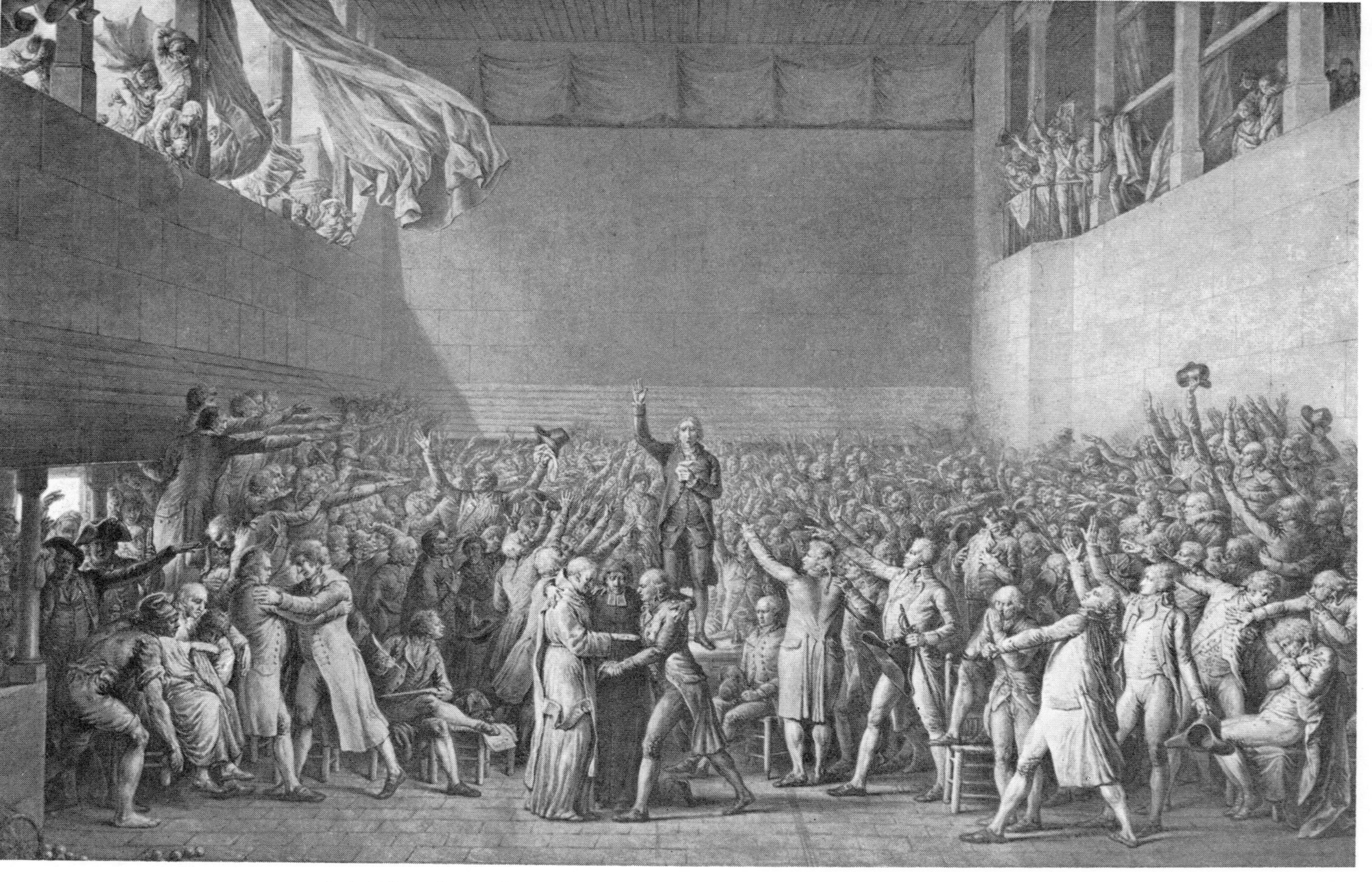

9. DAVID. Study for *The Oath of the Tennis Court.* *Fogg Museum of Art.*

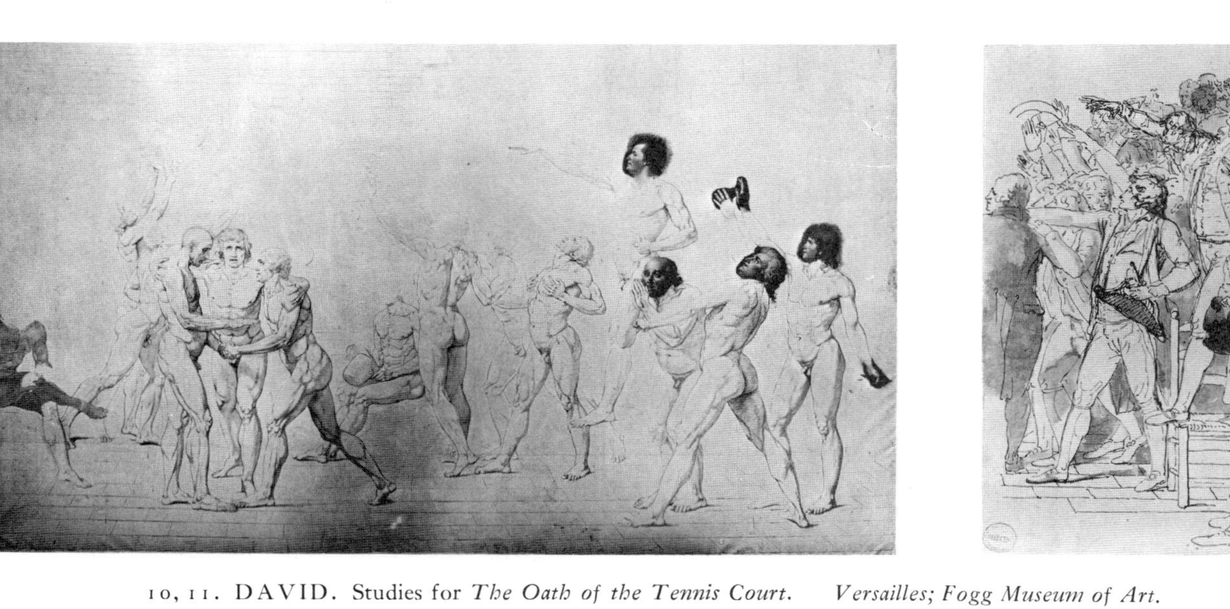

10, 11. DAVID. Studies for *The Oath of the Tennis Court.* *Versailles; Fogg Museum of Art.*

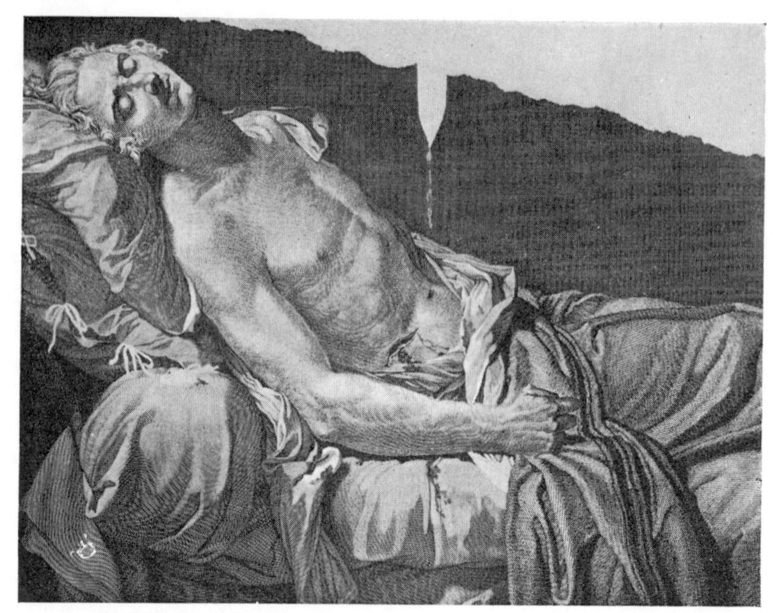

12. DAVID. *The Death of Lepeletier.* Engraving by Tardieu.

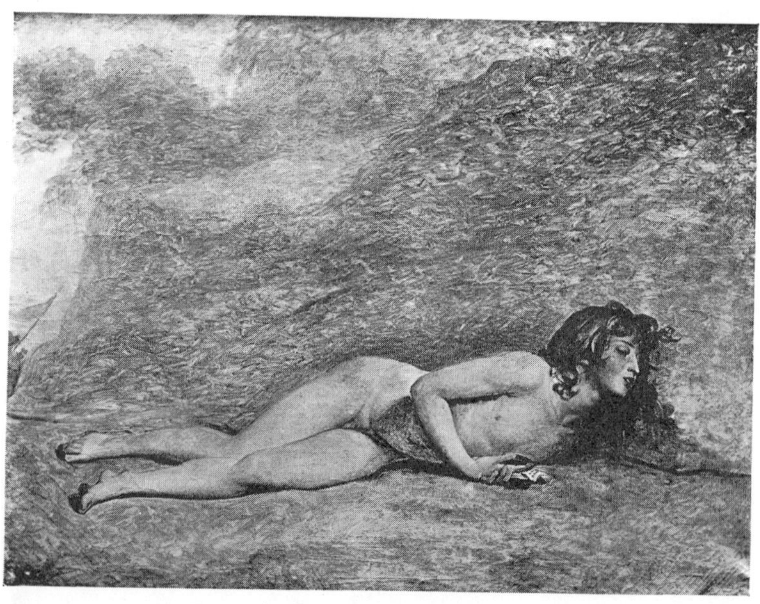

13. DAVID. *The Death of Bara.* *Avignon.*

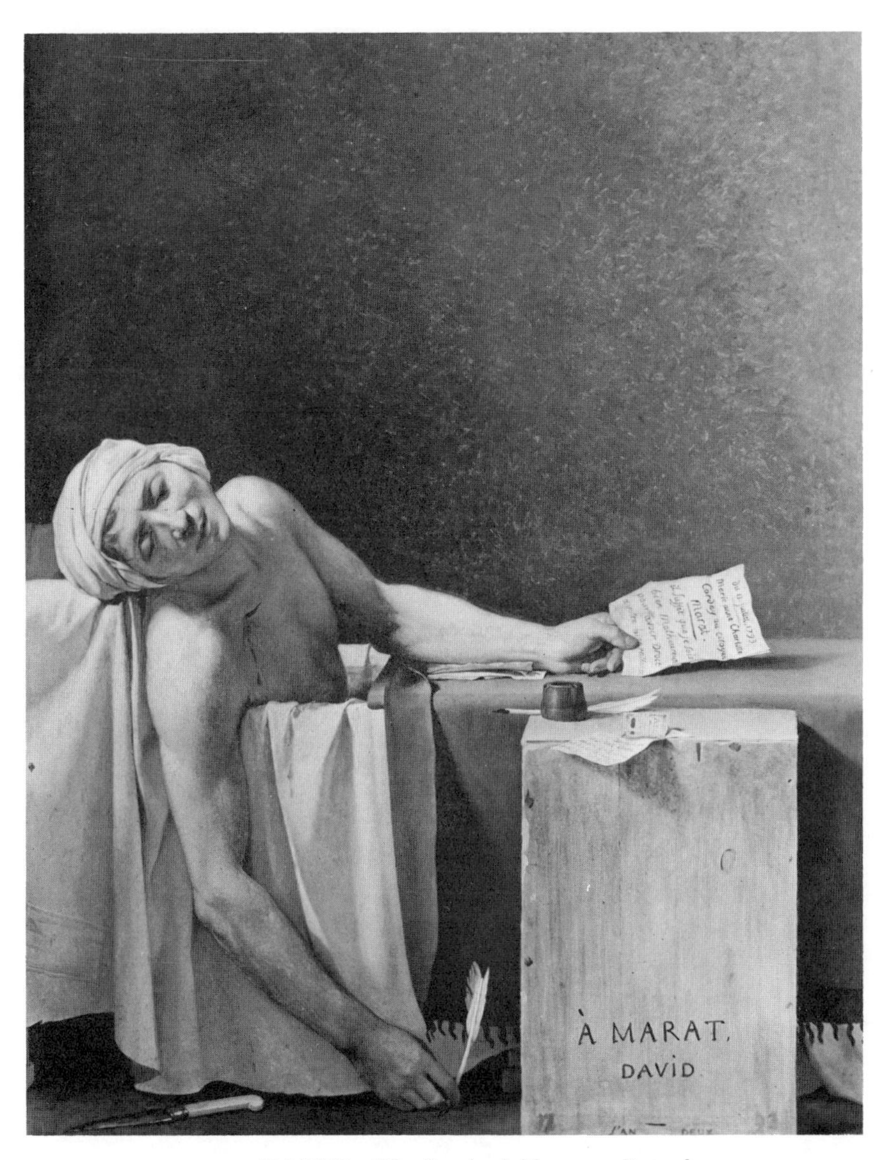

14. DAVID. *The Death of Marat.* *Brussels.*

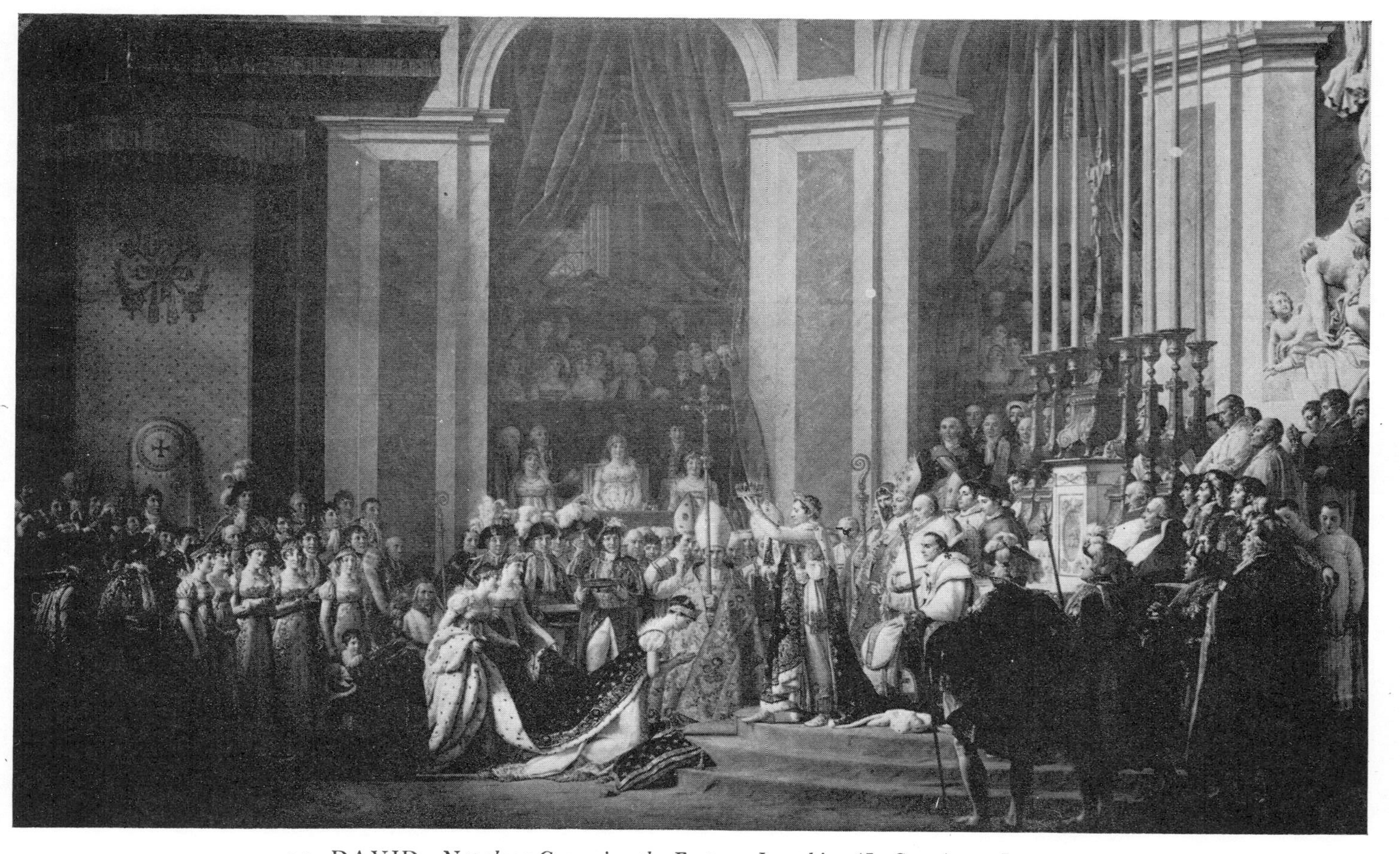

15. DAVID. *Napoleon Crowning the Empress Josephine (Le Sacre).* *Louvre.*

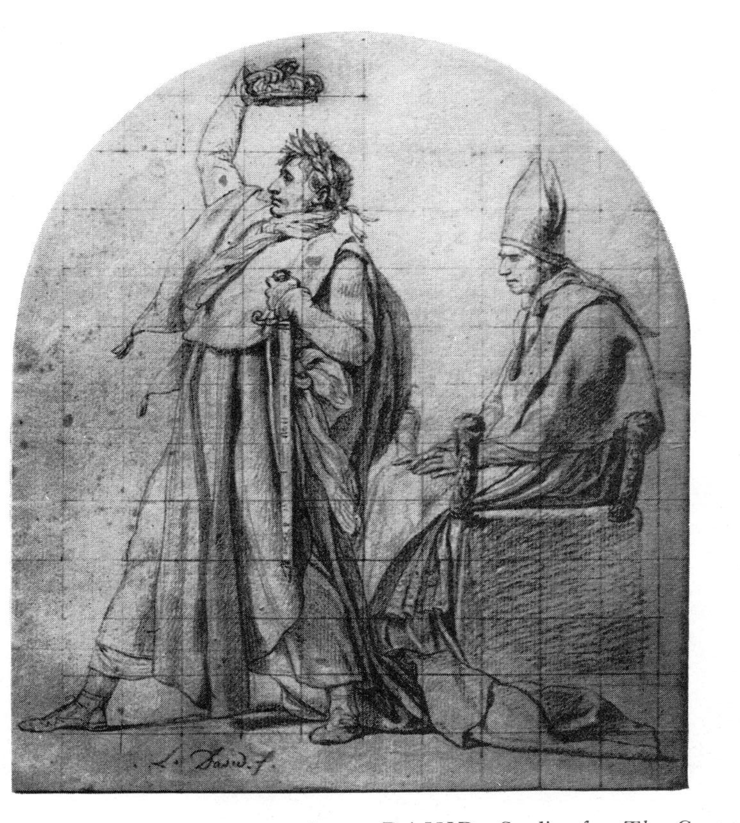

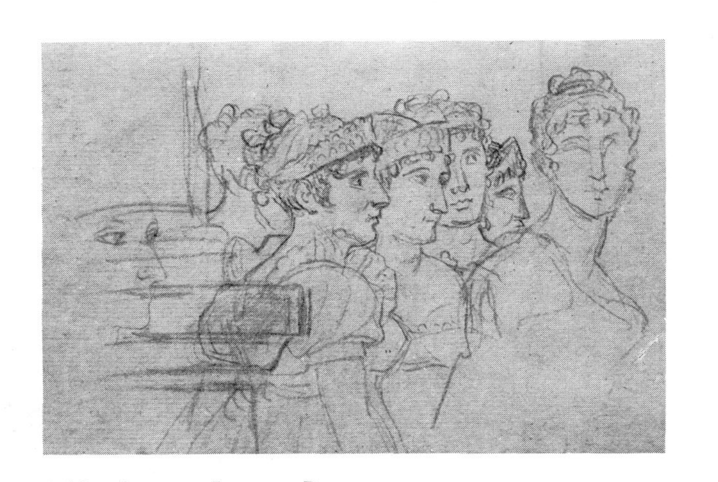

16, 17. DAVID. Studies for *The Coronation of Napoleon*. *Louvre; Besançon.*

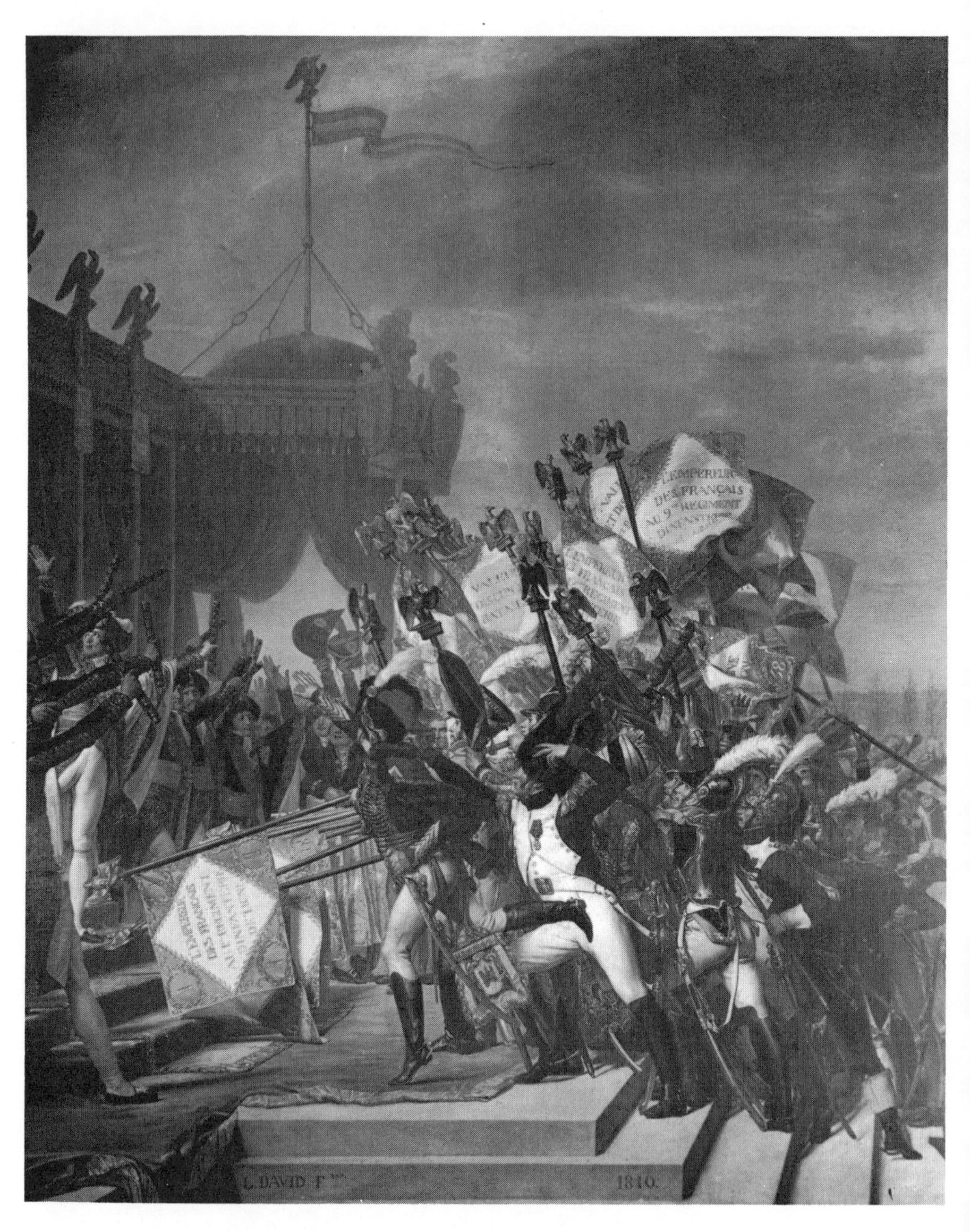

18. DAVID. Detail of *Napoleon Distributing the Eagles.* *Versailles.*

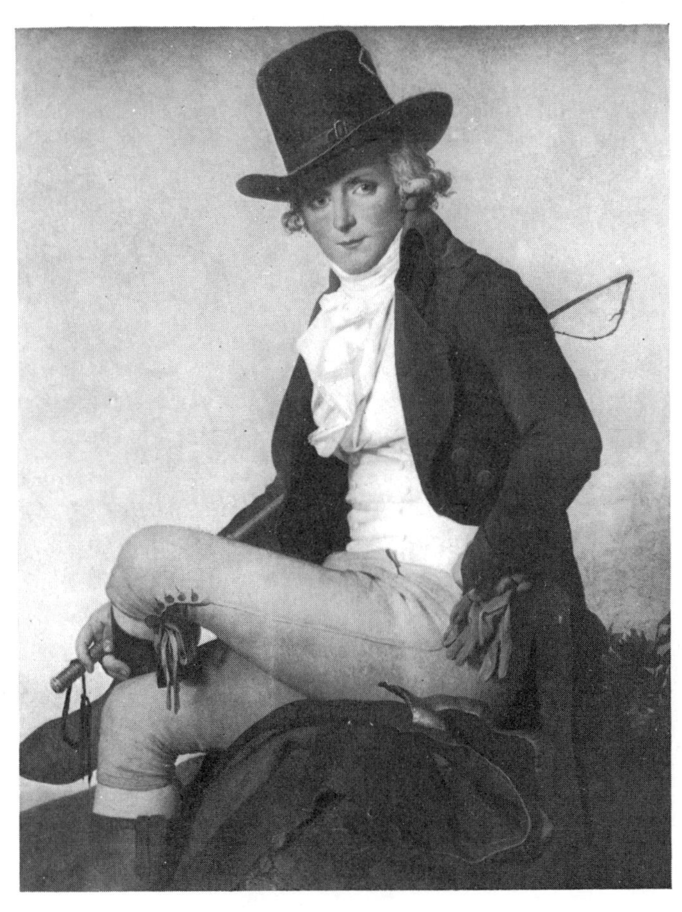

19. DAVID. *M. de Sériziat.* *Louvre.*

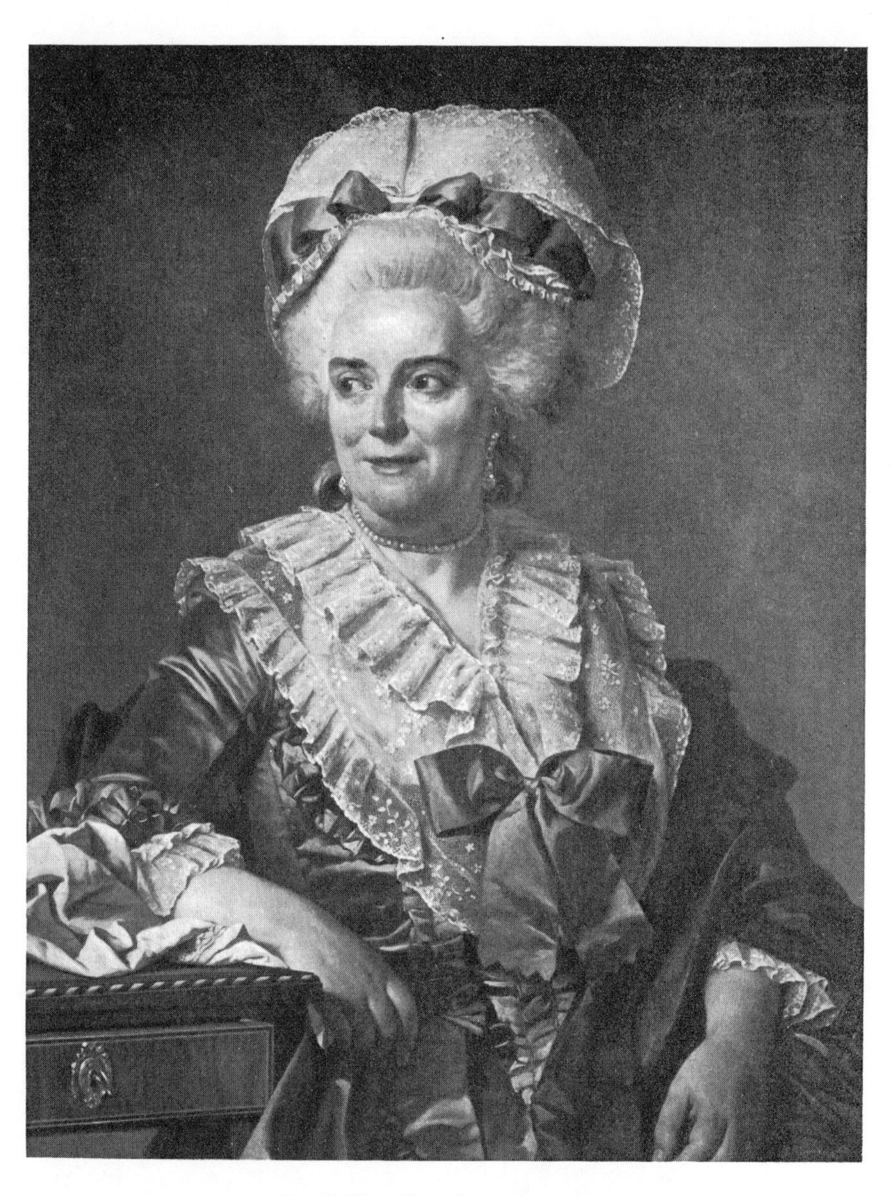

20. DAVID. *Mme. Pécoul.* *Louvre.*

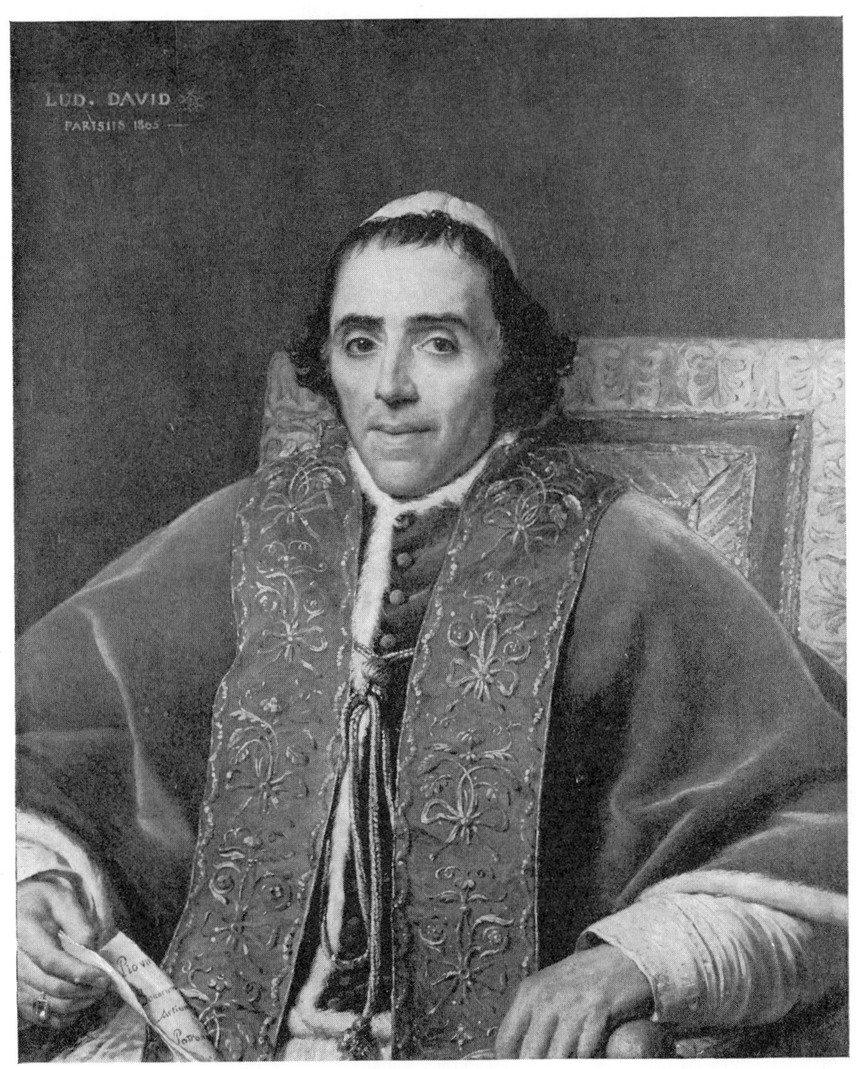

21. DAVID. *Pope Pius VII.* *Louvre.*

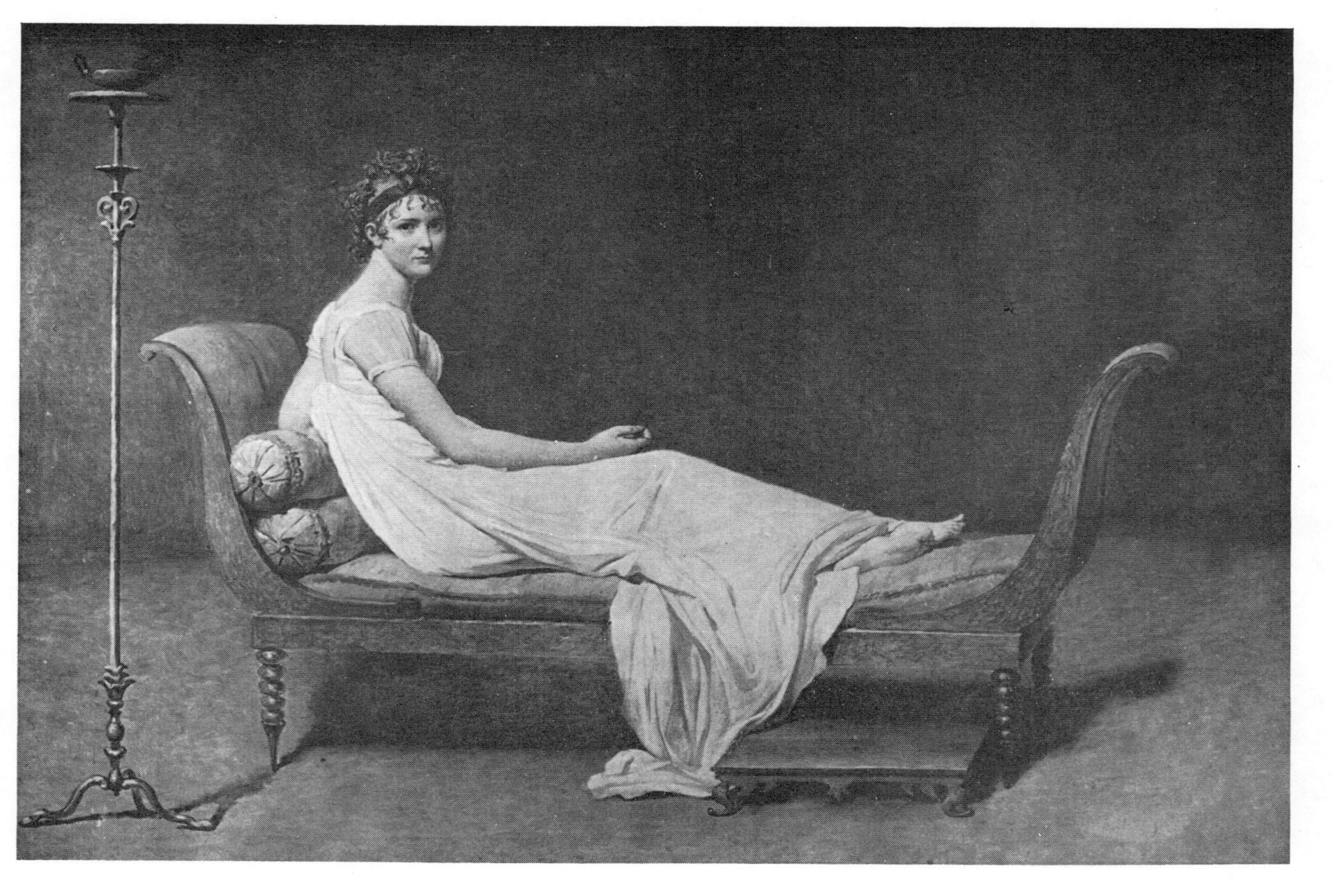

22. DAVID. *Mme. Récamier.* *Louvre.*

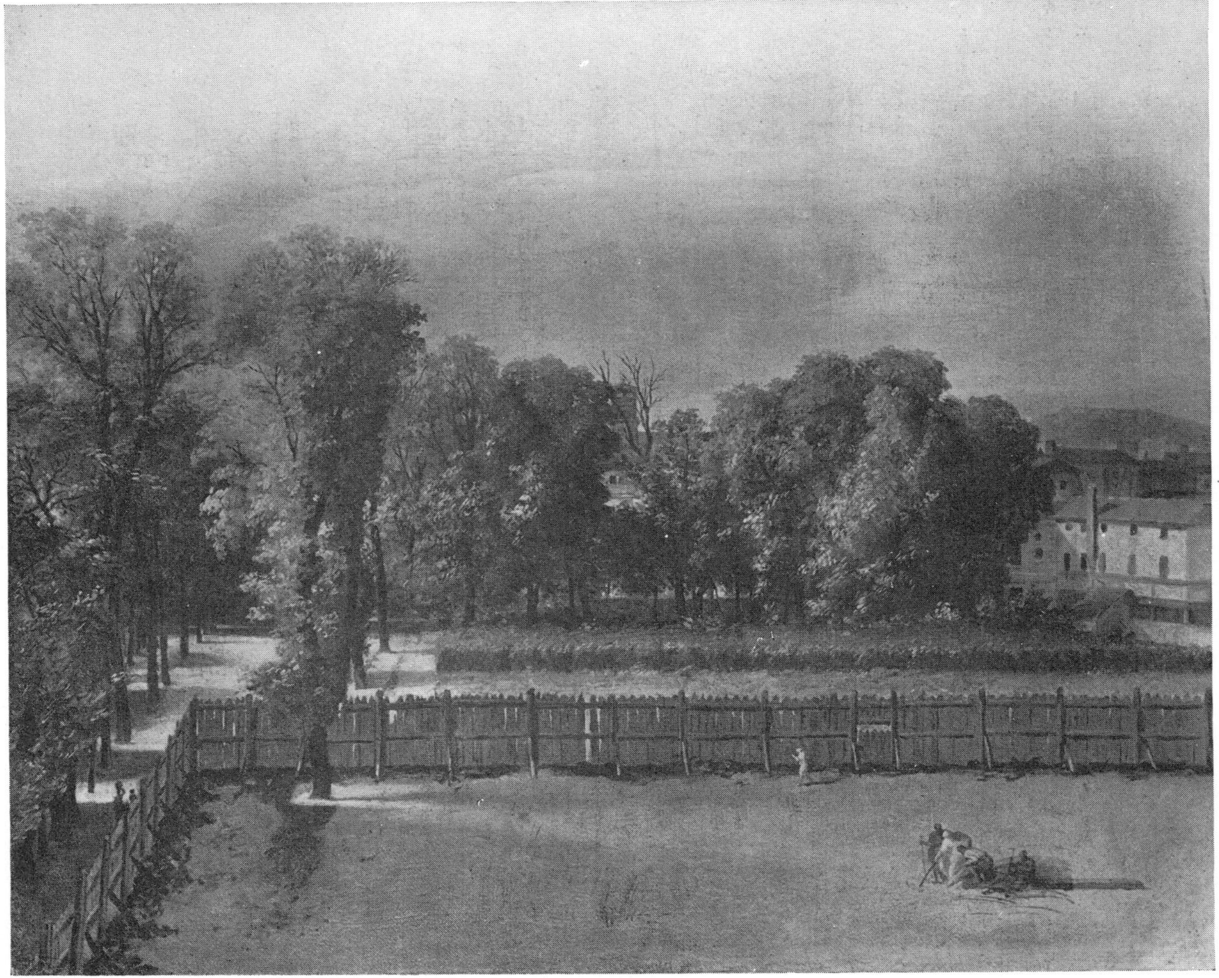

23. DAVID. *View of the Luxembourg.* *Louvre.*

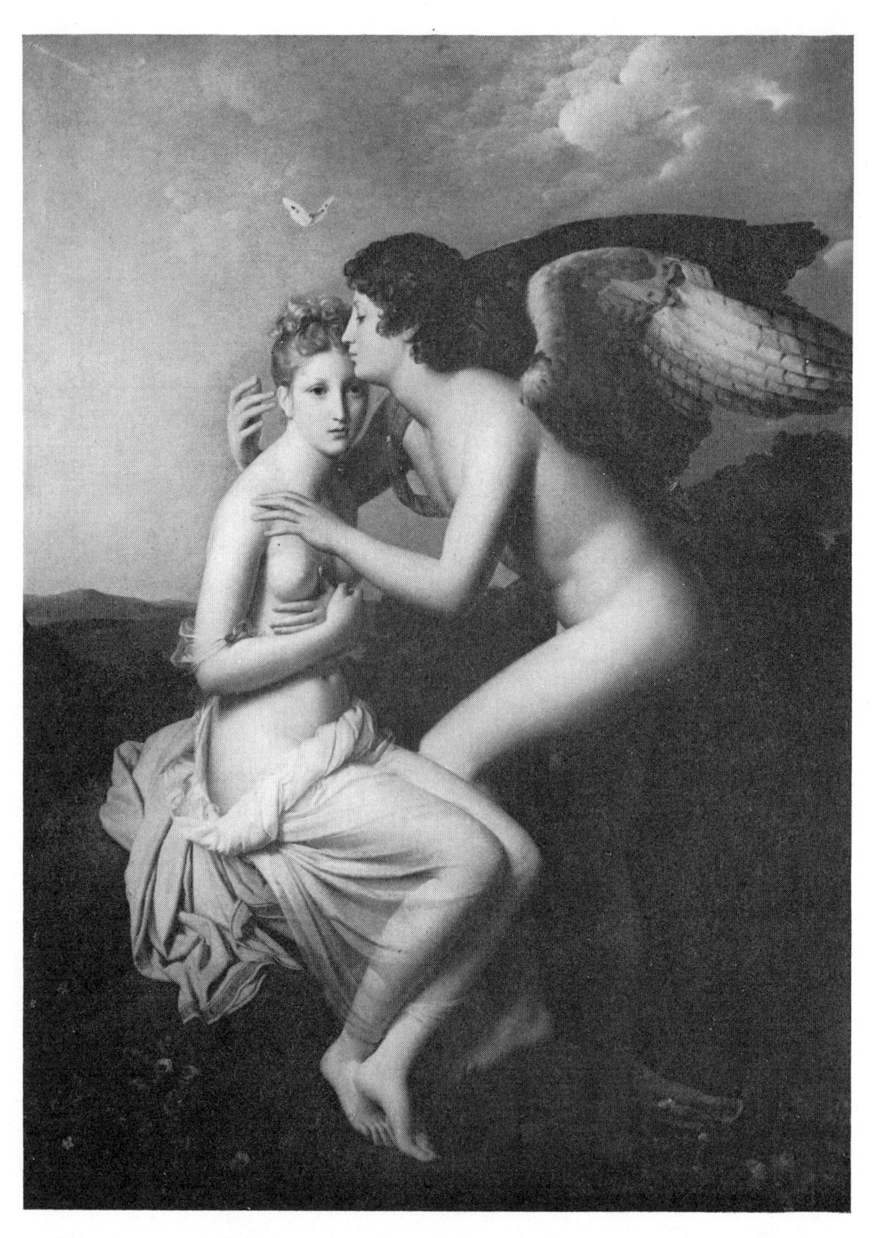

24. GERARD. *Cupid and Psyche.* *Louvre.*

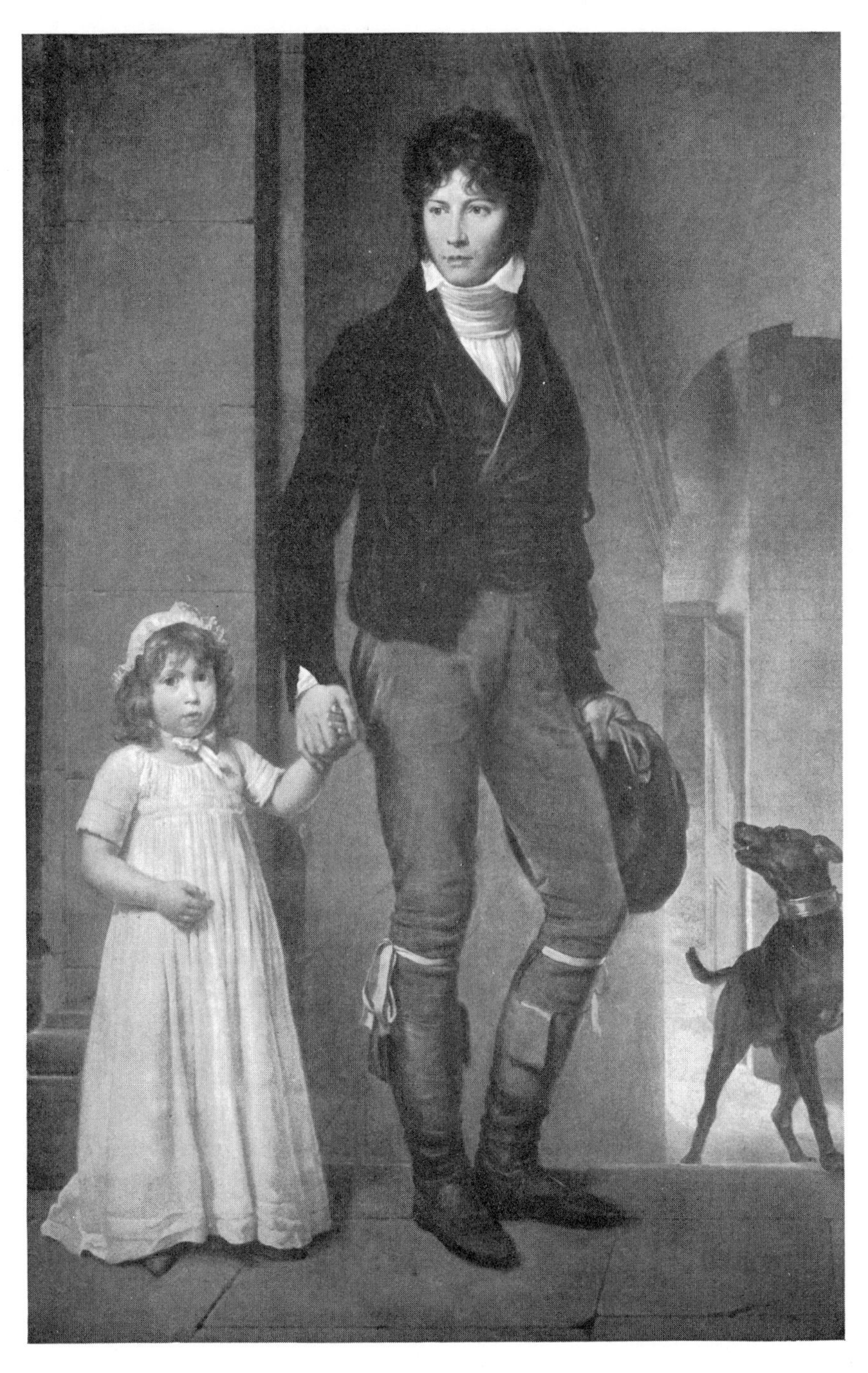

25. GERARD. *Isabey and His Daughter.* Louvre.

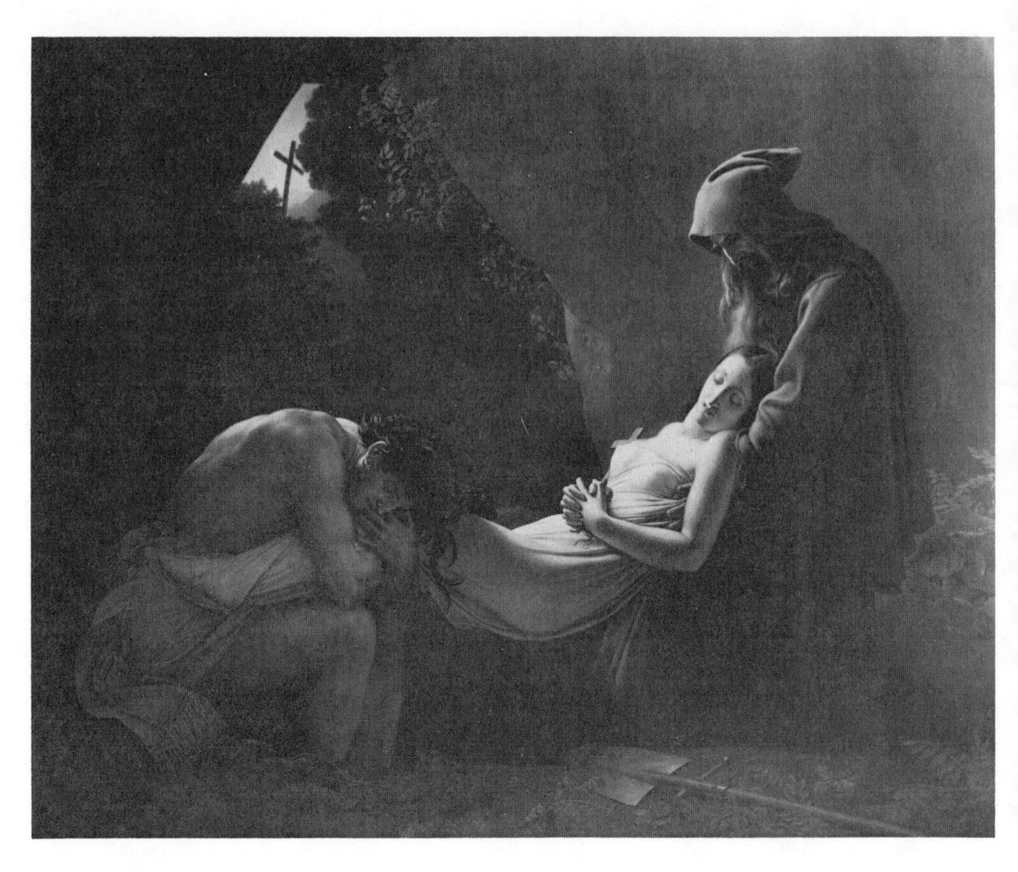

26. GIRODET. *The Entombment of Atala.* Louvre.

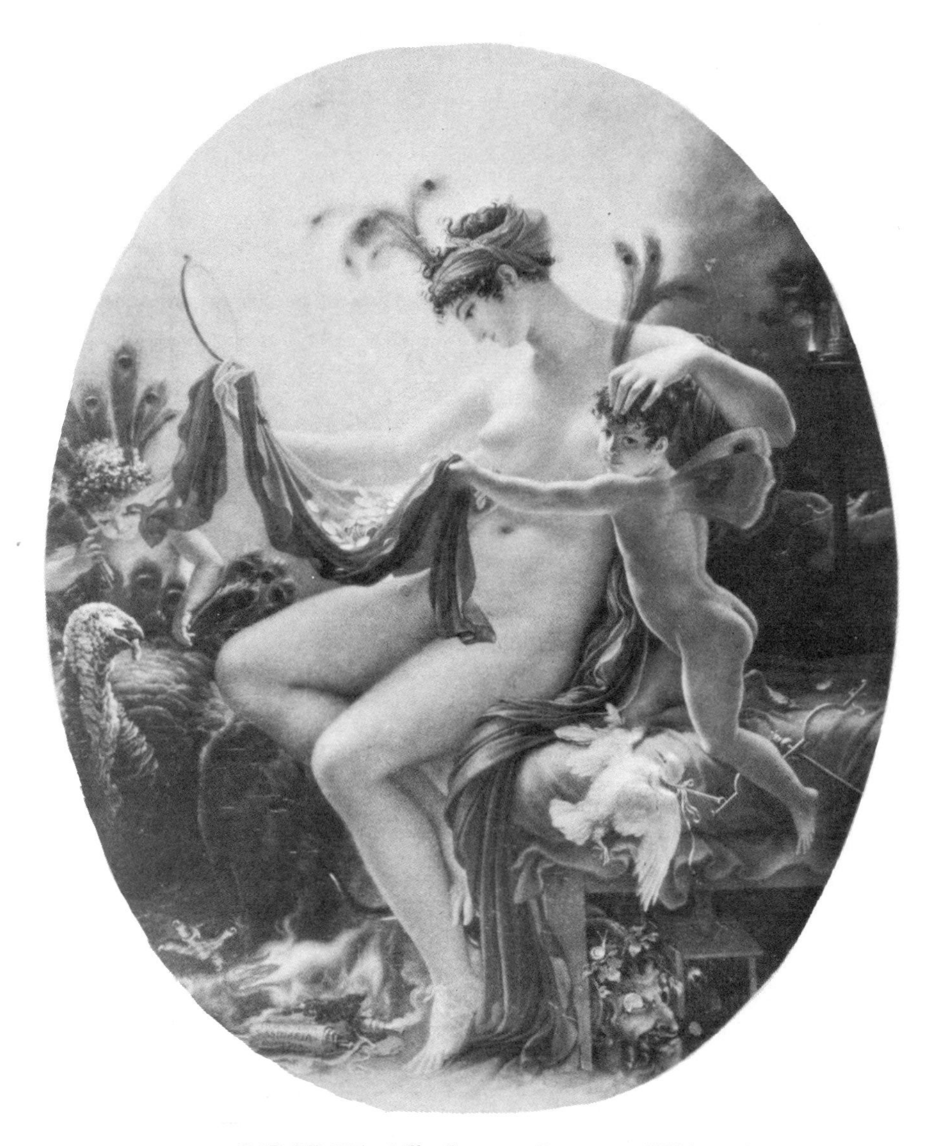

27. GIRODET. *Mlle. Lange as Danaë.* *Wildenstein.*

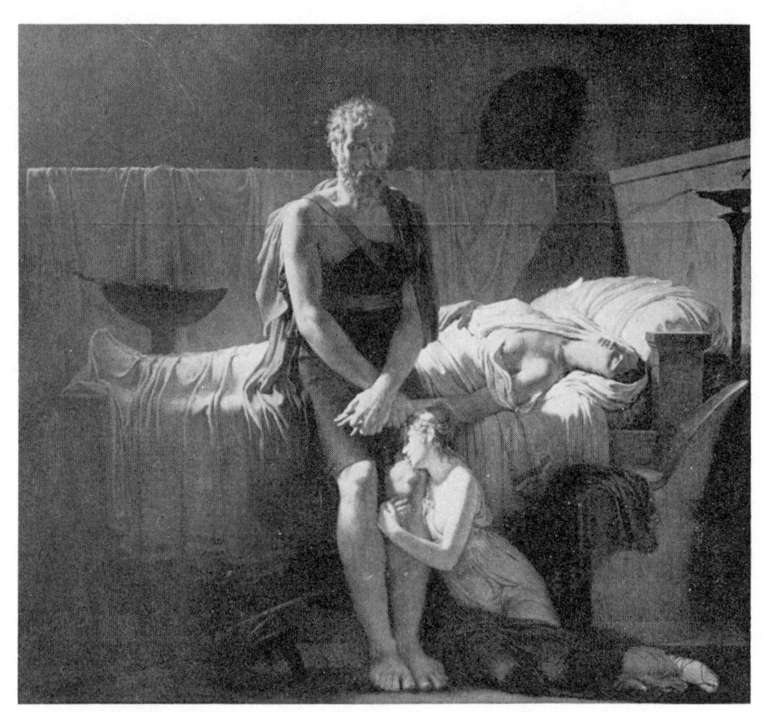

28. GUERIN. *The Return of Marius Sextus.* *Louvre.*

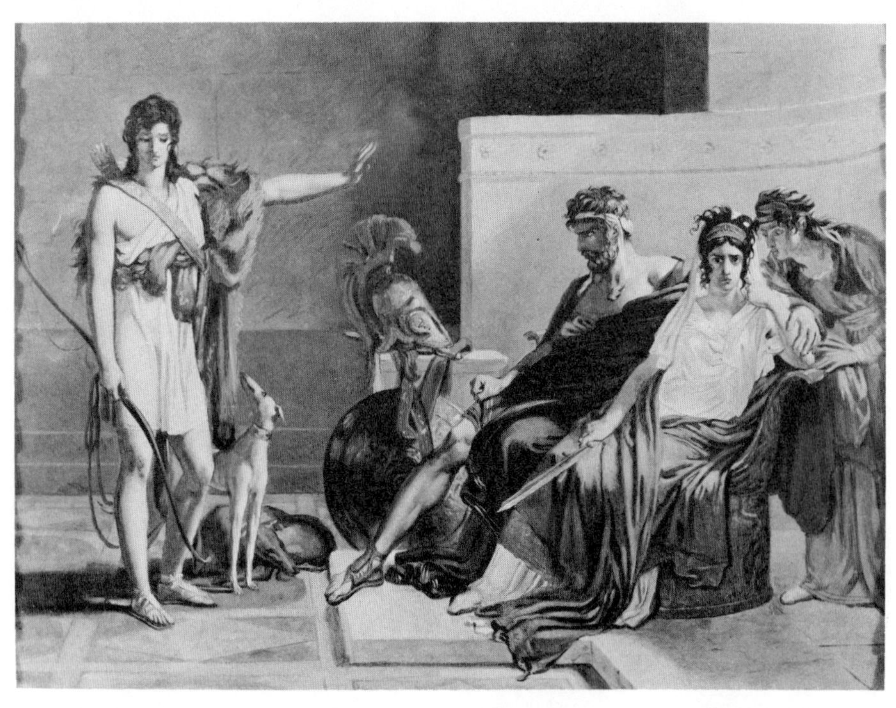

29. GUERIN. Study for *Phaedra and Hippolytus.* *Fogg Museum of Art.*

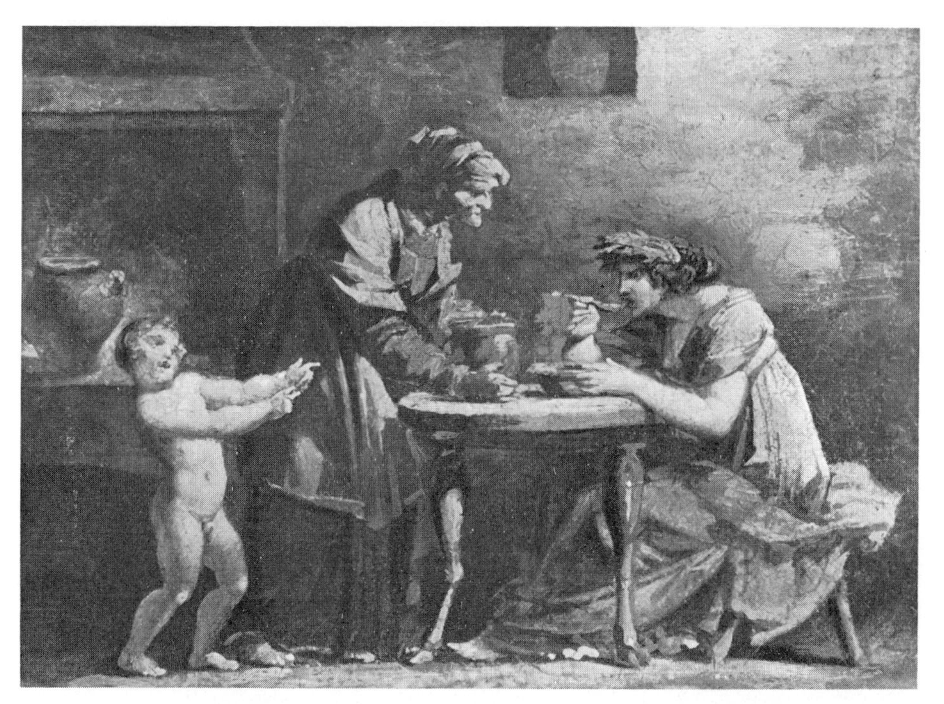

30. PRUDHON. Study for *The Vengeance of Ceres.* *Bayonne.*

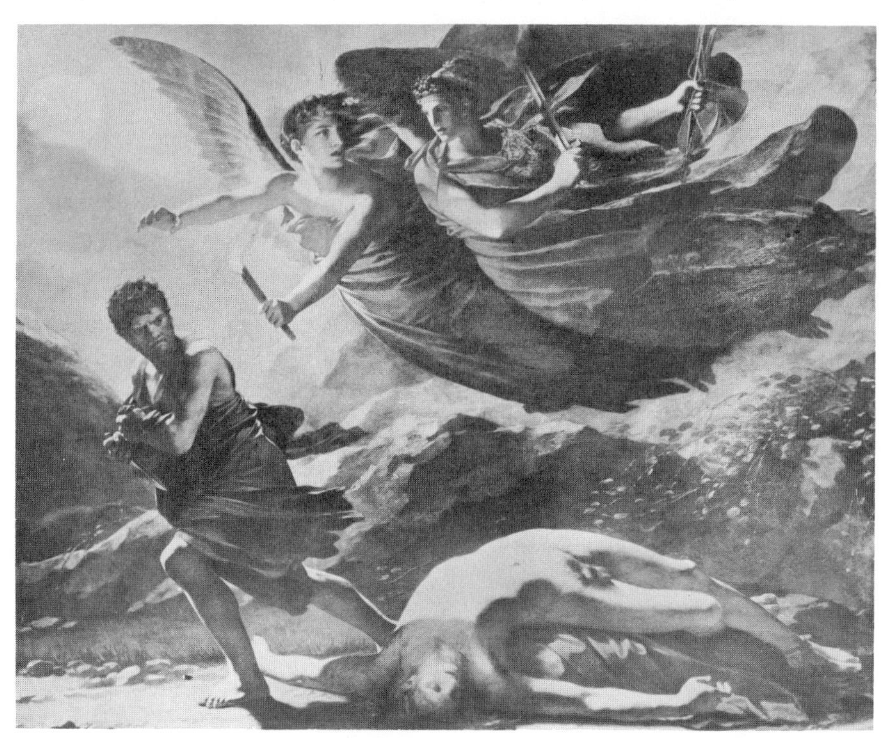

31. PRUDHON. *Vengeance and Justice.* *Louvre.*

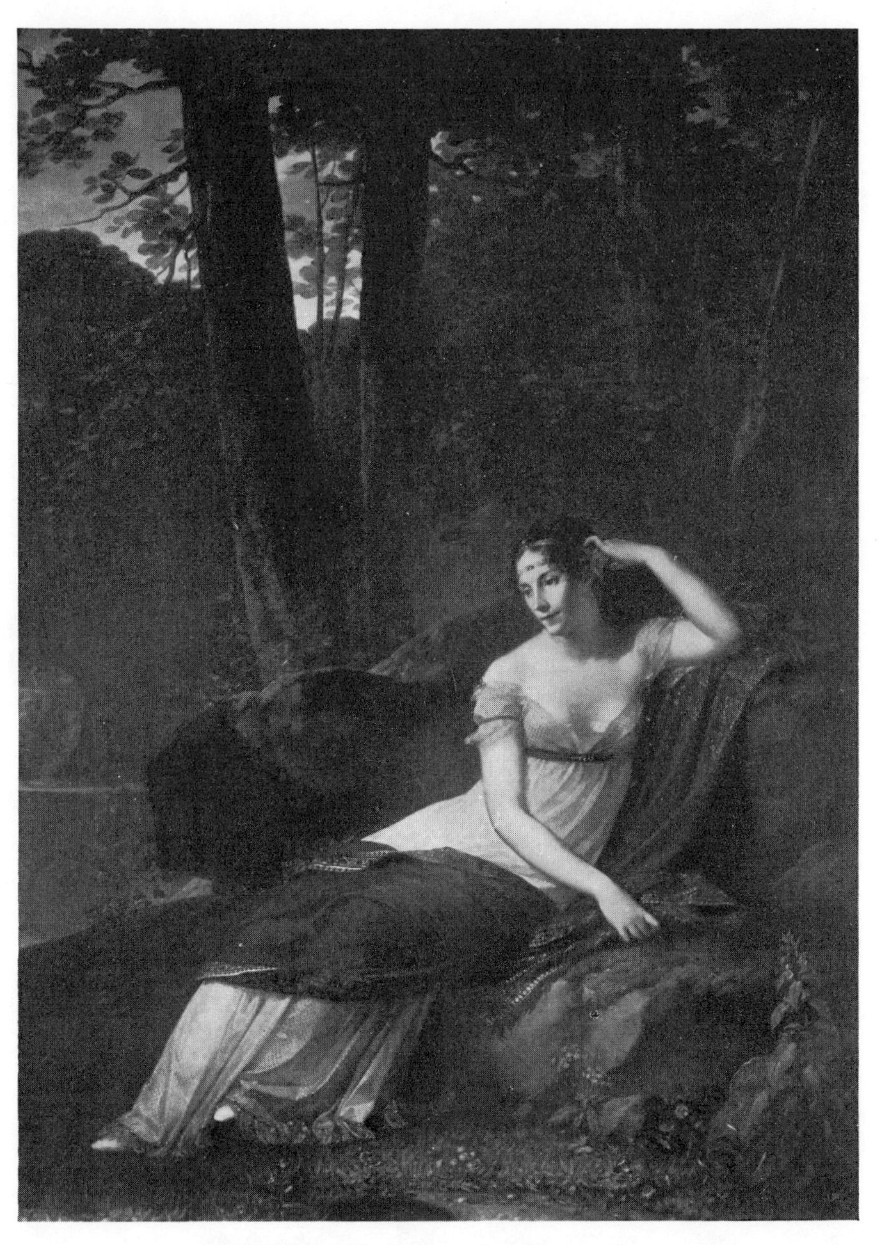

32. PRUDHON. *Empress Josephine.* *Louvre.*

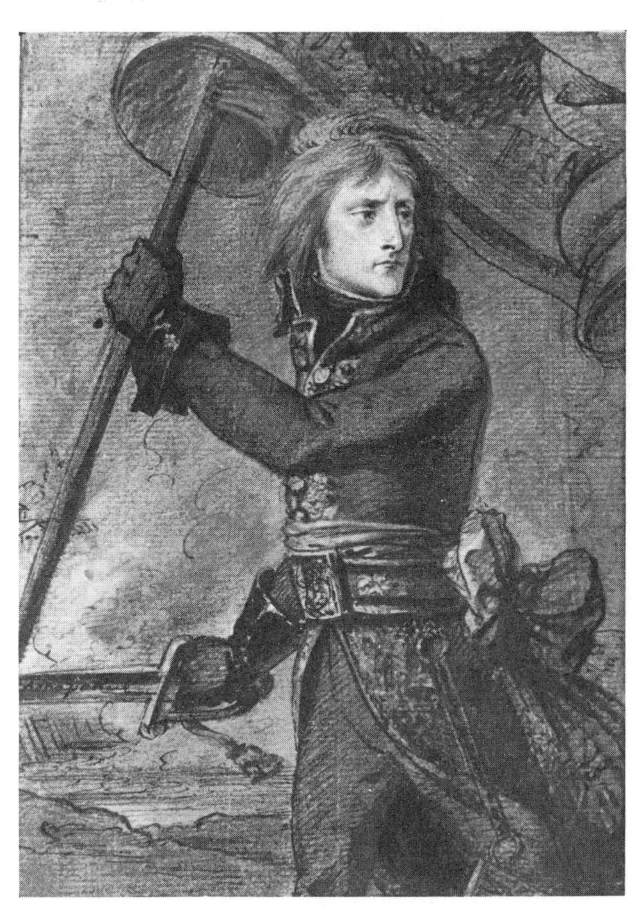

33. GROS. Study for *Napoleon at Arcole.* *Wildenstein.*

34. GROS. *Napoleon at Jaffa.* *Museum of Fine Arts, Boston.*

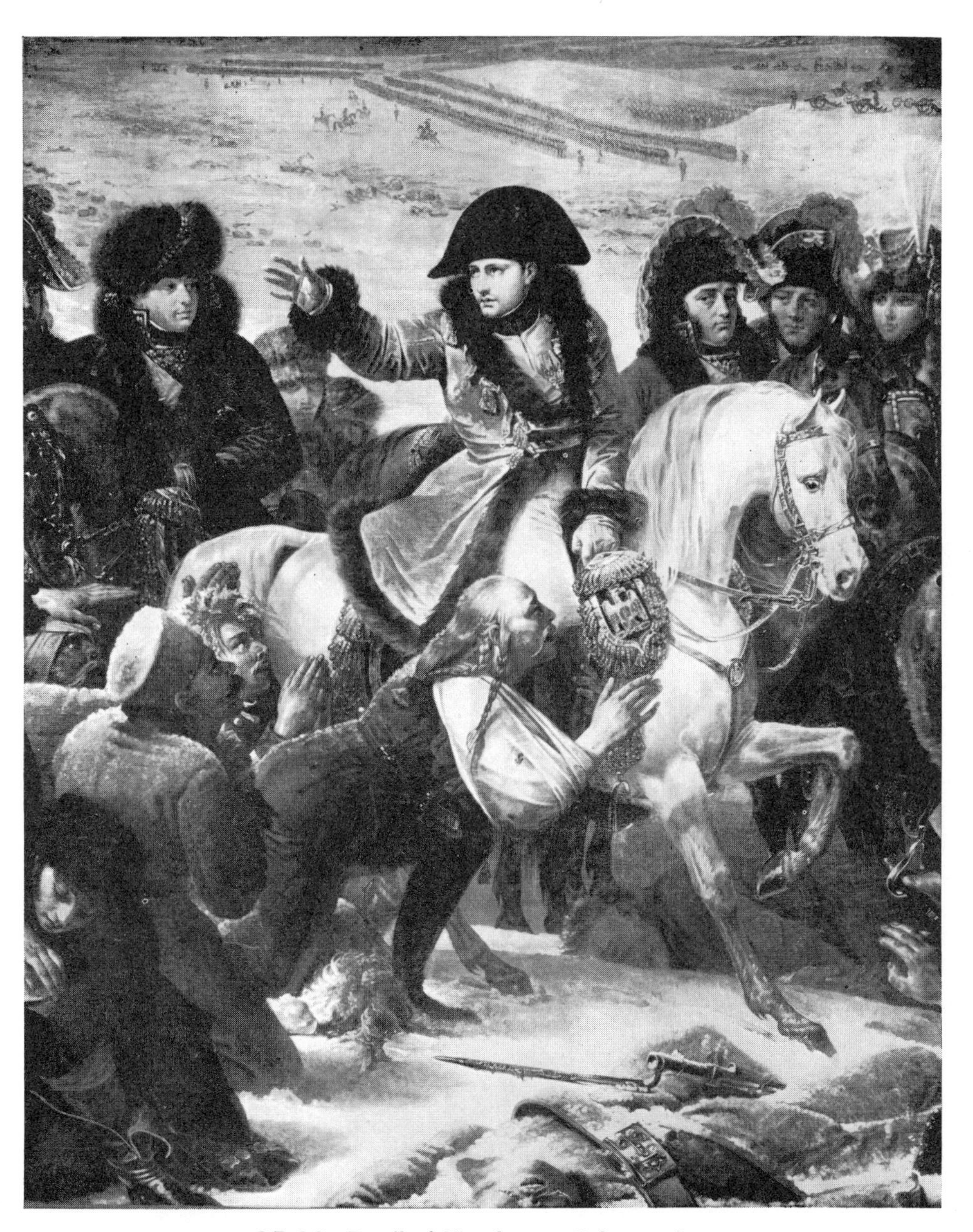

35. GROS. Detail of *Napoleon at Eylau.* *Louvre.*

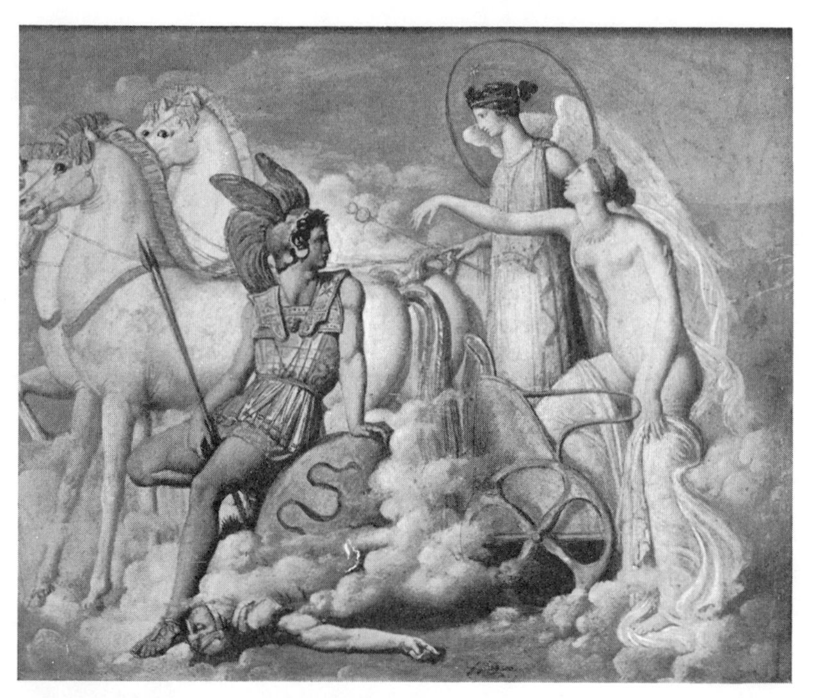

36. INGRES. *Venus Wounded by Diomedes.* *Private collection, Basel.*

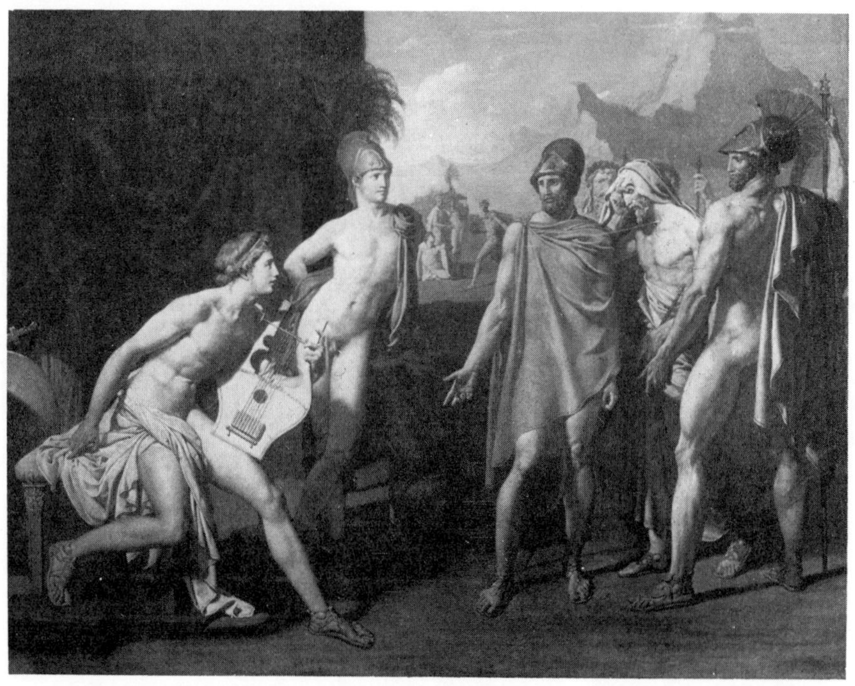

37. INGRES. *Achilles and the Greek Ambassadors.* *Ecole des Beaux-Arts.*

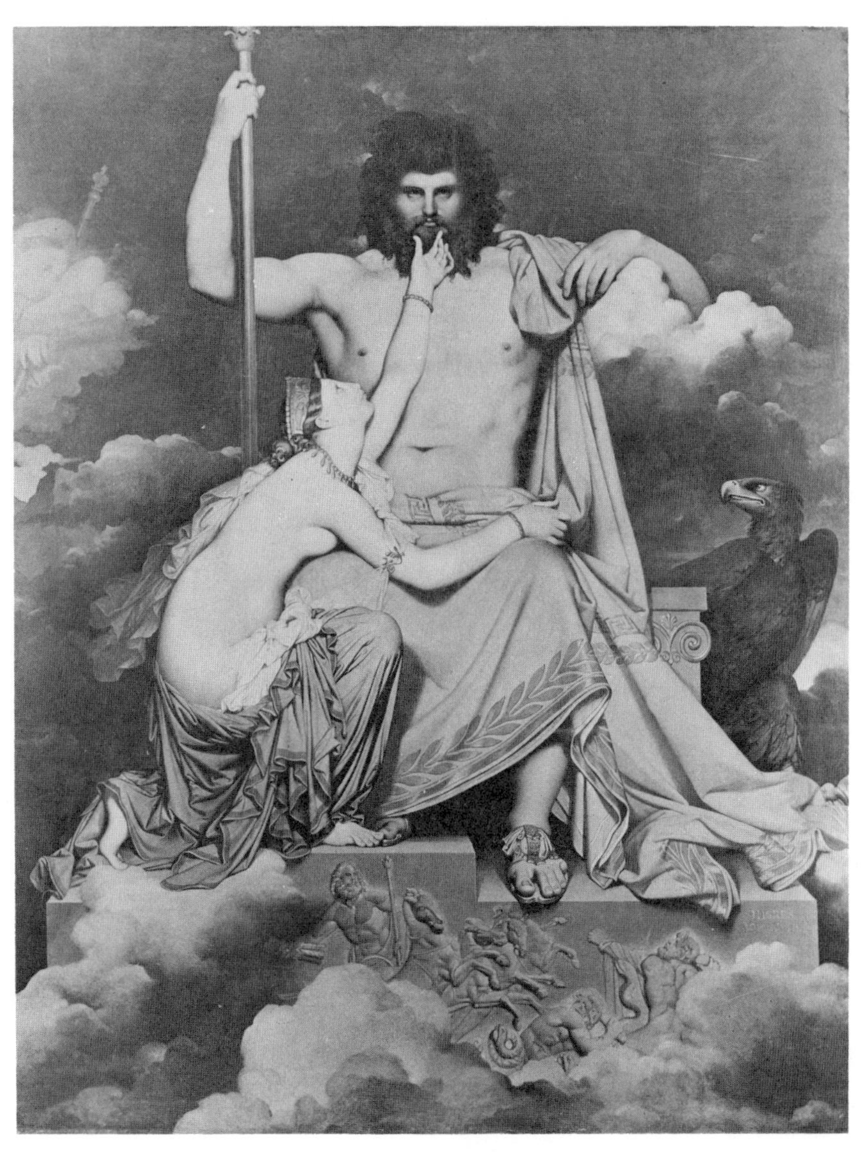

38. INGRES. *Jupiter and Thetis.* *Aix-en-Provence.*

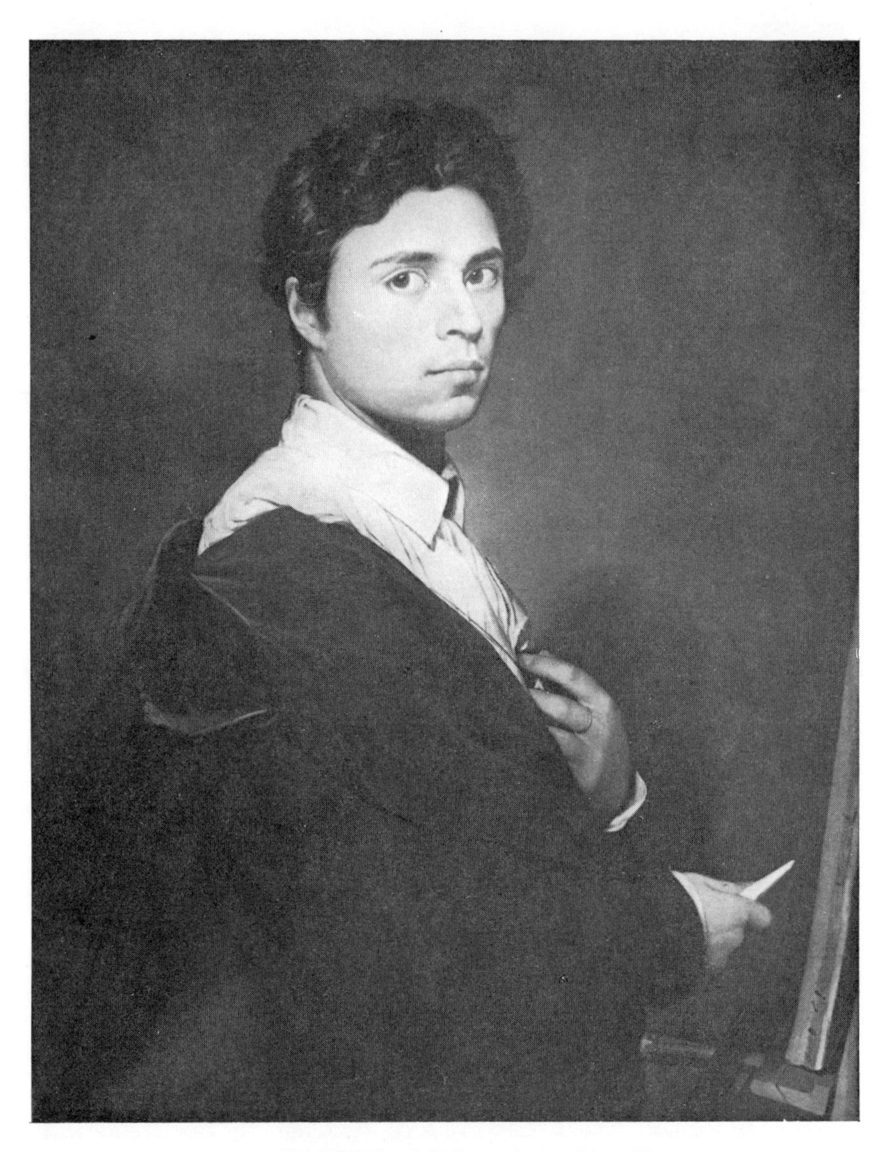

39. INGRES. *Self-Portrait.* *Chantilly.*

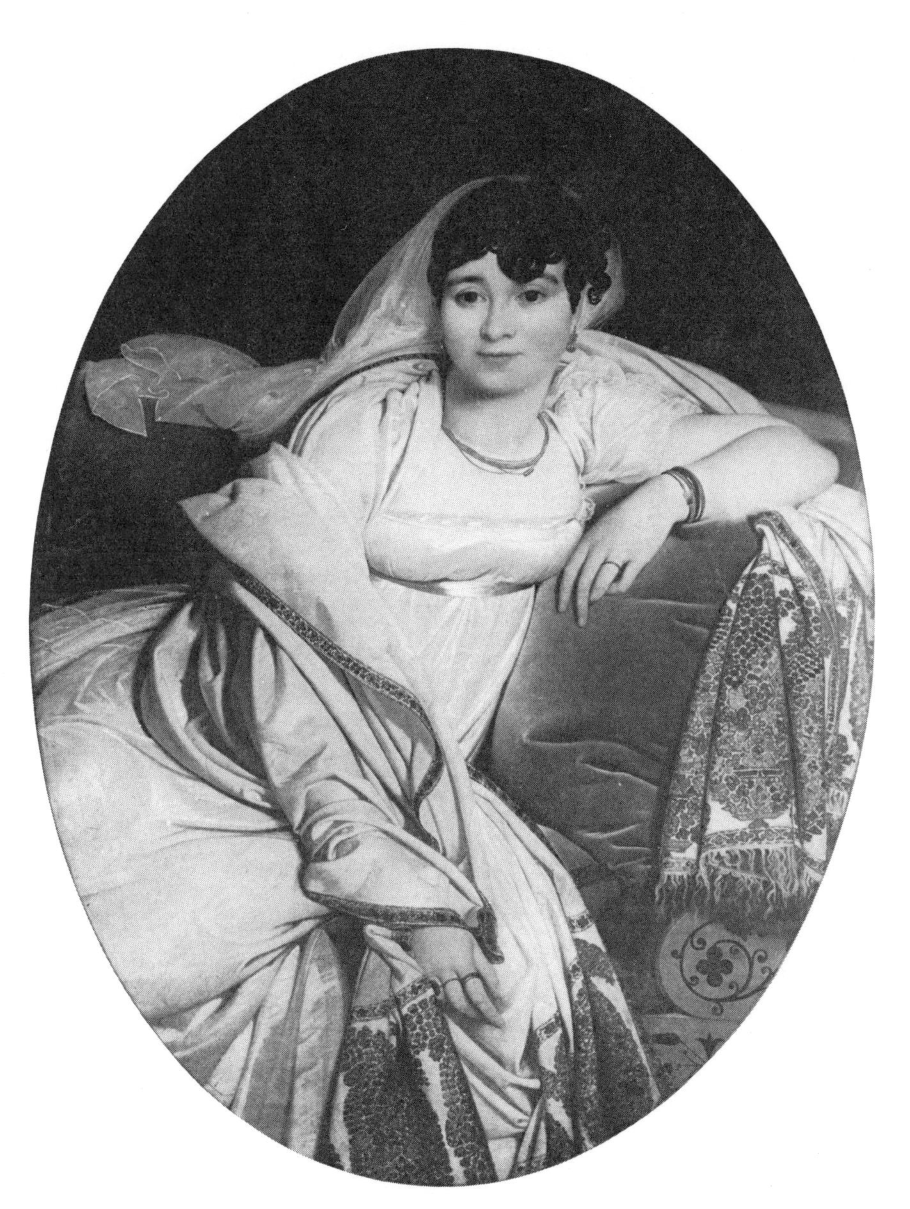

40. INGRES. *Mme. Rivière.* *Louvre.*

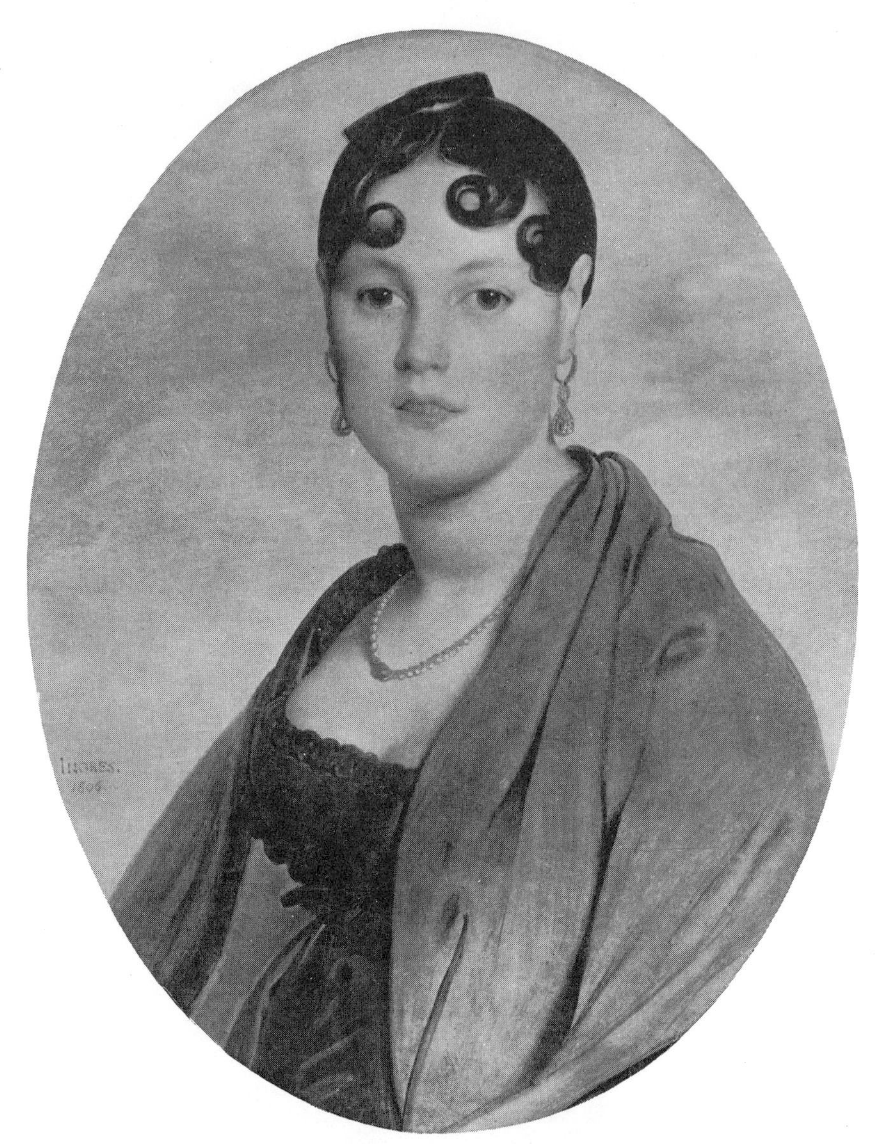

41. INGRES. *Mme. Aymon, "Zélie."* *Rouen.*

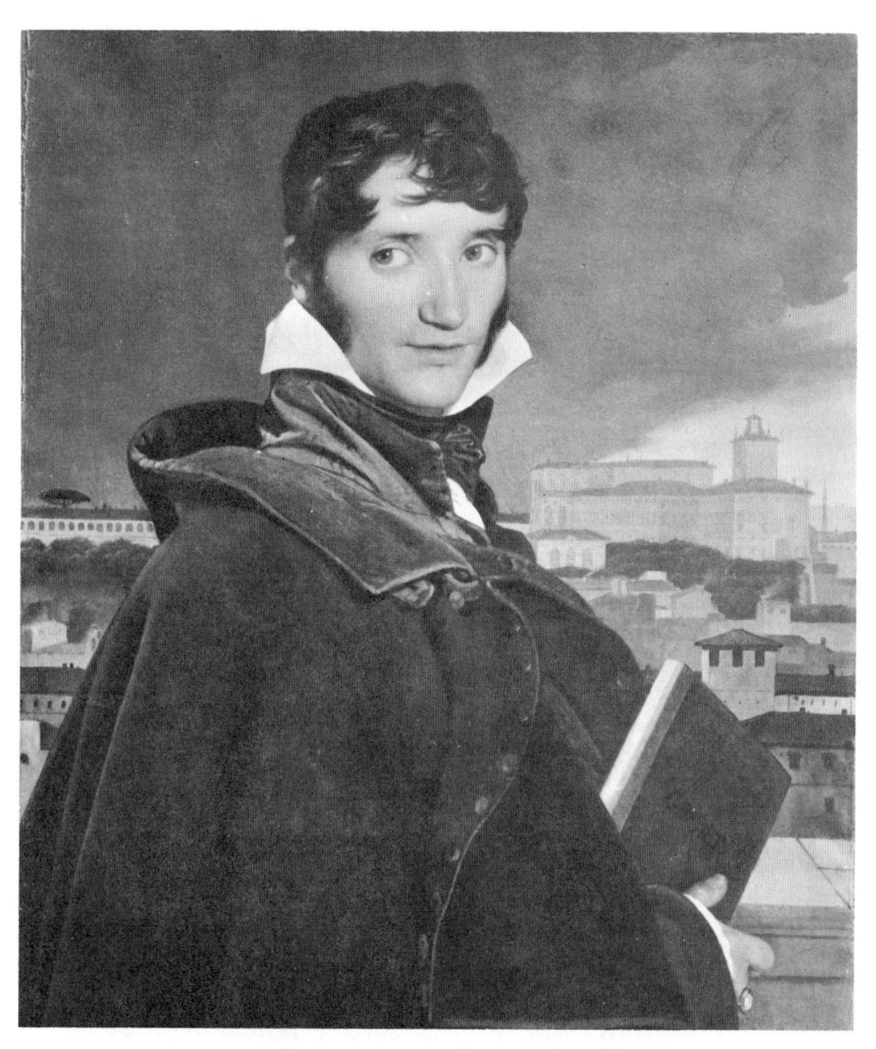

42. INGRES. *M. Granet.* *Aix-en-Provence.*

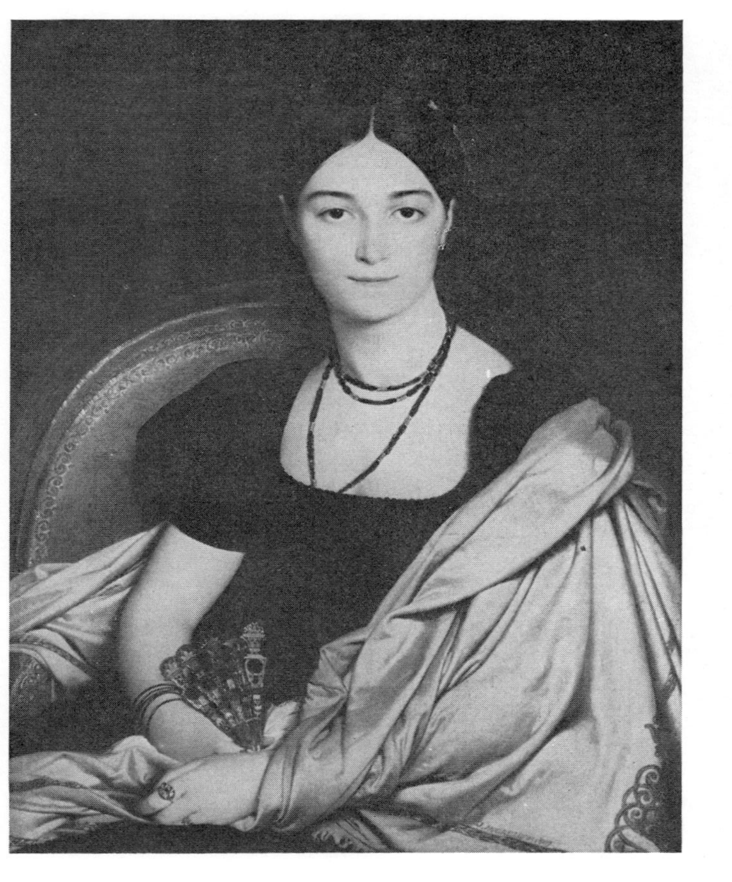

43. INGRES. *Mme. Devauçay.* *Chantilly.*

44. INGRES. *Mme. de Tournon.* *Henry P. McIlhenny.*

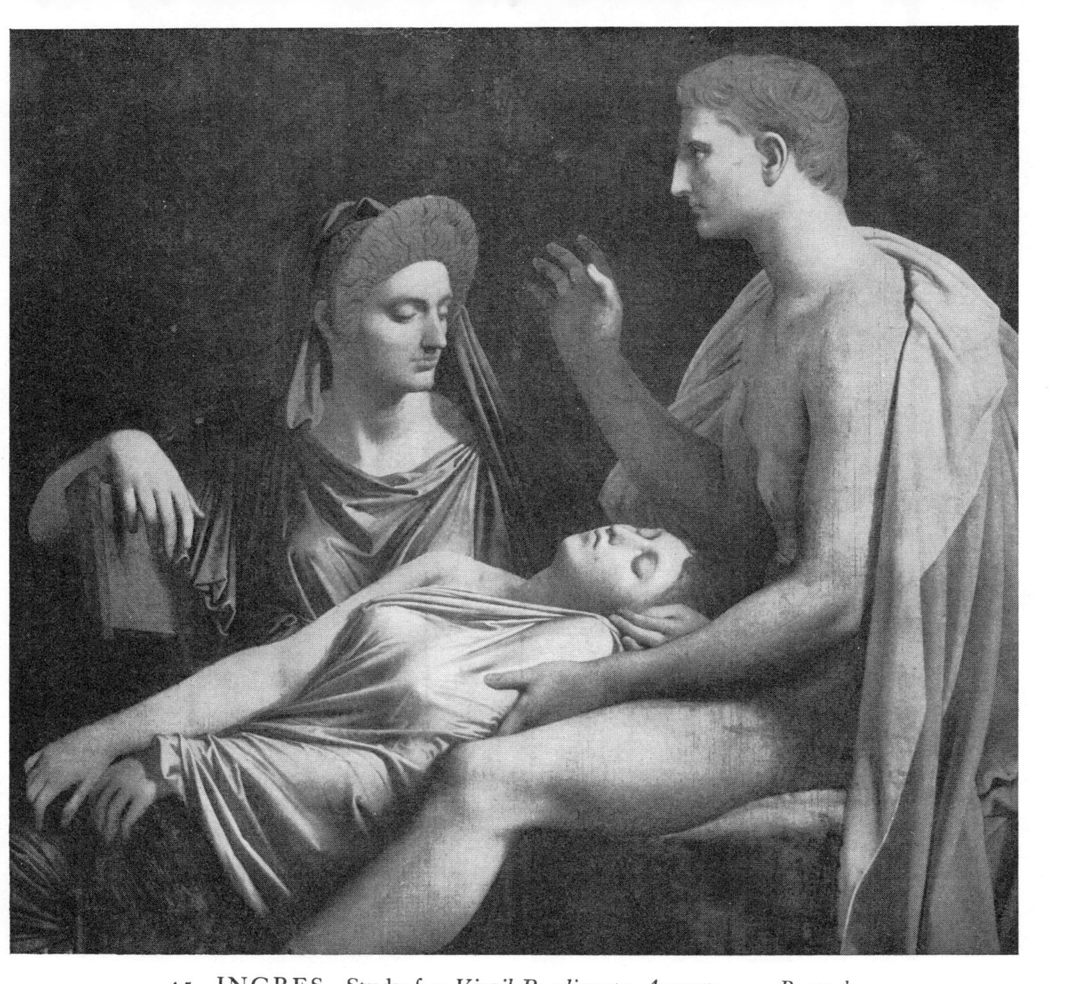

45. INGRES. Study for *Virgil Reading to Augustus.* *Brussels.*

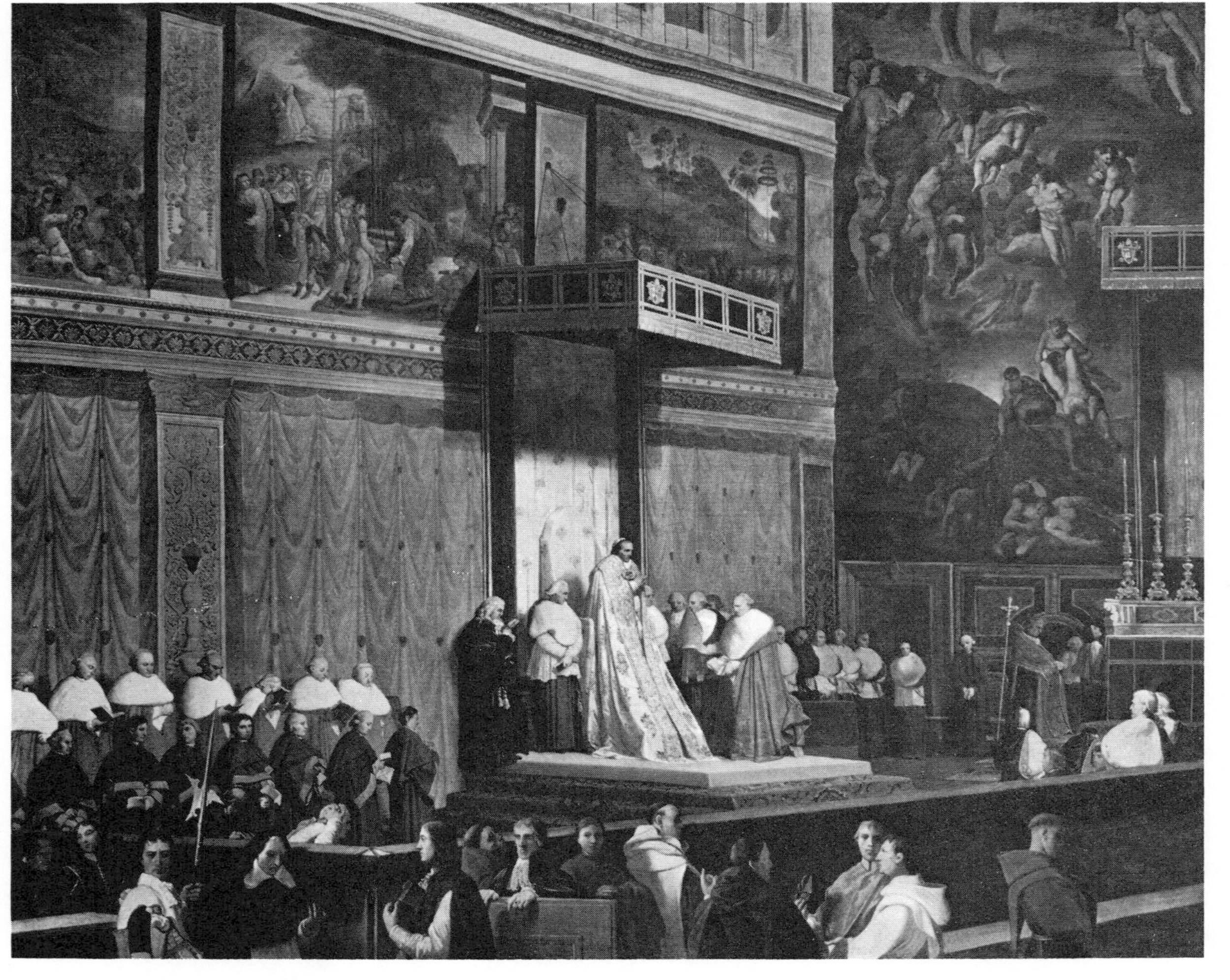

46. INGRES. *The Sistine Chapel.* National Gallery of Art, Washington.

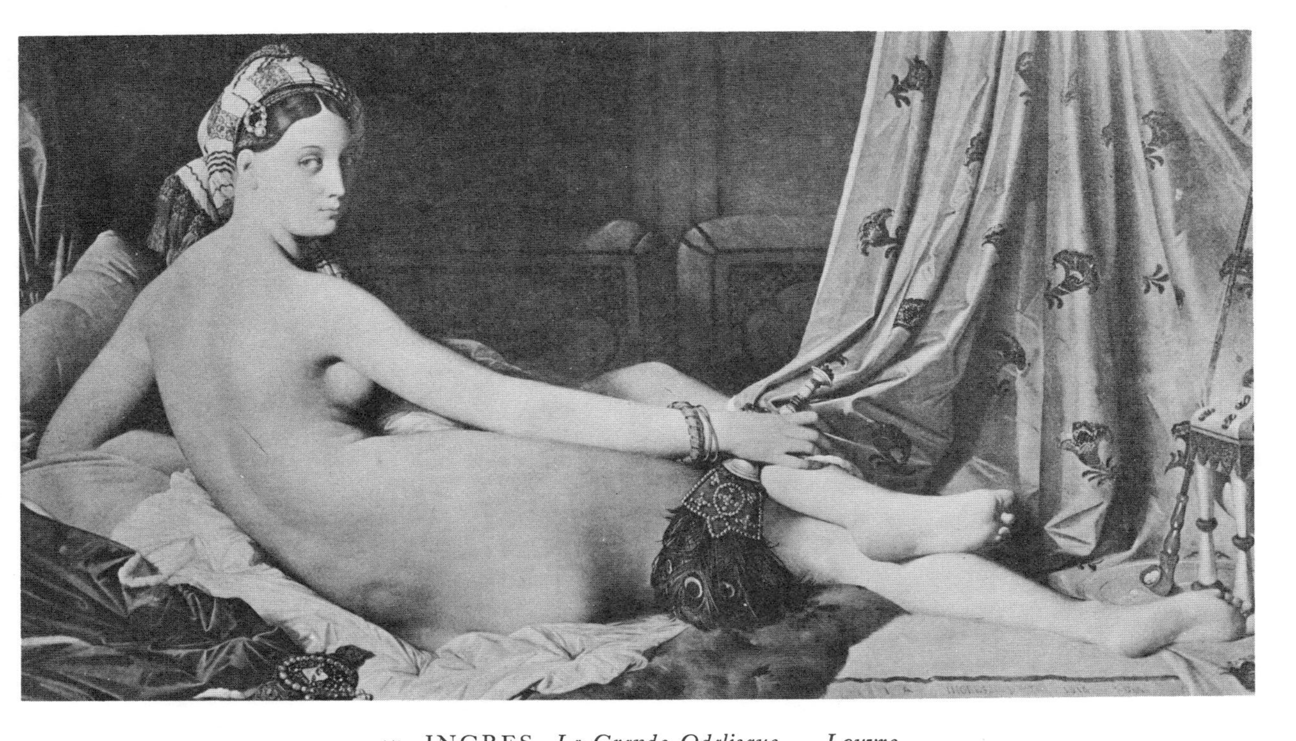

47. INGRES. *La Grande Odalisque.* *Louvre.*

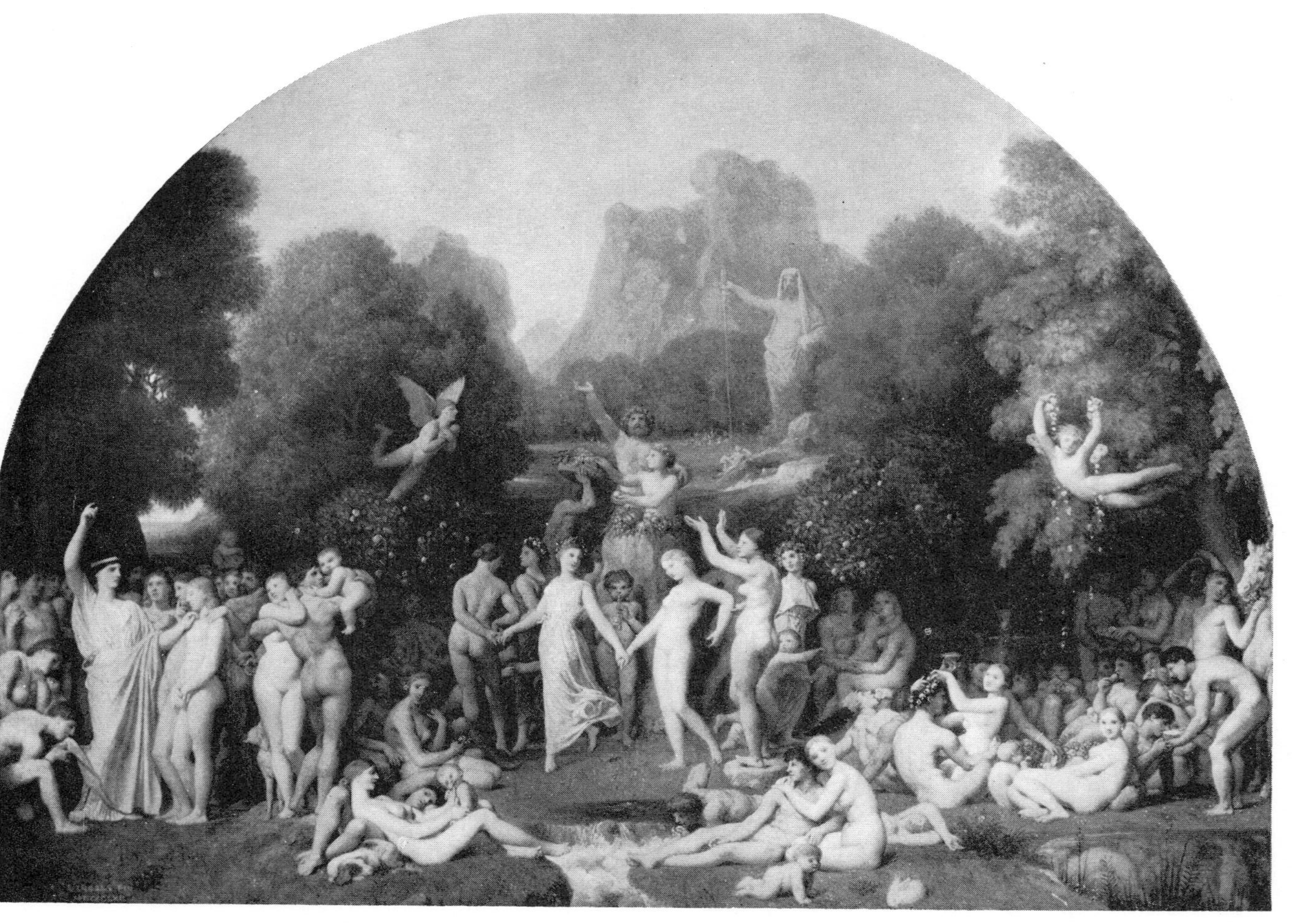

48 INGRES *The Golden Age* Fogg Museum of Art

49. INGRES. *The Turkish Bath.* Louvre.

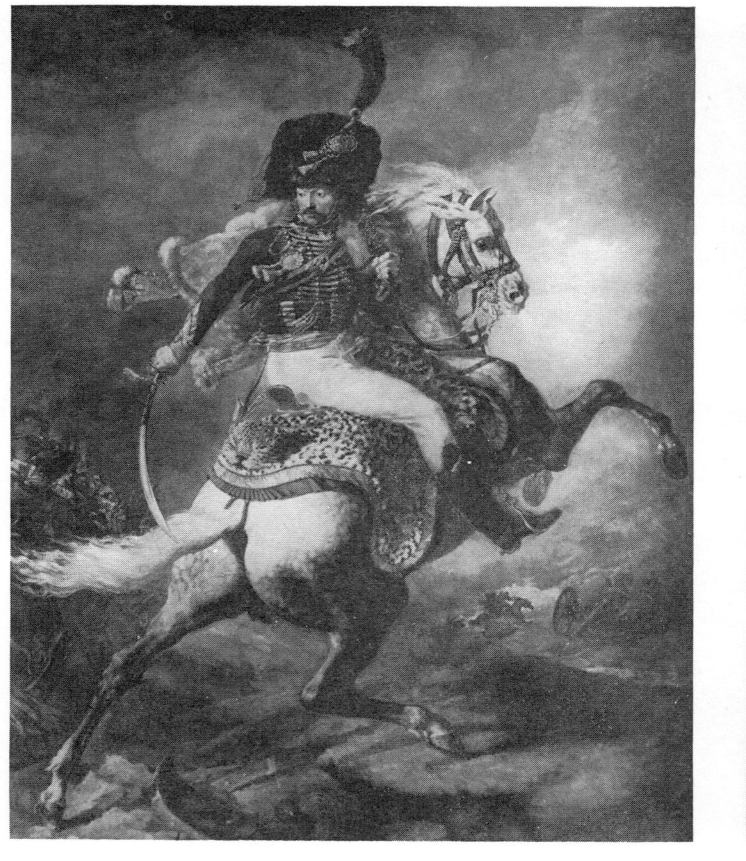

50. GERICAULT. *Officer of the Imperial Guard.* Louvre.

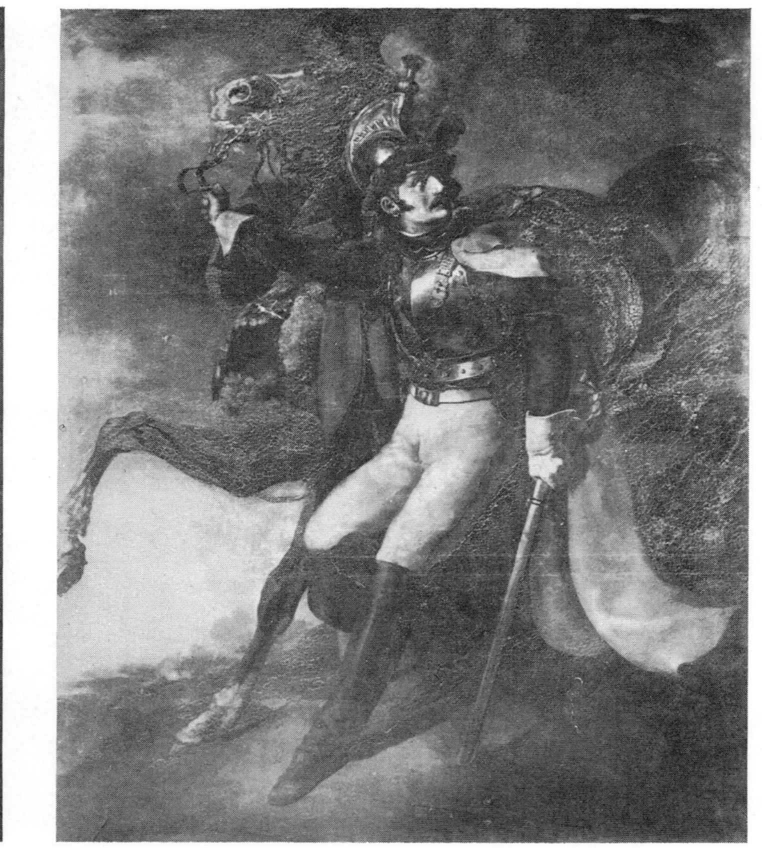

51. GERICAULT. *The Wounded Cuirassier.* Louvre.

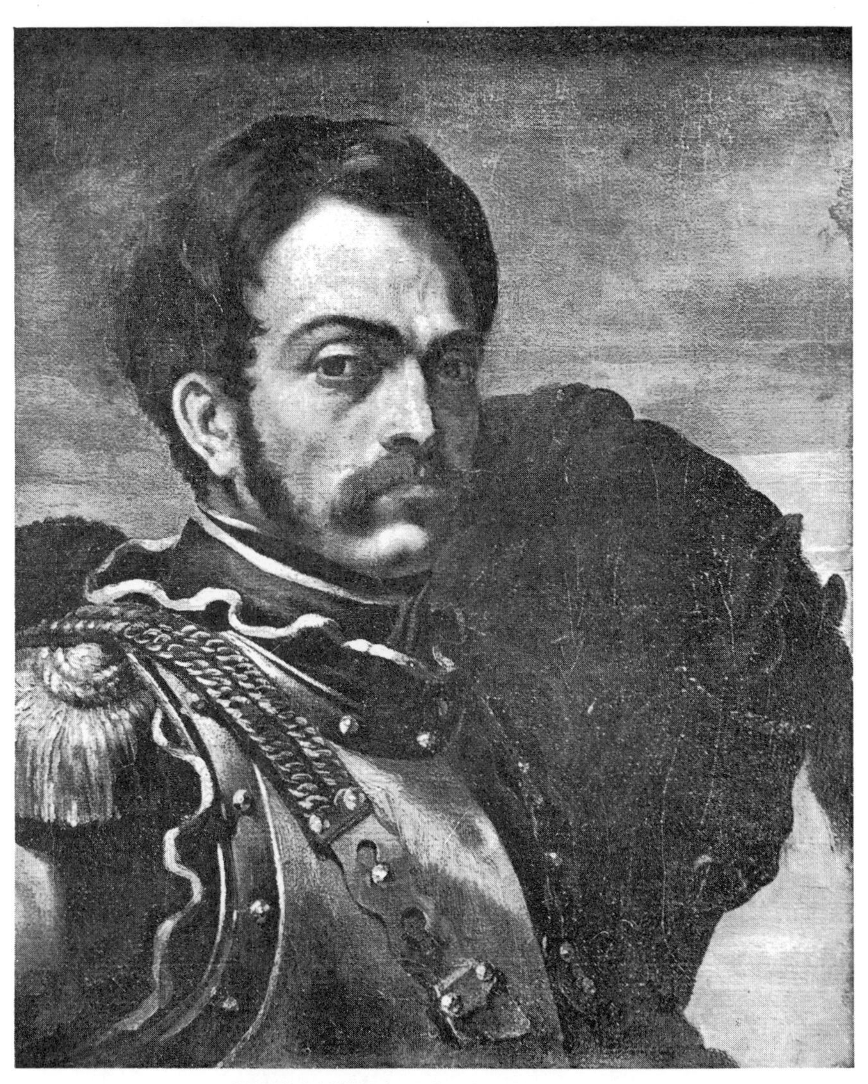

52. GERICAULT. *The Carabinier.* Rouen.

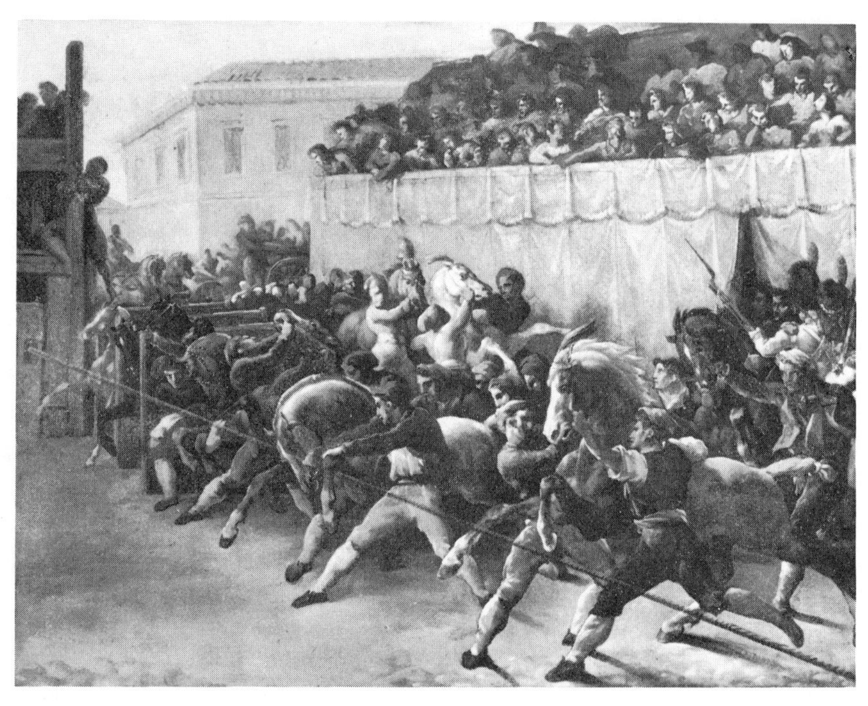

53. GERICAULT. Study for *The Córso dei Bárberi.* *Walters Art Gallery.*

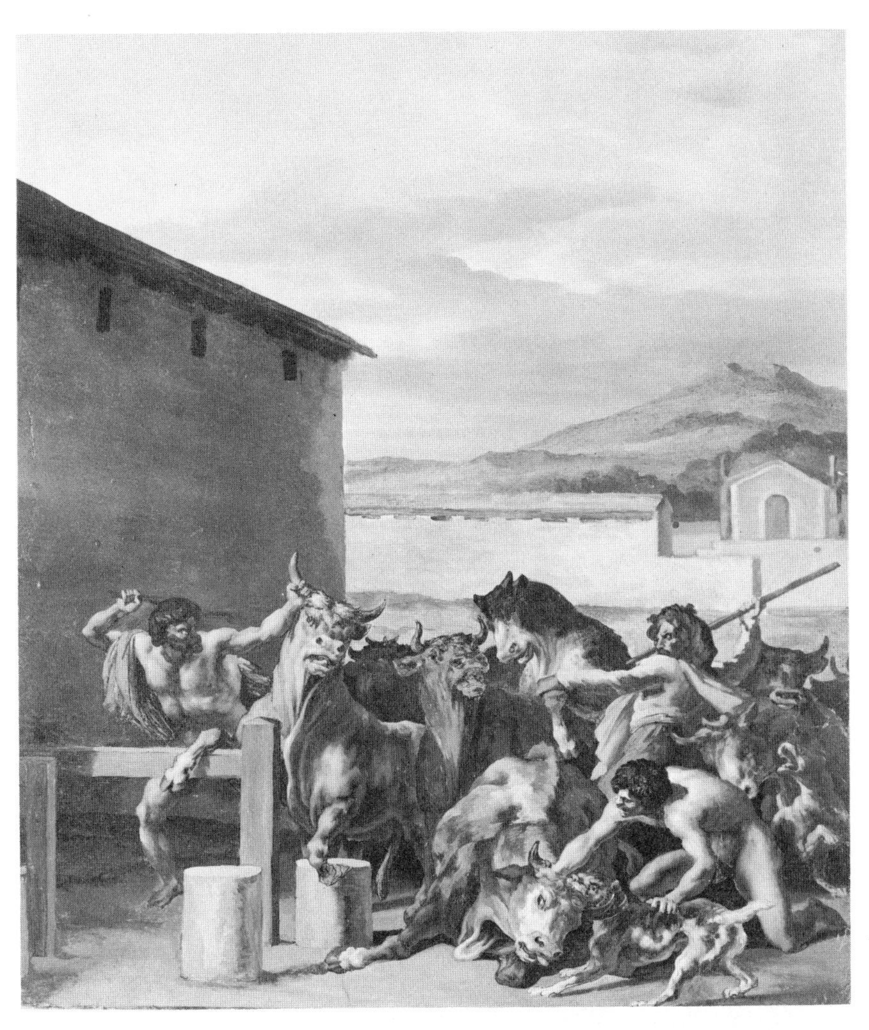

54. GERICAULT. *The Cattle Market.* *Fogg Museum of Art.*

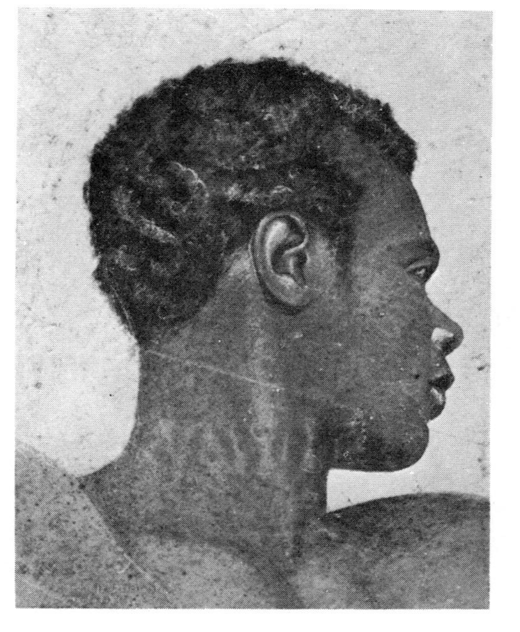

55. GERICAULT. *Negro.* *Rouen.*

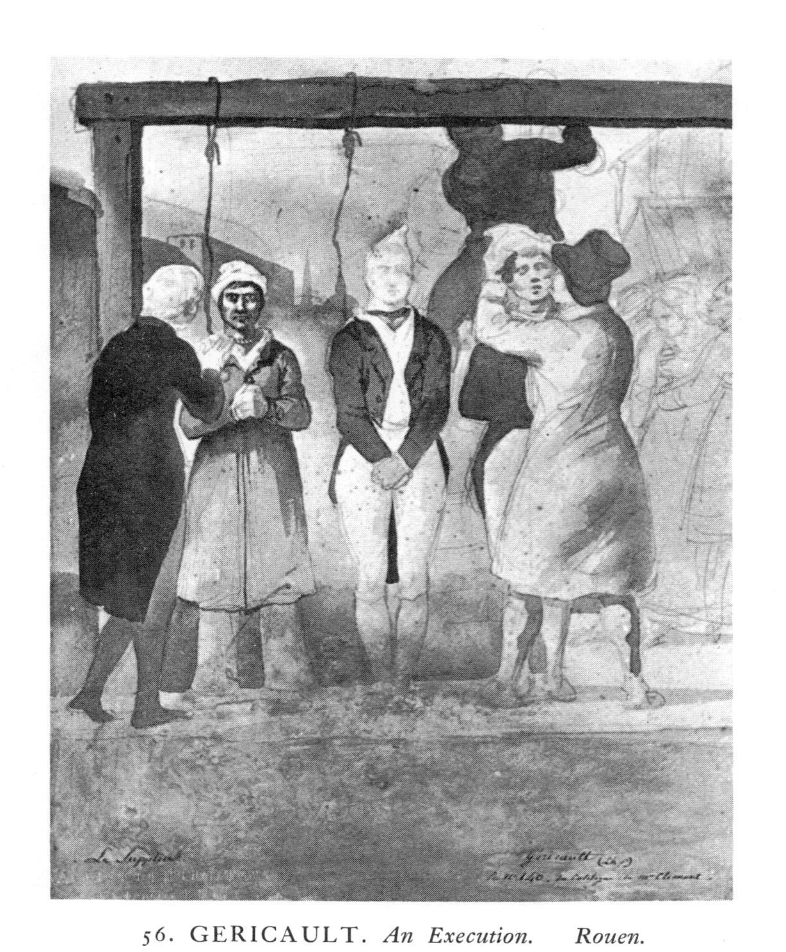

56. GERICAULT. *An Execution.* *Rouen.*

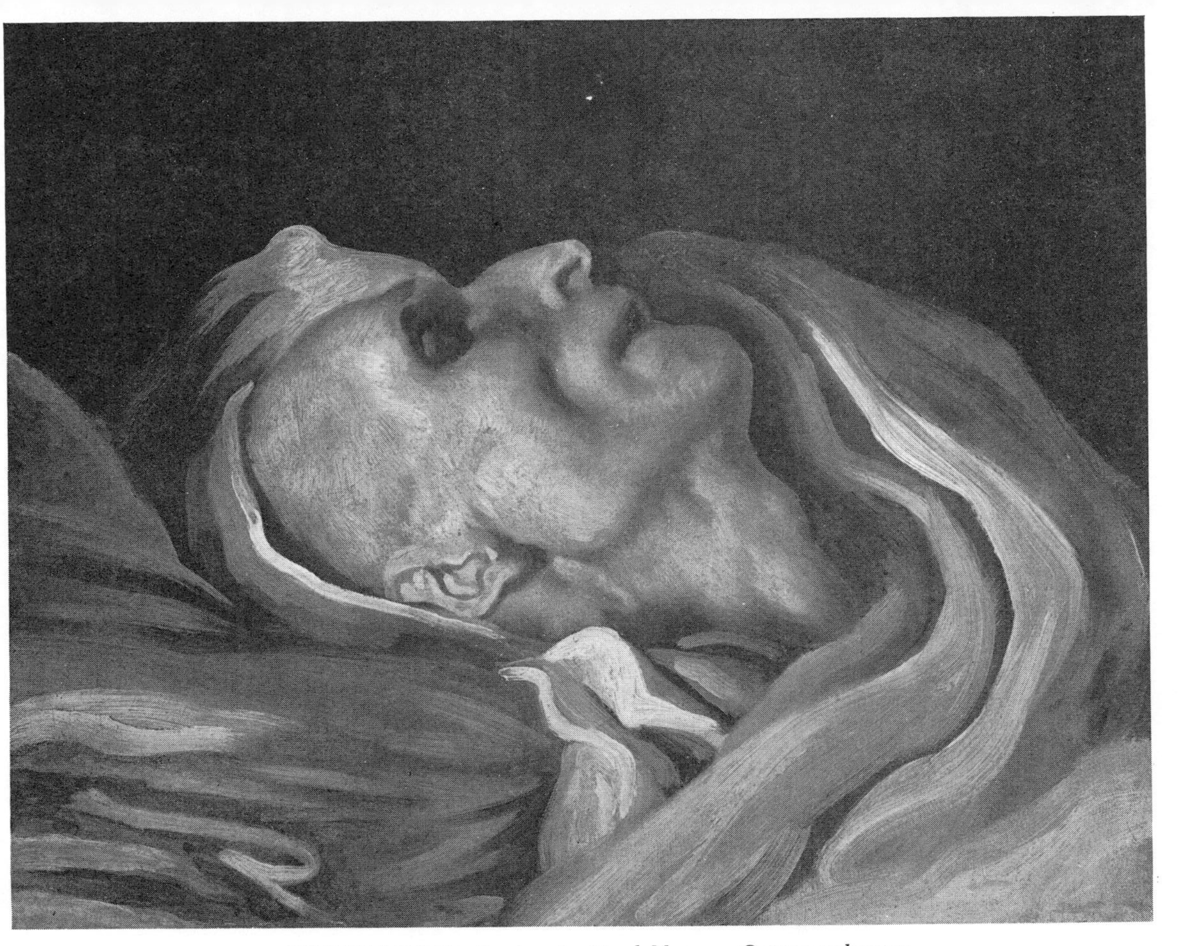

57. GERICAULT. *Study of a Dead Man.* *Owner unknown.*

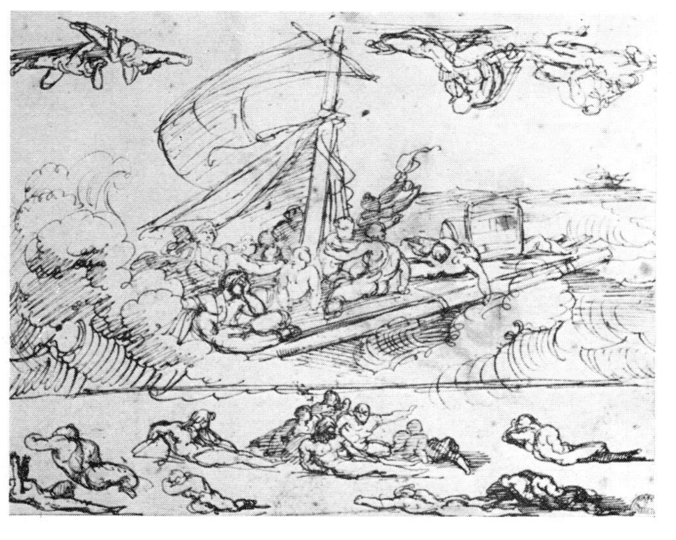

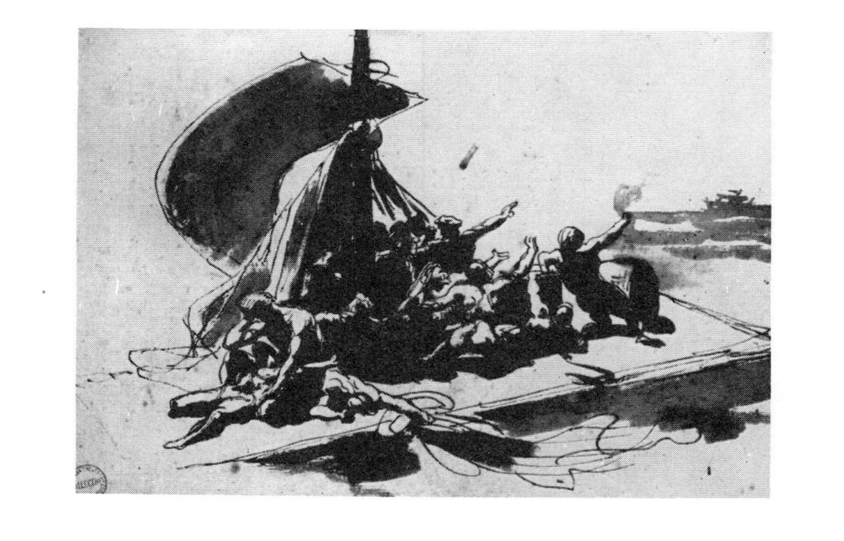

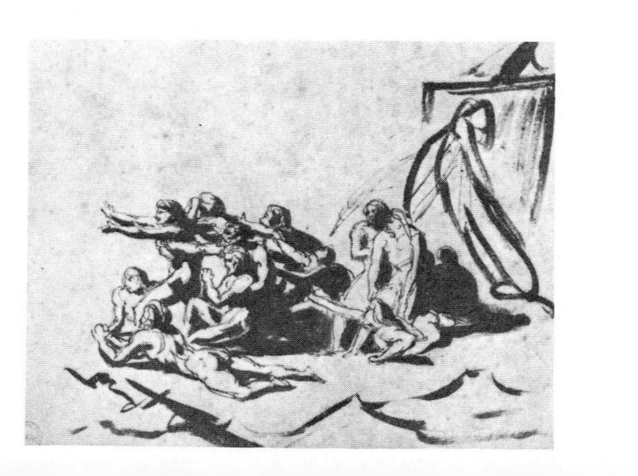

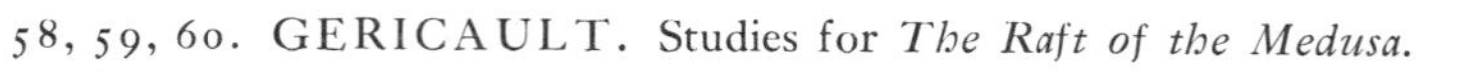

58, 59, 60. GERICAULT. Studies for *The Raft of the Medusa.* Rouen.

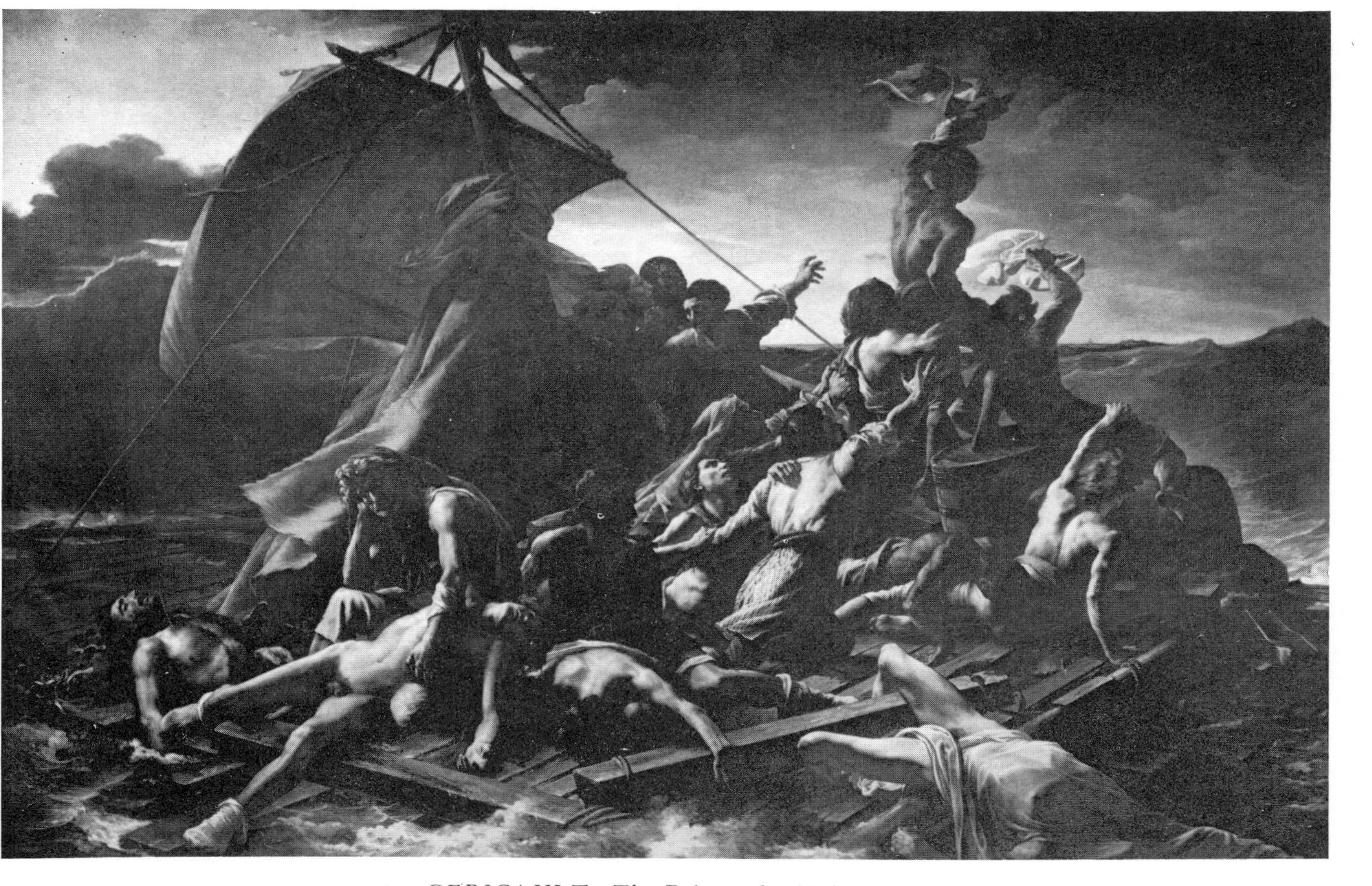

61. GERICAULT. *The Raft of the Medusa.* Louvre.

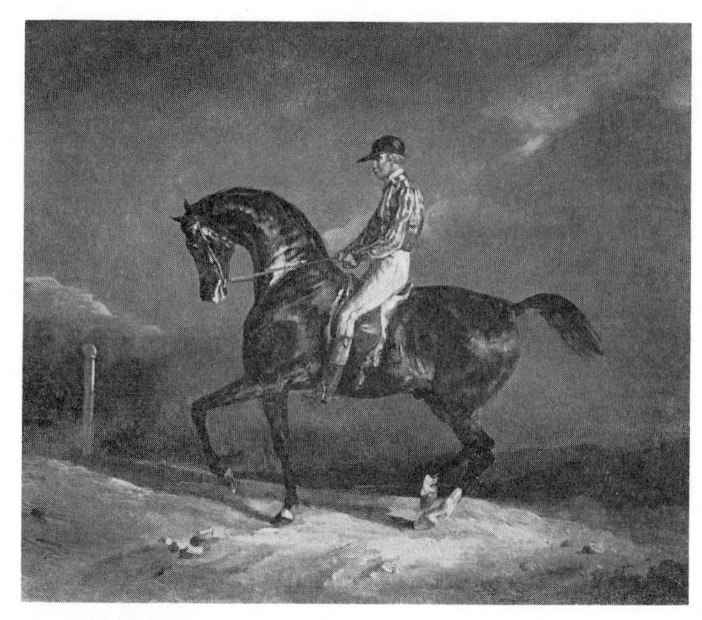

62. GERICAULT. *A Jockey.* *Wildenstein.*

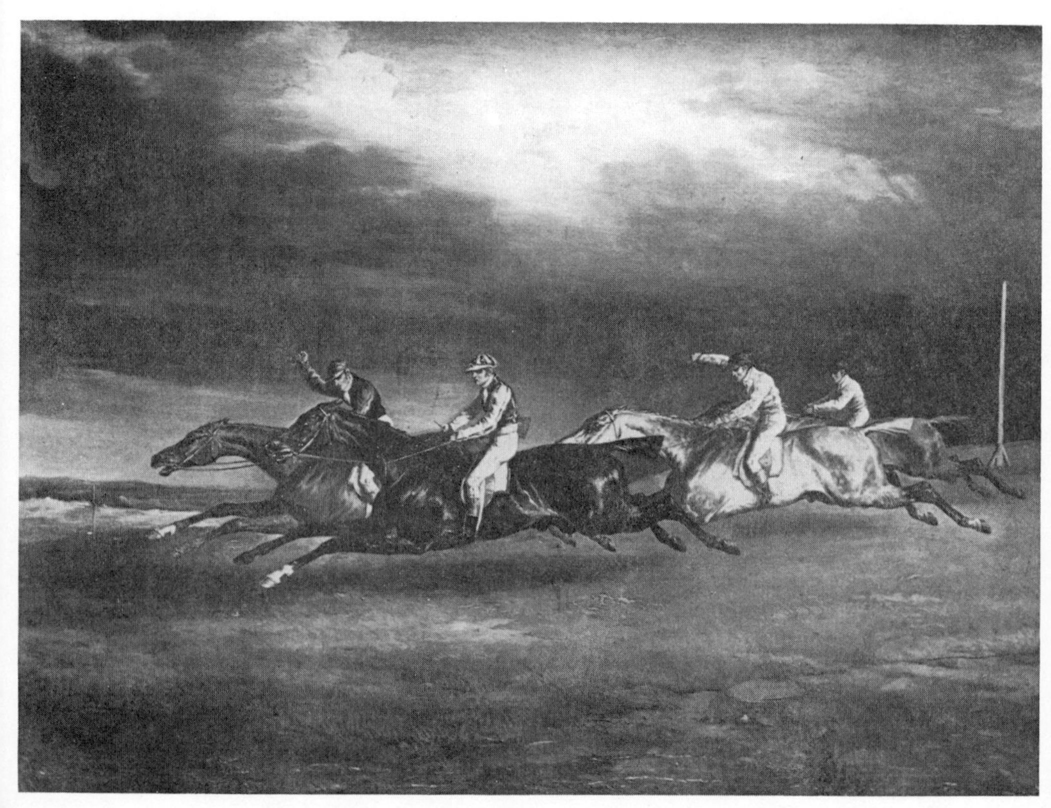

63. GERICAULT. *Racing at Epsom.* *Louvre.*

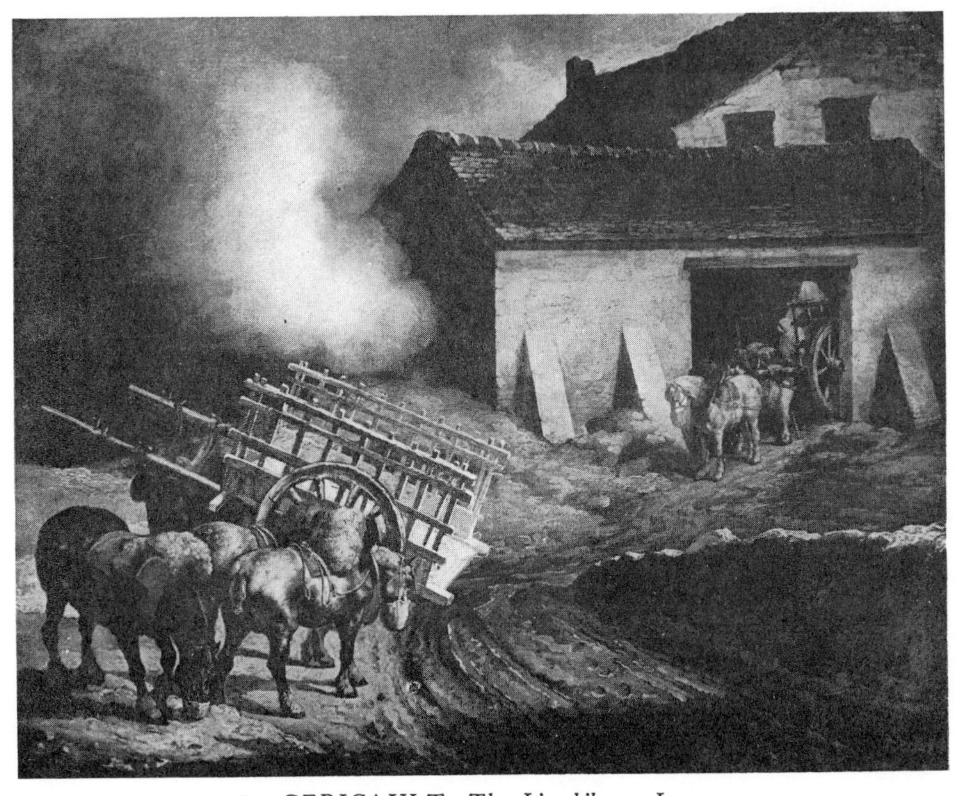

64. GERICAULT. *The Limekiln.* *Louvre.*

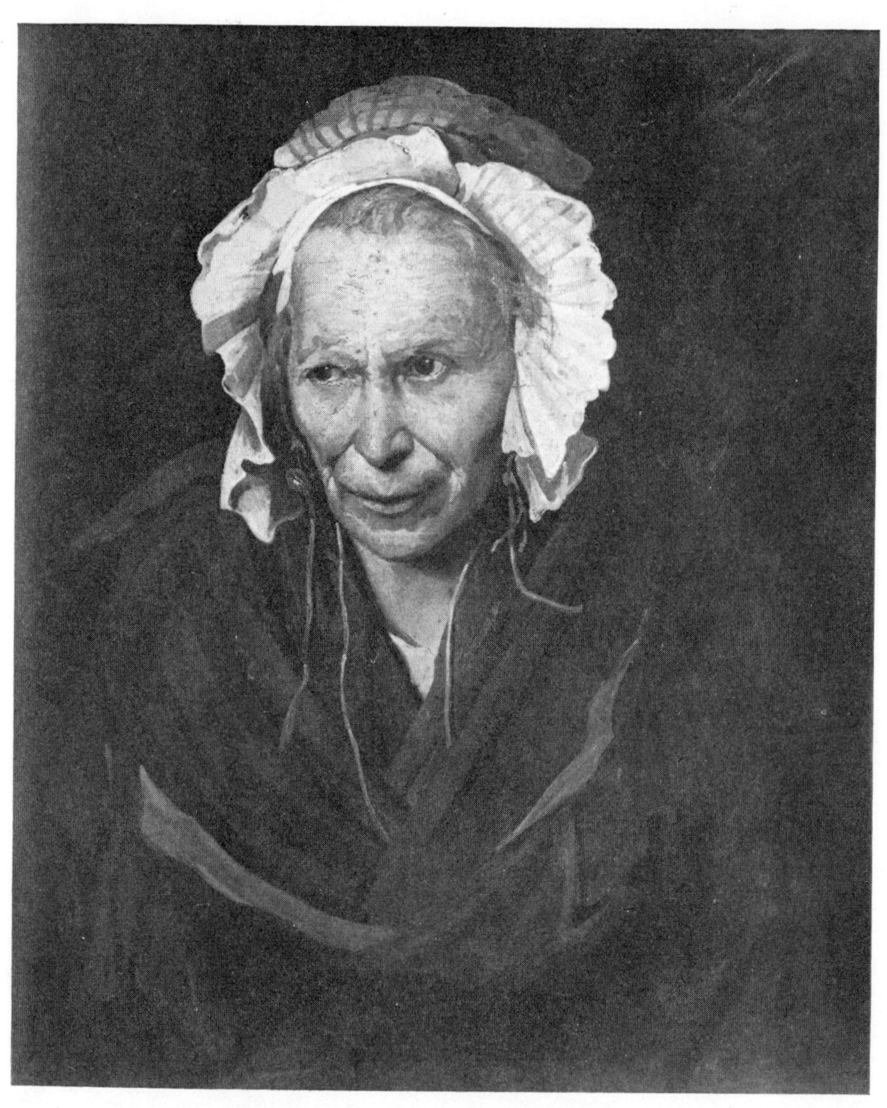

65. GERICAULT. *The Insane Woman.* Lyon.

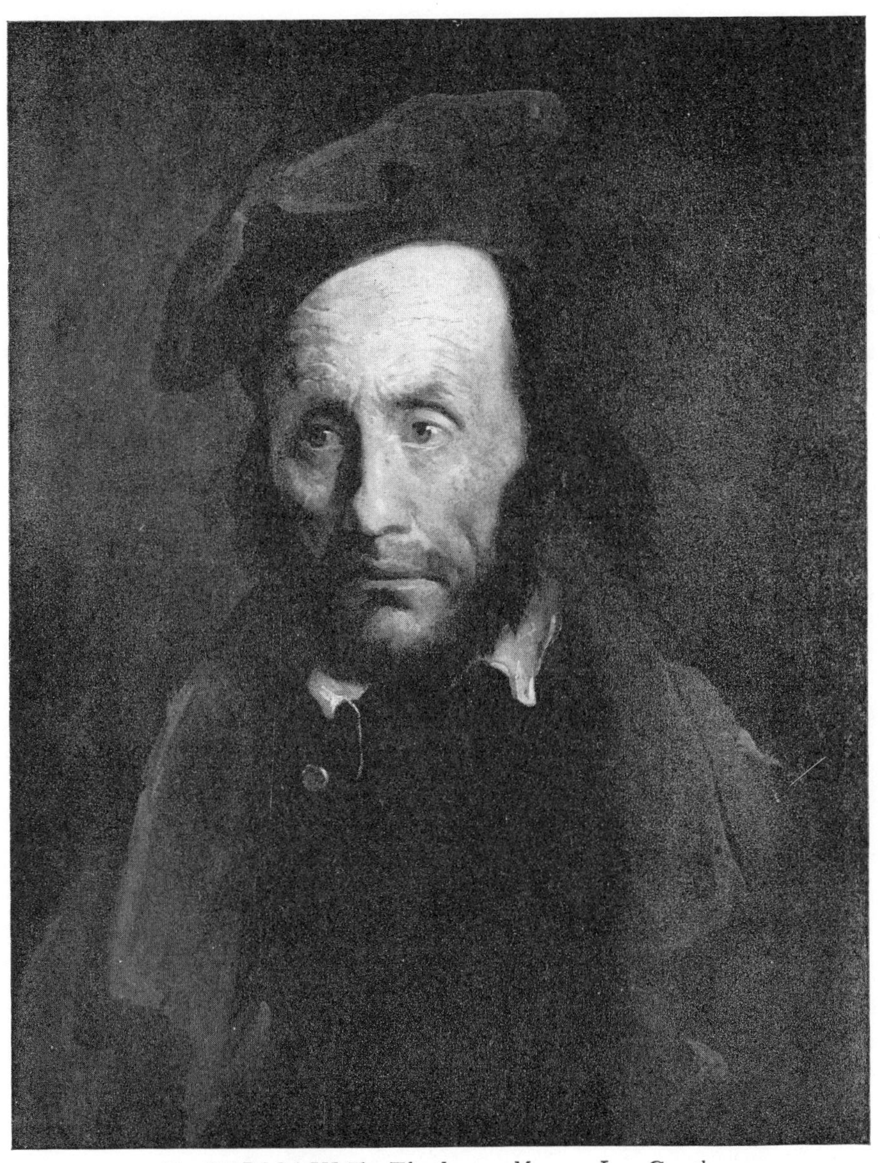

66. GERICAULT. *The Insane Man.* *Leo Gerstle.*

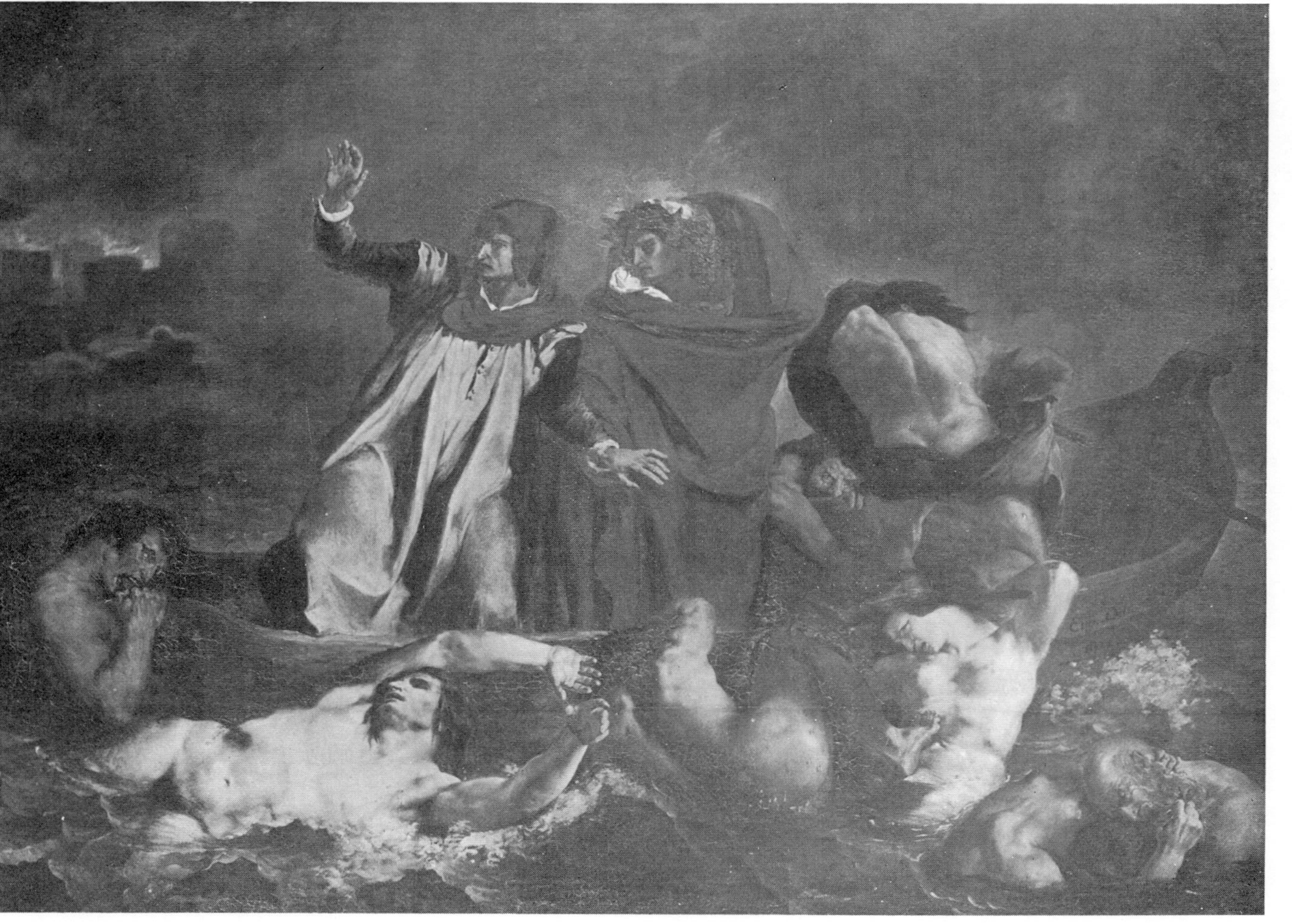

67 DELACROIX *Dante and Virgil in Hell* Louvre

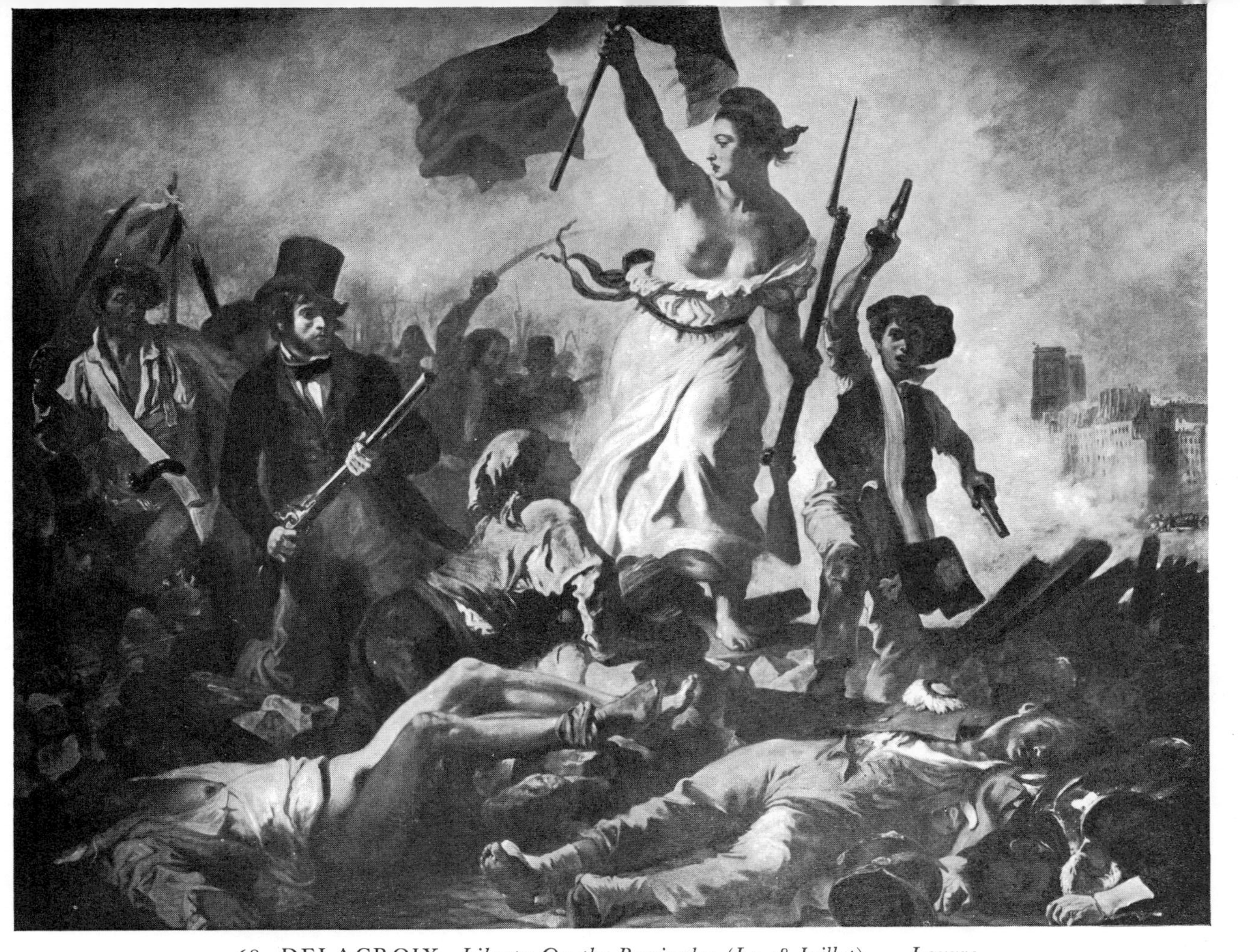

68. DELACROIX. *Liberty On the Barricades (Le 28 Juillet).* *Louvre.*

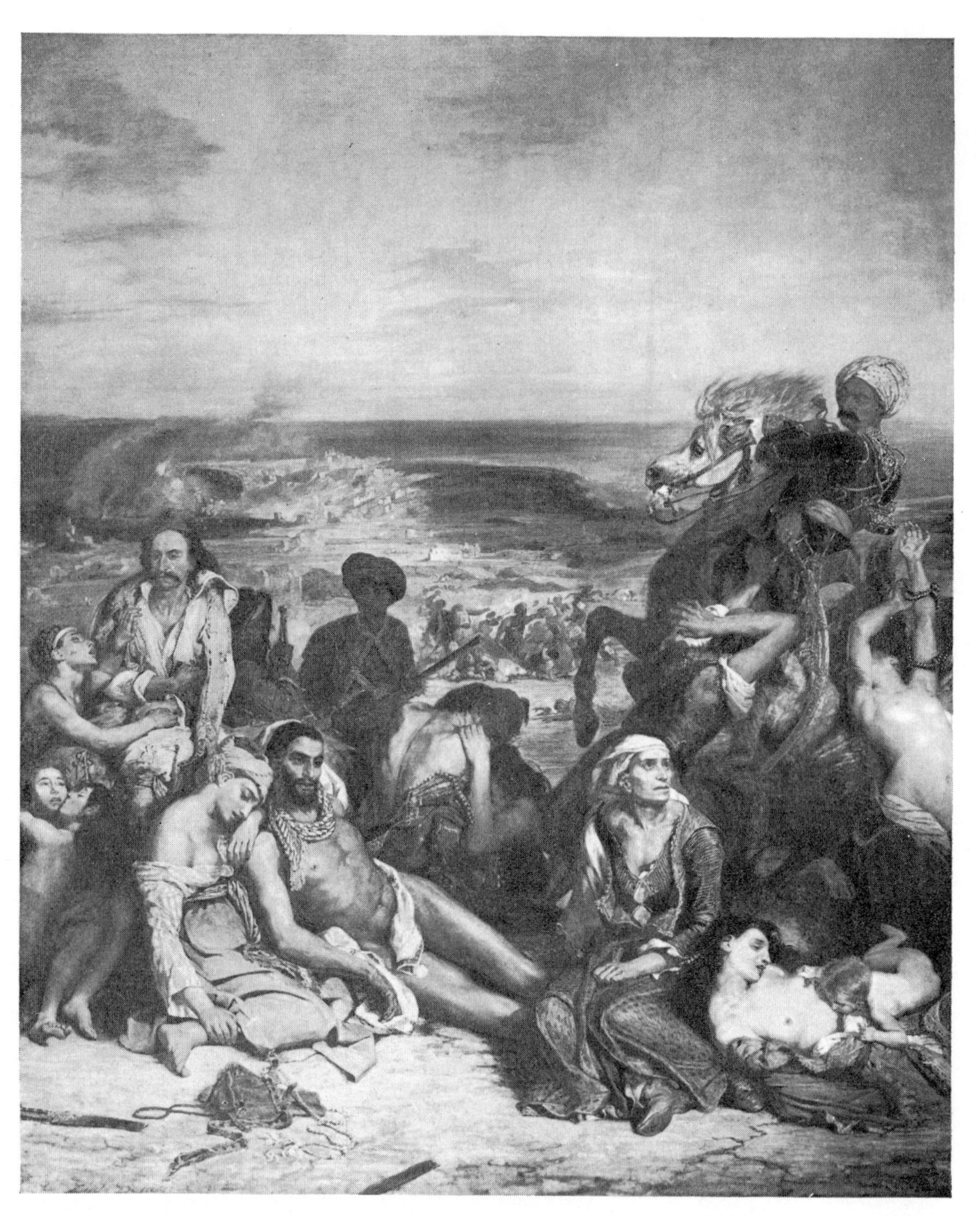

69. DELACROIX. *The Massacre at Chios.* *Louvre.*

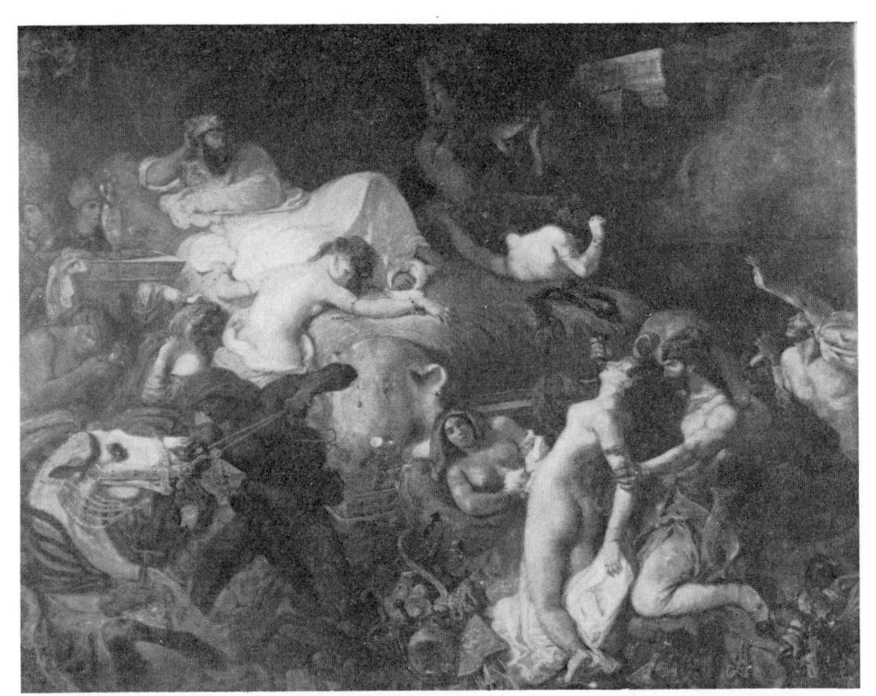

70. DELACROIX. *The Death of Sardanapalus.* *Louvre.*

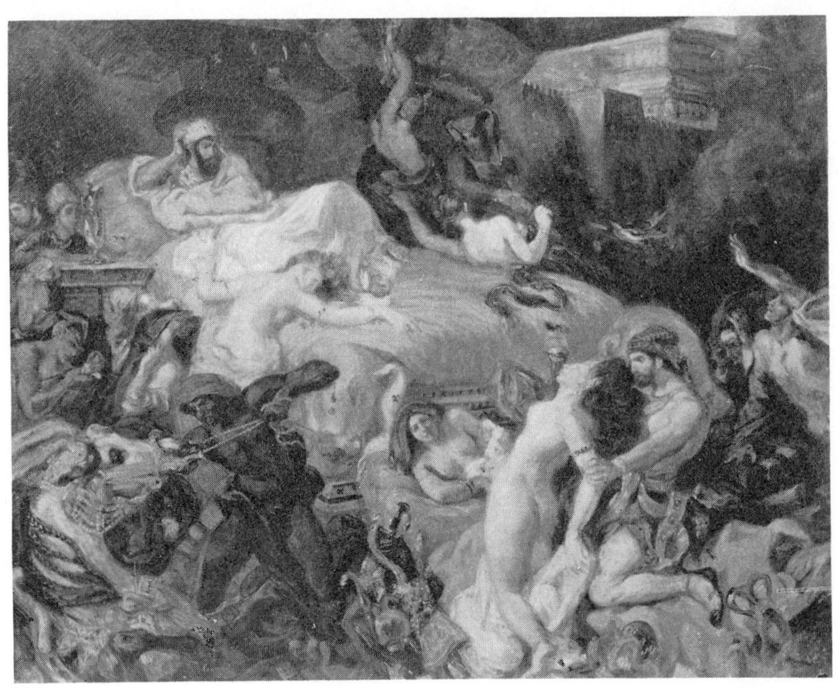

71. DELACROIX. Later version, *Sardanapalus.* *Henry P. McIlhenny.*

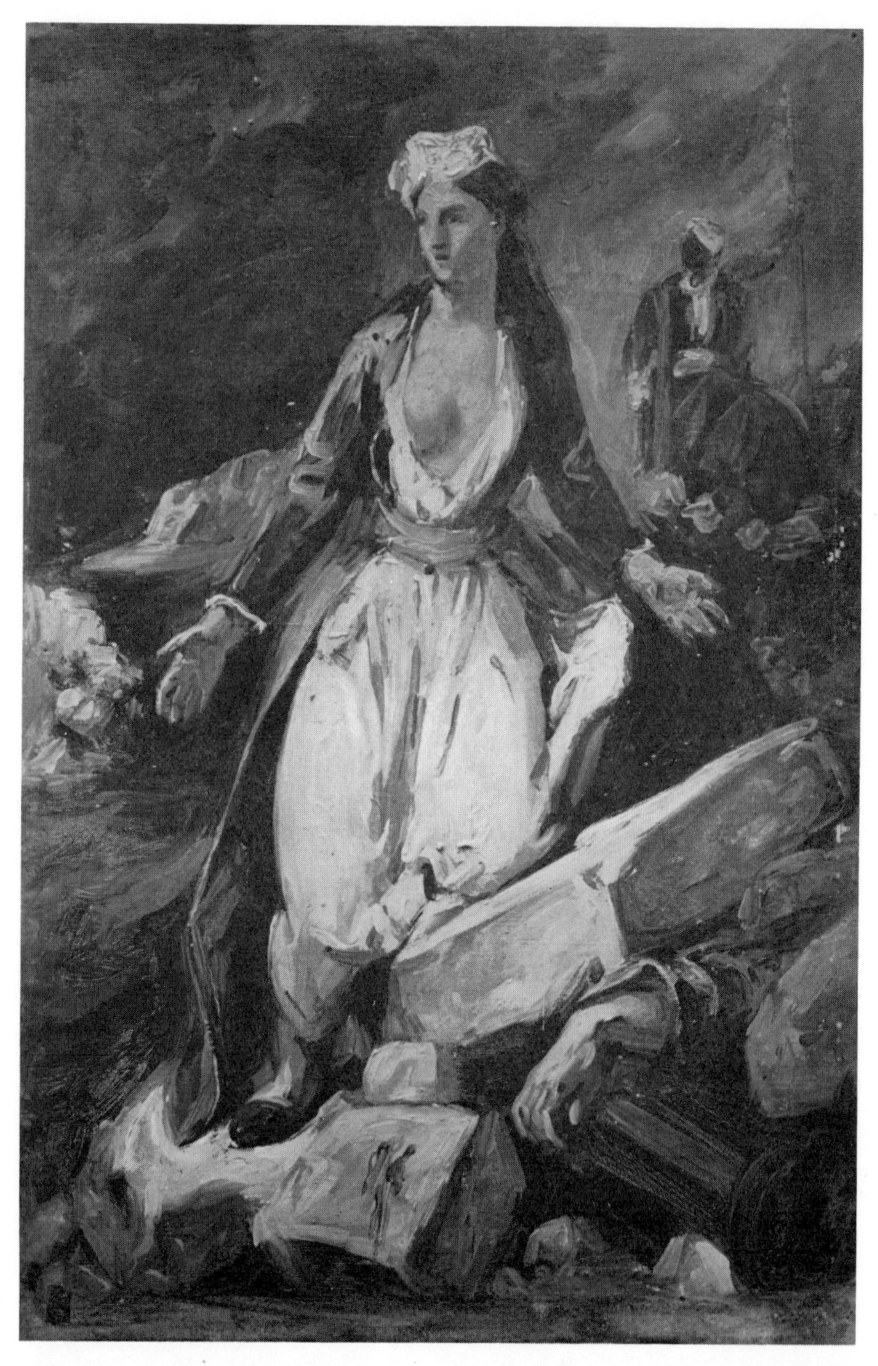

72. DELACROIX. *Greece Expiring at Missolonghi.* *Private collection.*

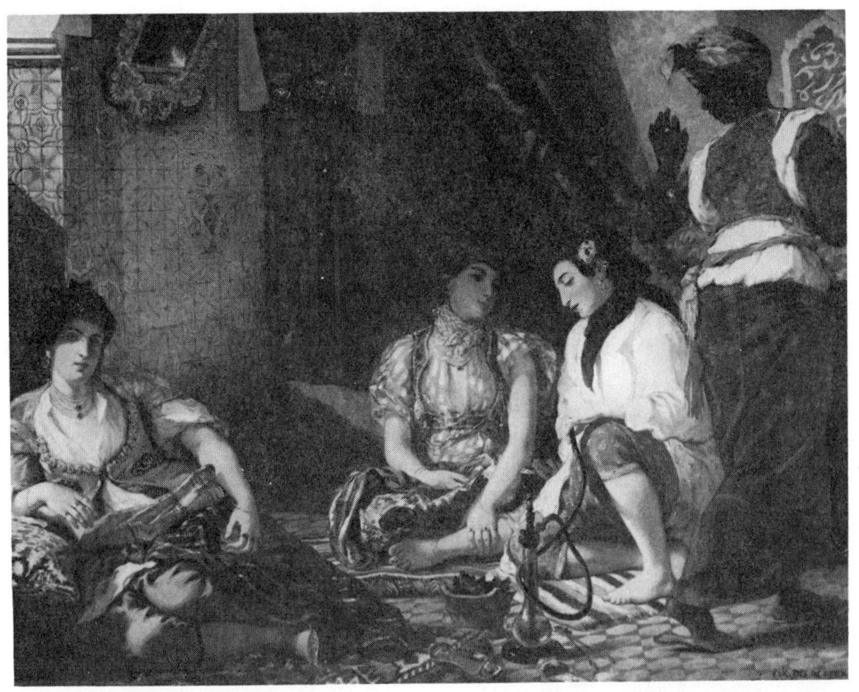

73. DELACROIX. *Algerian Women.* Louvre.

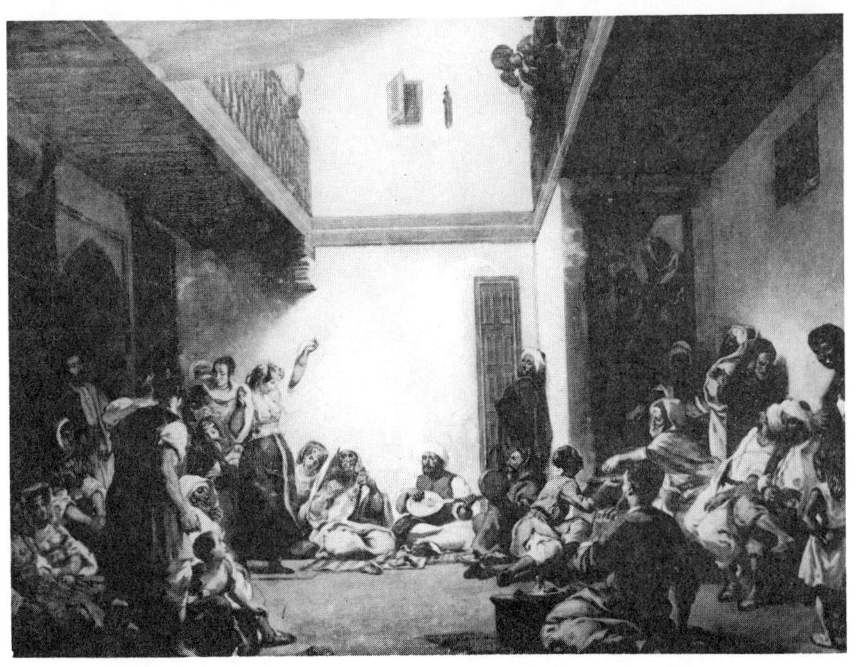

74. DELACROIX. *Jewish Wedding in Morocco.* Louvre.

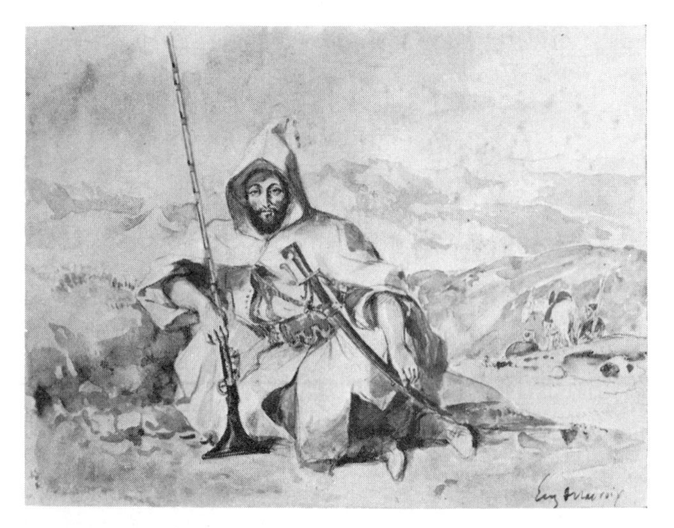

75. DELACROIX. *Soldier of the Sultan.* *Wildenstein.*

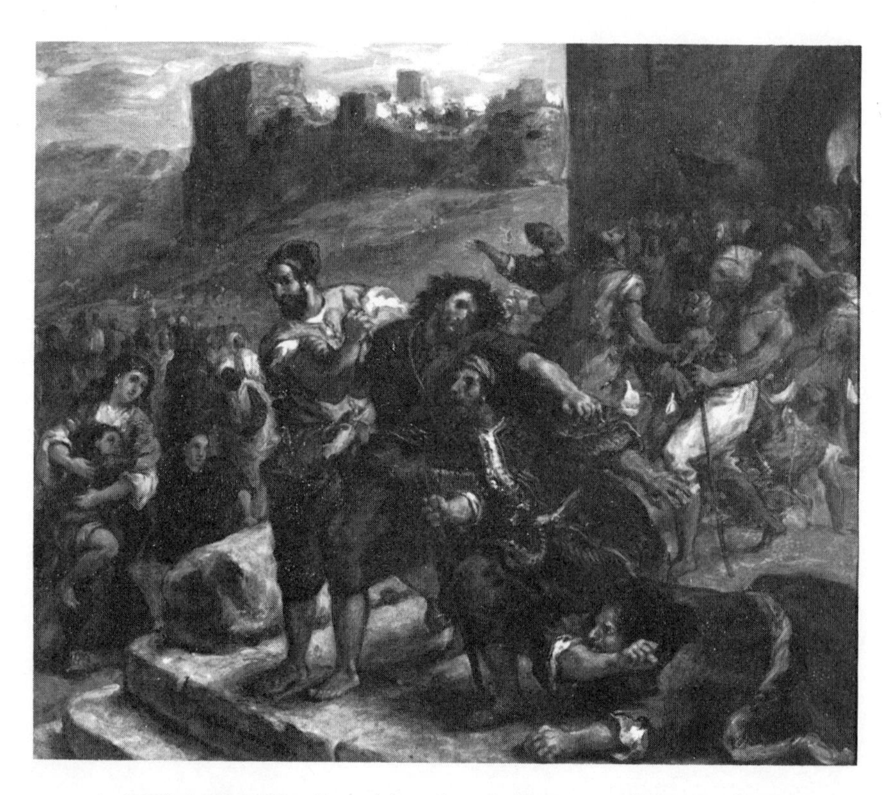

76. DELACROIX. *Convulsionnaires de Tanger.* *Private collection.*

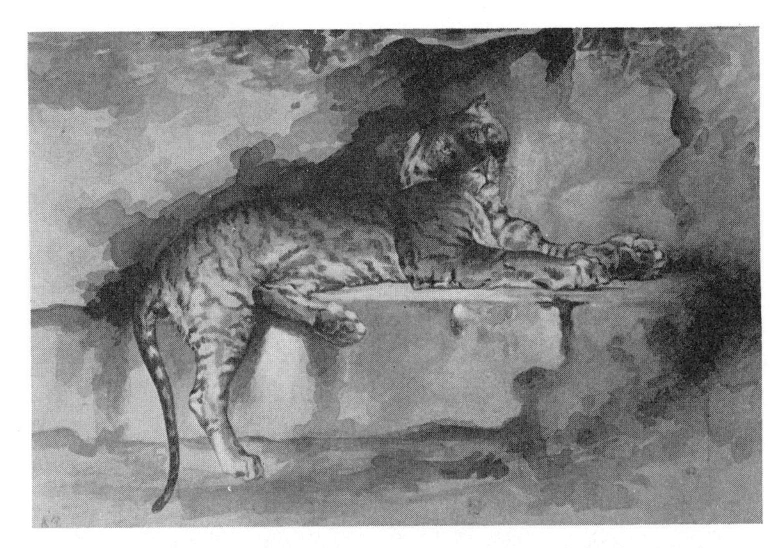

77. DELACROIX. *Tiger.* *Mr. and Mrs. Richard S. Davis.*

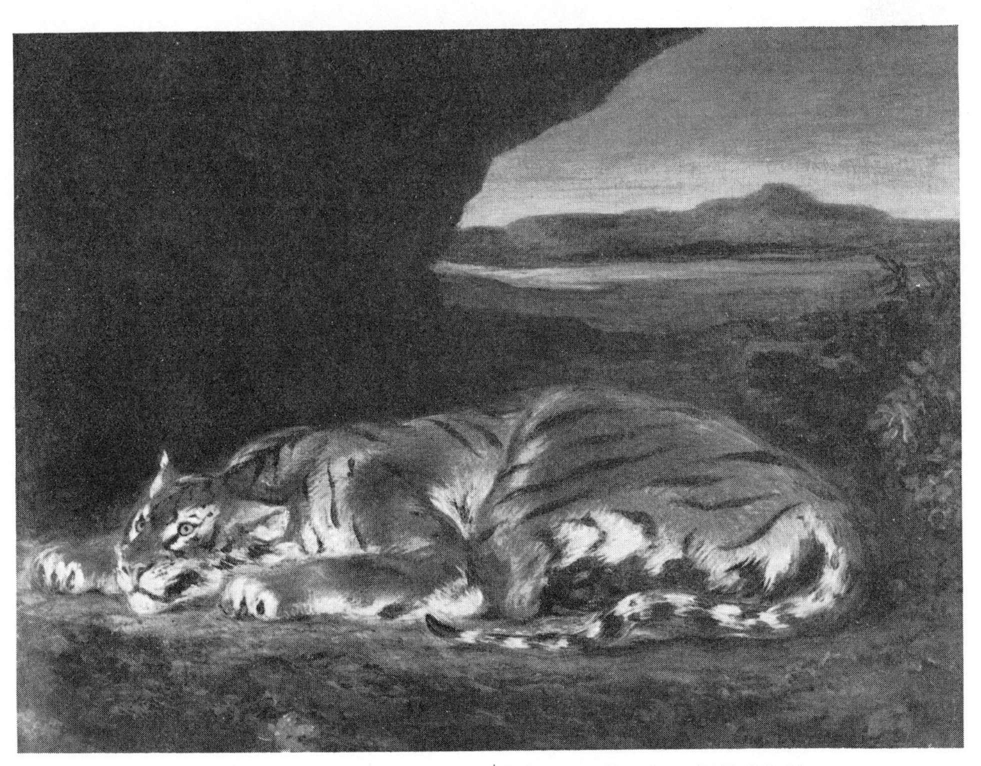

78. DELACROIX. *Tiger.* *Private collection, Philadelphia.*

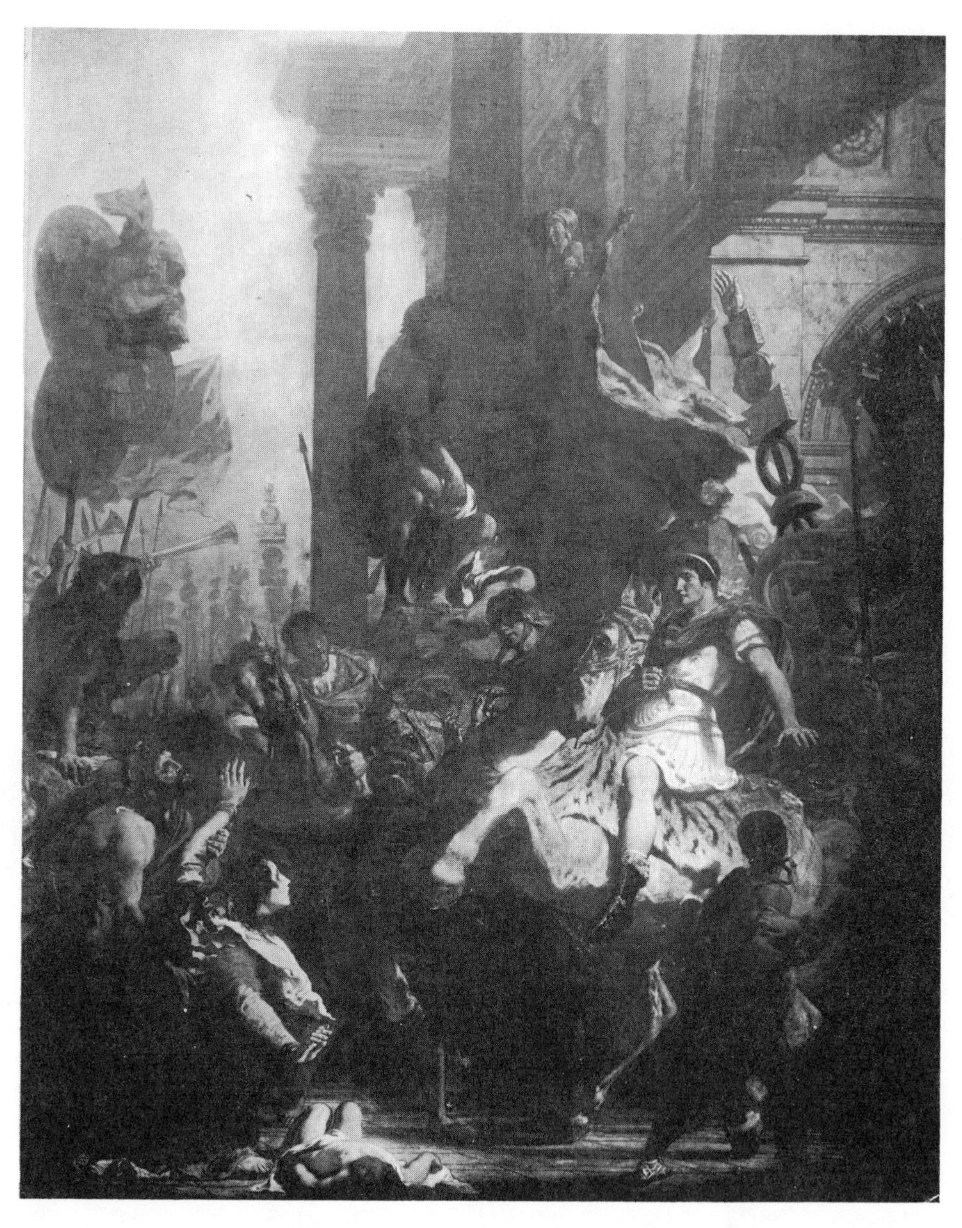

79. DELACROIX. *The Justice of Trajan.* Rouen.

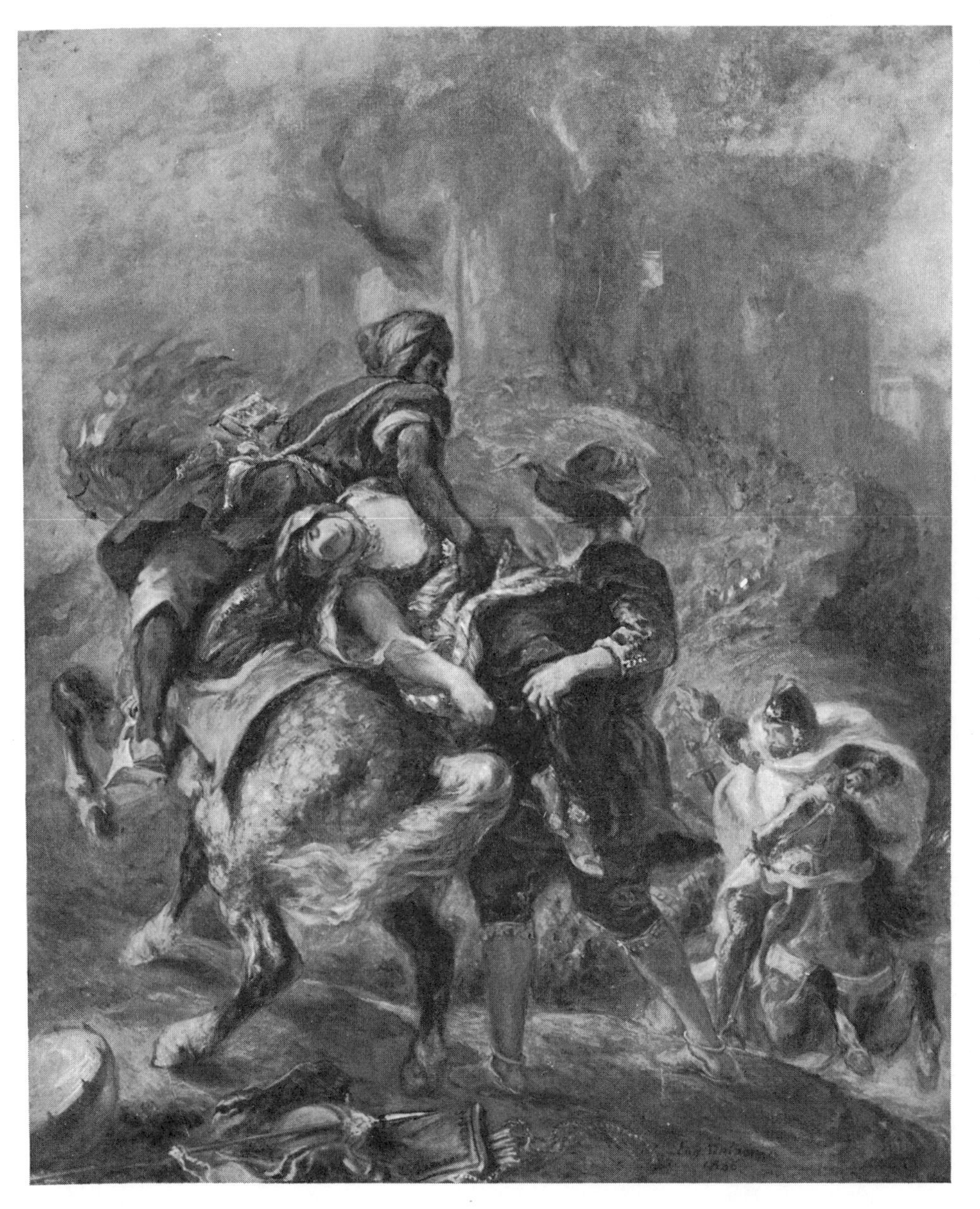

80. DELACROIX. *The Abduction of Rebecca.* *Metropolitan Museum of Art.*

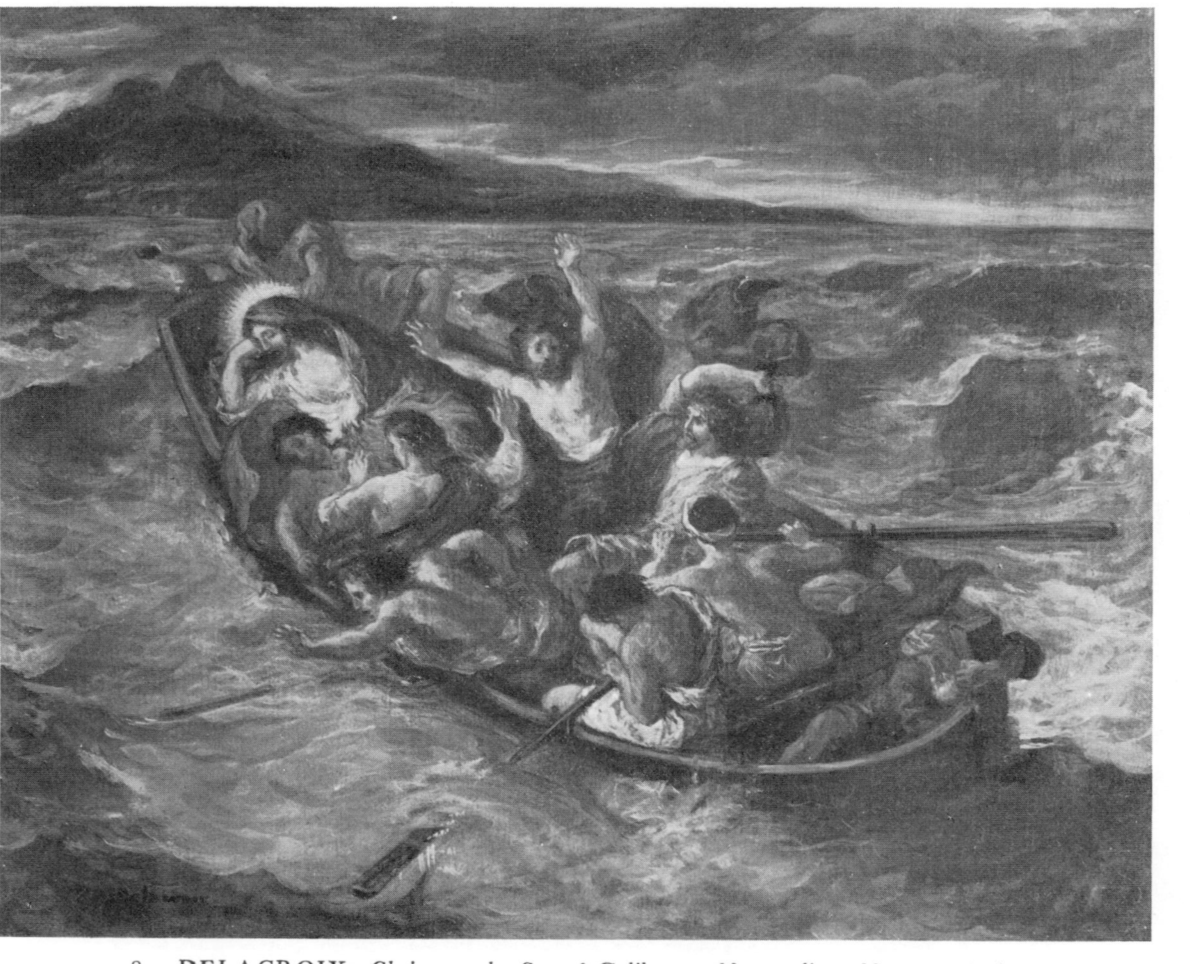

81. DELACROIX. *Christ on the Sea of Galilee.* *Metropolitan Museum of Art.*

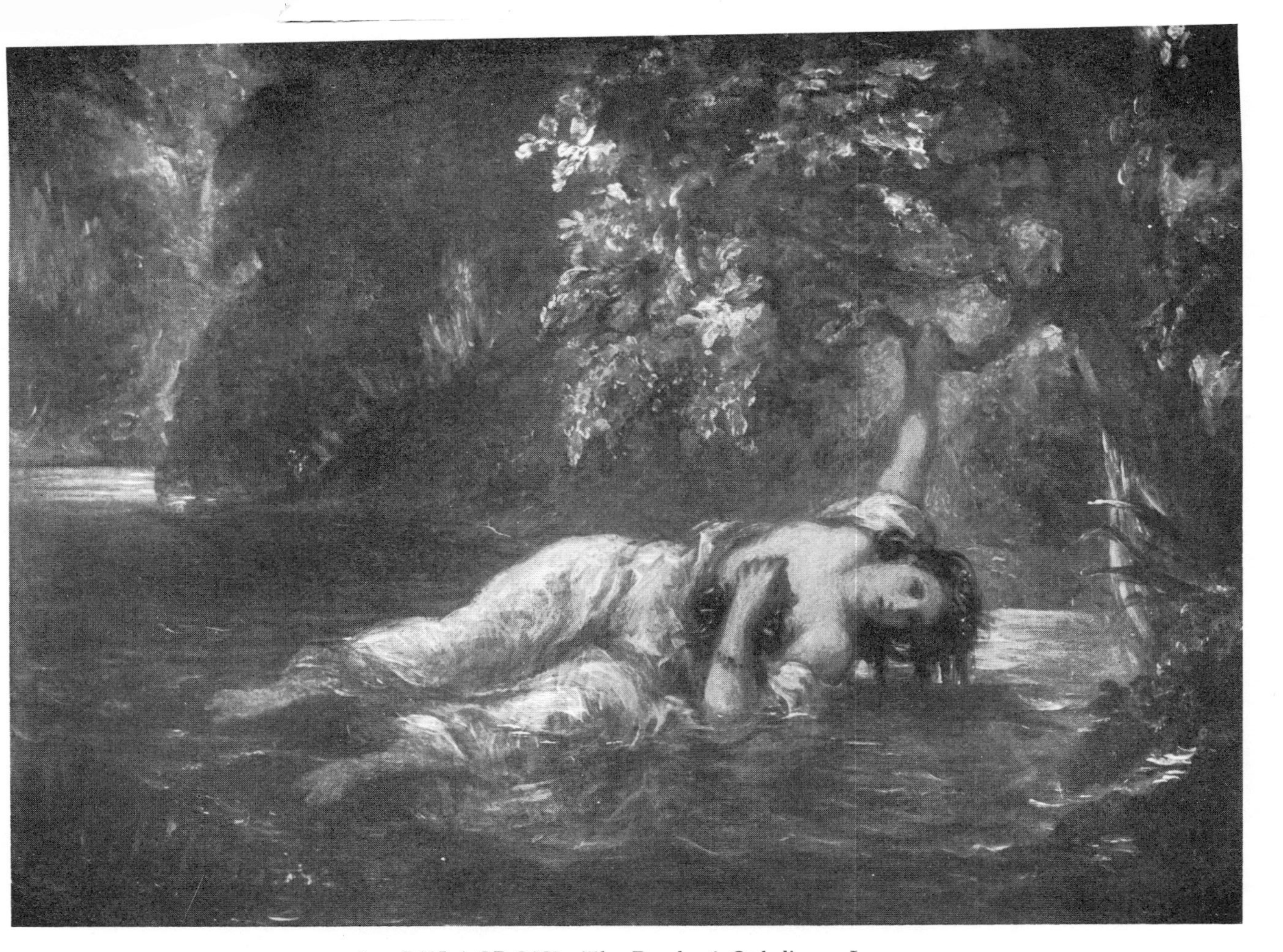

82. DELACROIX, *The Death of Ophelia.* Louvre.

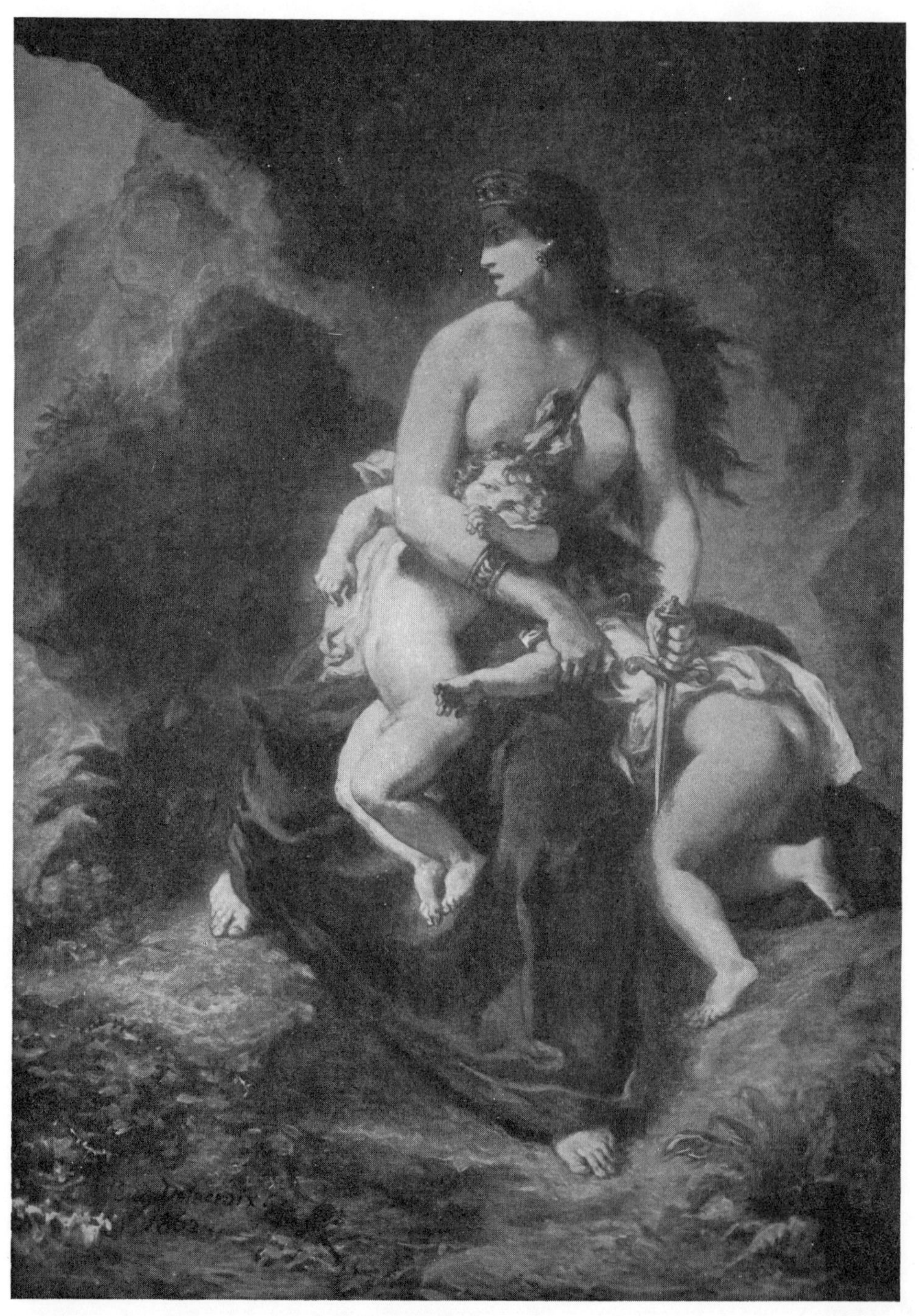

83. DELACROIX. *Medea.* *Louvre.*